The Sound Approach
To
English Grammar

الطريقة المثلى لقواعد
اللغة الإنجليزية

Devised by

Ibrahim A. Abu Anzeh

B.A in English - Cairo University (1967)
Education Diploma - Qatar University (1977)

Fourth Edition 2006
الطبـعـة الرابـــعـــة

(ردمك)ISBN 9957-05-031-1

رقم الإيداع لدى دائرة المكتبة الوطنية : ١٥٥١ / ٩ / ١٩٩٩

رقم التصنيف: ٤٢٥

المؤلف ومن هو في حكمه: إبراهيم عبد الرحيم أبو عنزه

عنوان الكتاب: الطريقة المثلى لقواعد اللغة الإنجليزية

الموضوع الرئيس: ١ - اللغات.

٢- قواعد اللغة الإنجليزية.

رقم الإجازة المتسلسل: ١٩٩٩/٩/١١٠٦

تم إعداد بيانات الفهرسة والتصنيف الأولية
من قبل دائرة المكتبة الوطنية .

الطبعة الأولى: ١٩٩٩م

الطبعة الثانية: ٢٠٠٠م

الطبعة الثالثة : ٢٠٠٤م

الطبعة الرابعة ٢٠٠٦م

عنوان المؤلف إبراهيم أبو عنزة

دولة قطر – الدوحة - ص.ب ٣٦٣١٧

هاتف : ٤٧٩٠٠٤٧ ٠٠٩٧٤

٠٠٩٧٤ ٥٨٢٩٢٥٩

E-mail: abuomar4667@hotmail.com

دار يافا العلمية للنشر والتوزيع

الأردن – عمان – الأشرفية - تلفاكس ٤٧٧٨٧٧٠ ٠٠٩٦٢ ٦

ص.ب ٥٢٠٦٥١ عمان ١١١٥٢ الأردن

E-mail: dar_yafa@yahoo.com

بسم الله الرحمن الرحيم

قال تعالى في سورة الروم :

﴿ ومن آياتِهِ خلقُ السماواتِ والأرضِ واختلافُ ألسنتكم وألوانكم . إن في ذلك لآياتٍ للعالمين ﴾

Allah says that the creation of the heavens and earth and the variety of your languages and colours testify to God's existence. These are signs for people who know.

Introduction to Fourth Edition

In view of the fact that the third edition has run out , I have planned the third edition in which I have included corrections, modifications, new language items and more drills so as to realize our goal : making learning English an easy , pleasurable process.

I catch this opportunity to thank all people who thanked me for this valuable book and   supplied me   with useful observations that I have considered when preparing this edition.

Author

مقد مة الطبعة الرابعة

الحمد لله الذي وفقنا لهذا العمل النافع. ونظراً لنفاد الطبعة الأولى والثانية والثالثة نتيجة للإقبال الكبير على الكتاب لسهولة التعامل معه ، فلقد رأيت أنه من الواجب أن أقوم بالتفكير في الإعداد للطبعة الرابعة. ولقد قمت بإدخال التصويبات والتعديلات اللازمة لتلافي بعض نواحي القصور في الطبعات السابقة، كما قمت بإضافة المزيد من اللغة والتمارين والأمثلة بغية إعطاء المتعلم المزيد من الممارسة والتدريب على استخدام قواعد اللغة. وإنني أرحب بأية أفكار تخدم الصالح العام لدارسي اللغة الإنجليزية. وفي الختام أرجو أن يلاقي هذا الكتاب المزيد من القبول والدعم.

ولا يفوتني أن أقدّم شكري لكل الأشخاص الذين اتصلوا بي مبدين إعجابهم بهذا الكتاب ومقدّمين بعض الملاحظات التي أخذتها بعين الاعتبار عند إعداد هذه الطبعة.

الدوحة
المؤلف

Introduction & Dedication

تقديــم وإهـداء

Allah has created the universe and populated it with peoples speaking different languages . The world's peoples have to communicate with each other , so it has become necessary for one to learn languages other than his mother tongue.

Arabic-speaking people find it necessary to learn other languages for the world is witnessing tremendous changes in the fields of knowledge and information , and access to these changes lies in English , a language spoken by millions all over the globe. It is logical that we learn English and command it so that we will be able to keep in touch with the outside world.

There have been several theories and methods regarding learning English as a second language , but I have found it useful to take Arabic into account while learning English. I am introducing a learning method that benefits people having problems with learning English by providing them with reasonable , practical solutions.

This method is based on two assumptions . Firstly , the learner should correctly pronounce words because this is the best way through which the learner can possess and continually increase his vocabulary. Secondly , the learner is supplied with certain structures that enable him to use vocabulary effectively. Through continuous practice the learner can command these structures , using the language with ease and confidence . I do not presume that this method is wholly perfect ; consequently, I welcome any constructive observations that can fill the gaps . However , a method is considered good when it proves successful in helping a large number of learners .

I have been applying this method to many learners , and the results have been excellent. Thanks to this method , many learners have become capable of using the language , thus gaining confidence and showing signs of daily language development.

I dedicate this book to whoever aspires to glory.

Author

مقدمة وإهـــداء

لقد خلق اللـه سبحانه و تعالى الكون و عمّره بأقوام ينطقون لغـات مختلفـة , و قضى ـ
سبحانه أن تقوم بين هذه الأقوام علاقات يسودها التفاهم حتى يصبح أعمار الكون ممكنًـا , و أن
وسيلة التفاهم تكمن في اللغة , و من هنا بات ضرورياً أن يتعلم الإنسان لغات أخرى غـير لغتـه
الأم .

إن العرب ينطقون اللغة العربية و تفرض طبيعة الحيـاة المعـاصرة علـيهم أن يتعلمـوا
لغات أخرى إلى جانب اللغة العربية لأن العالم اليوم يشهد ثورة معرفية و معلوماتية هائلة قائمـة
على اللغات الأجنبية تأتي الإنجليزية في مقدمتها . و لا أحد ينكر أهمية اللغة الإنجليزية اليوم إذ
أن ملايين الناس في أرجاء شتى من العالم ينطقون ويتفاهمون بها , و لـهذا ليس عيبًا أن نتعلمها
و نتقنها حتى يتيسر لنا السبيل الذي يؤدي بنا إلى تحصيل العلوم والمعارف النافعة .

ولقد طُرحت في ميدان تعلم الإنجليزية كلغة ثانية عدة نظريات و طـرق سـاهمت إلى
حد كبير في مساعدة الشعوب في تعلـم الإنجليزية , إلا أن وجود اللغـة الأم قـد يكون عائقـاً في
طريق إتقان اللغة ولهذا رأيت من المفيد أن نأخـذ اللغـة العربيـة بعـين الاعتبار لأنـه ليس مـن
مصلحتنا إغفال اللغة العربية ونحن نتعلم الإنجليزية . والطريقة التي أطرحها وفي نفس الوقت
أهديها إلى طلابي وطالباتي الذين كان لهم الفضل الكبير في ميلادها - تفيد كثيراً الجيل الذي تعلم
الإنجليزية في بيئة لم تـمكنه من تعلمها و إتقانـها, و لهذا فكّرت في طريقة تذلل لهم الصعاب و
تجعل تعلّم الإنجليزية ممكناً و سـهلاً و بالتـالي تـزول جميع همومهم المتعلقة بالإنجليزية, و
تعتمد هذه الطريقة على النطق السليم للمفردات التـي تشكّل عصب اللغة, وعلـى استخدام
الكلمات في جمل مفيدة حسب قوالـب لغوية متعارف عليها. و علـى المتعلم تقليدها بحيـث
يتمكن المتعلم من التعلم الذاتي , وتعتمد الطريقة أيضا علـى Speaking الحـديث و القراءة
reading والكتابة writing .

٦

ولقد قمت بتطبيق هذه الطريقة على عدد كبير من دارسي الإنجليزية ووجدت أنها تعطي ثماراً طيبة في زمن قياسي الأمر الذي أذهل الكثيرين و أخذ بأيديهم من حالة اليأس إلى وضع يستطيعون فيه إنجاز الشيء الكثير في مجال التعلم و هذا الشعور بالإنجاز يسرّع عملية التعلم لأن الدارس يرصد مدى تقدمه لحظة بلحظة .

و لابد لي أن اعترف بأن هذه الطريقة ليست المثلى , و لا بد أن يرى فيها البعض نواحي قصور لأننا بشر , و لا ندعي الكمال و لهذا فإنني أرحب بأية ملاحظات قد تسد الثغرات التي يراها البعض , و لا بد لي من القول أن الوسط الطلابي الذي تعاملت كان له الفضل في ميلاد طريقتي هذه لأن كان جل همي تذليل الصعاب ونزع اليأس من نفوسهم و زرع الأمل و إمكانية تعلم الإنجليزية و شاهدت الفرحة على وجوه غالبية الطلاب في المراحل الأولى من العمل بهذه الطريقة.

و في الختام أرجو أن أكون قد وفقت في تقديم طريقة تذلل الصعاب في مجال تعلم اللغة الإنجليزية وأريد أن أسجل أن قصدي هو خدمة قومي إرضاءً لرب العباد ,و أرجوا أن يتقبّل ربي هذا العمل و الحمد لله رب العالمين و الصلاة و السلام على سيد المرسلين و إمام المعلمين سيدنا محمد صلى الله عليه و سلم . كما أنني أسعد بإهداء هذا الكتاب إلى كل الطامحين إلى المجد.

المؤلف
إبراهيم عبد الرحيم أبو عنزة

Sound Pronunciation

النطق السليم

لكي نتعلم الإنجليزية لا بد من نطق الكلمة بشكل سليم , و في الإنجليزية يوجد لكل حرف هجـاء أكثر من صوت واحد , و أقدّم بعض الإرشادات التي تساعد على نطق الكلمة بشكل جيـد و عـلى كتابتها بدون أخطاء إملائية, وهذه قواعد عامة تنطبق على غالبية المفردات , و لا بد مـن التنويـه من أن هناك استثناءات .

We have to pronounce words correctly if we want to learn English properly.

It is important to know that each alphabet has more than one sound , which confuses the learner and hinders his language development. I am supplying some general pronunciation tips that , if followed , can solve , to a great extent, many language problems , namely vocabulary acquisition and spelling.

* أولا : تنطق الـ a /أيه/ في ثلاث حالات:

1- a - e

ate, fate, late متأخر , hate يكره , mate زميل , made صنع
mare, wave - يلوح بـ موجة, save ينقذ، يوفر،يقتصد في , cave كهف lame أعرج , flame -
لهب name ,same , fame شهرة, plane طائرة care رعاية،يهتم , take يأخذ, make يصنع,
wake up يوقظ/يستيقظ
cake , for the sake of من أجل, bake , bare عارٍ, fare الأجرة rare نادر, dare يجرؤ, safe
خزانة، آمن , tame مروض- يروض , game لعبة frame إطار , crane , flare , glare , snare
يصطاد - فخ - شرك snake ثعبان , skate يتزلج .

٨

2- ai

maid خادمة , mail بريد , hail يرحب ب , rail , fail يرسب - يفشل ,
sail يبحر , tail ذيل , wail يبكي , wait ينتظر, bait الطعم ,
faint يغمى عليه , paint يدهن , pain وجع- ألم , painful مؤلم ,
painless غير مؤلم , explain يفسر , rain مطر- تمطر , brainدماغ,
drain , fair عادل- شقراء معرض .

3- ay

play يلعب , pray يصلي , pay يدفع, say يقول , stay يمكث , lay يضع ,
slay يذبح , ray أشعة, day يوم , may ربما , way طريق، طريقة
clay طين-صلصال , hay, bay ,

* نلاحظ أنه في وجود e أو i أو y يتم نطق a /أيه/ وذلك في عدد كبير من الكلمات.

* ثانياً : أما في غياب e أو i أو y يتم نطق a /آ/ مثل/آن/

ran , fan مروحة , man رجل , mat حصيرة , mad مجنون , lad فتى , bad سيء , sadحزين ,
car , sat جلس , can يستطيع-علبة يملك has , had كان لديه, ban/بان/ , ركض
van , start , star , dark , dam back , sack , park , art فن, rank رتبة, tank خزان- دبابة
part جزء ,
party طرف/حفلة/حزب , smart أنيق , rat فأر , pack يحزّم حزمة-سرب ,
farm مزرعة , swan ألوز , bang فرقعة-خبطة, sang (أغنية)غنى , rang اتصل ,
hang يتدلى - يعلق .

لاحظ النطق في هذه الكلمات :

far / فار /بعيد , fair عادل ، شقراء ، معرض , fare الأجرة ,
man / مان/رجل , main / مين / رئيسي , mane عرف الديك أوالحصان ,
plan / بلان / خطة , plane طائرة , plain سهل – سادة .

في المجموعة الواحدة تجد الحرف a له أكثر من صوت واحد و نجد أننا حصلنا على كلمات أخرى بإضافة "e" أو "i" و لها معاني جديدة ... إننا نستطيع أن ننطق جيدا و أن نحصل على كلمات أخرى بسهولة و أن نكتبها دون صعوبة .

نأخذ أمثلة أخرى تساعدك على اكتساب المزيد من المفردات بسهولة و على الارتقاء بالإملاء لديك.

mad / ماد / مجنون , made / ميد/ صنع , maid / ميد / خادمة
hat قبعة , hate يكره , can علبة / يستطيع , cane عصا,
tale حكاية , tail ذيل, male ذكر, mail بريد ,
sail يبحر , sale مبيع , tail ذيل , tale حكاية ,
rate سعر-معدل-نسبة , rat فأر

إن الخطوة الأولى تتمثل في النطق السليم للكلمة , ثم وضع الكلمة في جملة .

اقرأ الجمل التالية مراعياً قوانين النطق السابقة .

It is too far .   My maid is fair .   She has got fair hair.
إنها بعيدة جداً   إن خادمتي حسناء   إن لديها شعر أشقر

The man with fair hair has paid the fare .

إن الرجل ذا الشعر الأشقر قد دفع الأجرة.

This maid is mad , so I want another maid .

هذه الخادمة مجنونة ، و لهذا فإنني أريد خادمة أخرى .

* ثالثا : تنطق الـ a مثل / o / في الحالتين التاليتين :

1- a / o / all جميع -كل , ball كرة/بول- , المرارة gall ,
mall مجمع تجاري-مطرقة خشبية

طويل tall ,صغير/سمول/ small- ينادي- يسمي -يتصل بـ – call

, wall حائط , pall غطاء النعش

fall هبوط-يهبط - يسقط , hall قاعة- صالة

اقرأ الجمل بصوت عالٍ و لاحظ طريقة النطق و ركّز على النطق والمعنى.

It is fair that you play and pray .   من العدل أن تلعب وتصلي.

It is fair that you pay the maid a good salary .

من العدل أن تدفع للخادمة راتبا جيدا .

It is mad that you pay the maid a bad salary .

من الجنون أن تدفع للخادمة راتباً سيئا .

If you play , I will stay on .   إن تلعب ، فإنني سوف أستمر في البقاء .

If you play ball in the hall , you will pay .

إن تلعب الكرة في الصالة ، فانك سوف تدفع .

The hall is too small .   إن الصالة صغيرة جدا .

*****

2- al → chalk طباشير/تشوك , talk حديث- يتحدث -,

, stalk ساق النبات - يطارد - اصطبل

walk يمشي- مشوار مشي

١١

We can walk to the small hall , and we can talk there .

نحن نستطيع المشي إلى الصالة الصغيرة و يمكننا أن نتحدث هناك .

* al = / a: / ⟶ half / ha:f / هاف نصف-منتصف ,

a month and a half شهر ونصف , half ⟶ halves (

(الجمع) , Half the girls are there. Half the house is for
sale.

A half egg (√) , half an egg (√) ,

calf / كاف /

عجل , calves عجول .

* رابعاً: تنطق e /ئي/ :

bet /بت/ ابت , let /الت/ يراهن , يؤجر /الت/ يدع , wet /وت/ رطب-مبلل , bed - فراش

سرير , set /ست/ طقم - مجموعة , fed أطعم, led قاد,

well بئر-بخير, wed يتزوج- يزوج , hell جهنم, bell جرس, fell هبط-سقط خلية, cell

sell يبيع., web شبكة-غشاء .

في حالة ee يتم مد /ئي/ إلى الأسفل كما هو الحال في الكلمات التالية:

seed /سيد/بذور, feet /فيت/أقدام, feed /فيد/يطعم-يغذي, weep يبكي. need حاجة-يحتاج,

deep عميق, peel يقشر, seem يبدو, deem , weed عشب ضار, heed

, wheel/ويل/عجل .

أنطق هذه الكلمات:

keep يحفظ , kept حفظ, meet يقابل, met قابل , weep يبكي ,

wept بكى , sleep ينام , slept نام , creep يزحف, crept زحف ,

feel يشعر, felt شعر.

۱۲

يتم نطق ea مثل ee في بعض الحالات: <u>ea = ee</u>

meat / , يأكل eat, تسرب-سيلان/ليك leak , قمة peak , يتكلم speak

لحم ميت / meal / ميل / وجبة seat, مقعد , beat يضرب , يهزم

heat, حرارة / neat مرتب ,

beak   clean / كلين / ينظف bead خرزة , treat/يعامل-يعالج/تريت

. مدير مدرسة-منقار الطير

يتم نطق ea مثل e في الحالات التالية:

ea = e : head /هد / رأس , يترأس , يرأس ,
               bread, خبز , read (الماضي من يقرأ)
               death / دث / الموت , الوفاة , dead ميت
               deaf أصم , wealth الثروة
               health /هلث / الصحة , breath/برث/النفس .

* خامساً : ١- c يتم نطقها / سِ / إذا جاء بعدها أحد هذه الحروف : e, i , y

كما هو في الحالات التالية:

مهذب decent , السنت cent , يتسابق, سباق race , وجه face
/ديموك رسي/ democracy , decency, central , مركز centre, مدينة / سيتي / city , قلم رصا ص pencil
, سياسة / بولسي / policy, غير رحيم merciless رحيم merciful , الرحمة mercy , الديمقراطية, pharmacy /فارماسي/ صيدلية democracy /ديموك رسي/, agency وكالة /ديسنسي/الحشمة
منشأة- مرفق-تسهيل /فاسيليتي / facility

١٣

* **Read these sentences :**

I can take you to my neat city . إني أستطيع أن أخذك إلى مدينتي النظيفة .

The man is dead , so we can talk to the fat doctor .

I met a tall man in the city centre .

We can speak and eat in the hall . It is fair to

have democracy and a pharmacy in the small city . من العدل أن يكون عندنا
ديمقراطية و صيدلية.

٢- تنطق c مثل k في الكلمات التالية:

scare مهمل careless , حذر - مهتم - يهتم careful , رعاية - يهتم care , سيارة / كار / car
يرعب , came جاء , black اسود , lack قلة- يفتقر إلى , cat قطة, sack كيس-
, clean نظيف , corner زاوية , creep يزحف , crack شرخ , يطرد/ساك/
crop محصول , crescent / الهلال /كرسنت , cross , craft
, picnic يتنـزه -نزهة flock , block, sock , mock , pock , dock , deck , peck , lick, pick
picnicking التنـزه, panic يصاب بالخوف , panicked خاف- خوف .

٣- cc ينطق الحرف الأول k والثاني حسب الحروف اللاحقة له:

, accident حادث accept / أك سبيت / يقبل , accent / أك سينت / اللهجة ,
concentrate/كون سنت ريت /يركز , succeed / ساك سيد / ينجح , accede يعتلي
accelerate /يعجل, access (to) , accessible مدخل- منفذ , سهل الوصول إليه ,
account /أكاونت/ حساب-بيان , accord/ أكورد/ اتفاق , *
accommodation /أكوموديشن/ مسكن -توفيق ,
accompany / أكامباني /يصاحب- يرافق , accomplish ينجز.
soccer /سوكر/ كرة القدم , sceptic /سكبتك/ متشكك *

* Read these sentences : اقرأ هذه الجـمل

* It is better for you to accept this job.

من الأفضل لك أن تقبل بهذه الوظيفة.

* The black man came to this place to take part in the race.

جاء الرجل الأسود إلى هذا المكان ليشترك في السباق.

* I have just opened a bank account.

لقد افتتحت لتوا حساباً في البنك.

* He had an accident because he was driving carelessly.

* The accord is important.   إن الاتفاق مهم.

* I can concentrate on democracy .   .

أستطيع أن أركز على الديمقراطية

* I don't care at all .   إني لا أبالي على الإطلاق .

* I hate careless people   إني اكره الناس المهملين .

* We can sit with careful people and talk a lot .

* You can succeed if you concentrate .

إنك تستطيع أن تنجح إذا أنت تركز.

* If you don't concentrate, you will fail .

إذا لم تركز، فإنك سوف ترسب.

* I can accept that; it is fair.   أني أستطيع أن أقبل ذلك.

* I can't agreeيوافق; it is mad   لا يمكنني أن أوافق. إنه جنون .

******

* ch = / tsh اتش /

reach يصل إلى , teach يدرس /تيتش/ , beach شاطئ /بيتش/

breach خرق , each كل preach يوعظ , chart خريطة ,

charm يسحر- شيء فتّان – سحر -تعويذة ,

charter حافلة أو استئجار طائره- ميثاق , cheese جبن ,

chess لعبة الشطرنج , choice خيار , choose يختار , cheat يغش ,

١٥

صدقة- مساعدة   charity , واجب-عمل ضروريchore, يراجع-يفحص-يدقق check , رخيص cheap
الفقراء –جمعية خيرية
(كبير الطباخين / شف / chef , / برا نش / فرع branch *)

*****

* ch = / k ك /

ديك/ كوك/ cock , يتألم– ألم / أيك / ake / ache , مدرسة /سكول/ school
, شخصية character , ساعة clock , معدة /ستوماك/ stomach , مهندس معماريarchitect
, مادة كيماوية chemical , فجوة chasm
, مجموعة المنشدين /كوايار/ choir , حبل-وتر chord , كيمياء chemistry

* يجدول- جدول / شد يول- سكيجول/ schedule

****

* cia , cie , cio = / sh / /ش/

social اجتماعي /سوشال/ , efficient / افيشنت / كفء ,
commercial تجاري/كوميرشال/ , ancient قديم / delicious ديليشس / , precious لذيذ
/ شاس بري / ثمين ,
vicious رذيل , sufficient كافٍ , sufficiency اكتفاء-كفاية , deficiency نقص , racial عنصري .

● **Read the sentences :**

It is good to teach and preach, but it is better that you apply what you preach.   .
من الخير أن تعلّم و توعظ , و لكن من الأفضل أن تطبق ما توعظ به

We cannot accept any breach of decency.

إننا لا يمكننا أ ن نقبل أي خرق للحشمة.

١- ننطق الـ g مثلما ينطق أهل القاهرة كلمة جمال.

go يذهب , got حصل على , get يحصل على , gate بوابة , game لعبة , goal هدف ,
goat ماعز , fog ضباب , hog خنزير-شخص قذر و طماع , sing يغني , song أغنية ,
glass زجاج , grass عشب , green اخضر .

٢- ننطق g /ج / كما ننطق كلمة الجزيرة:

age العمر , page الصفحة , rage الغضب , wage أجر ,
sage fridge إسفين-وتد ,wedge سياج, hedge جسر,bridge رقيق gentle , نبات الميرامية -عاقل
صفة /جين/ gene , جنس (المذكر/ المؤنث في النحو) gender , يولد generate /ثلاجة/فردج/ ,
genius /جين ياص/ إنسان عبقري -نبوغ- عبقرية , /موروثة ,
geology /جيولوجيا /جيولوجي . علم الجيولوجيا

٣- ننطق g كما ينطق أهل القاهرة "جمال" مع عدم نطق حرف u كما يلي:

guard / قارد / يحرس , حارس / guide /قايد مرشد , دليل , guarantee / قارنتي / - يكفل
vogue ضمانة - يضمن , vague / غامض , guilt /قلت / جرم- ذنب guilty /قِلتي / مذنب ,
موضة , guess يخمن , guest ضيف / guise /قايز / ثوب- هيئة- .

٤- ننطق gh /ف f/ في الحالات التالية:

laugh /الاف/ يضحك , rough /رَف/ فظ خشن , tough /تف/ شديد - يابس , draught
/درافت/ تيار هواء , cough / كف / كحة - يسعل- يكح , touch / تا تش / لمسة - يلمس ,

٥- لا يتم نطق gh كما في الكلمات التالية:

الليل , night , محق - حق , right , خفيف- ضوء / لايت / light
, اشترى / بوت / bought , ساطع- لامع bright , يرعب frighten , الرعب fright , يحارب / fight
sought / سعى / سوت , caught , fought , brought.

* **Read these sentences following the pronunciation rules:**
*   The food is delicious, so you can eat a lot.
*   We **care for** نهتم بـ the social اجتماعية affairs شؤون of
    people.
*   The song الأغنية you sang scared me **a lot.** كثيراً
*   You are **guilty** مذنب ; you killed the fair maid .
*   You can **frighten** a careless man , but you can't **scare**
    a **bright** man .

    إنك تستطيع أن ترعب رجلا مهملاً ولكنك لا تستطيع أن ترعب رجلاً ذكياً.
*   We are lucky to have democracy in this country.

    إننا سعداء الحظ في أن لدينا ديموقراطية في هذا البلد.
*   Democracy means freedom of choice. الديموقراطية تعني حرية الاختيار.
*   You are free to do and say what you like, but you are
    not free to **offend others.** (يسيء إلى الآخرين) .

سابعاً: ١- ننطق h /هـ/ كما في الحالات التالية:

ضار / هارم فل / harmful , يؤذي - ضرر / هارم / harm , يكره hate , قبعة / هات / hat
, يملك / هاف / have , هو he , هو him , يضرب hit , حار hot , غير ضار harmless ,
has / هاز / يملك , hammer مطرقة , haven ملاذ , happy ,
ham , home , harvest يحصد الحصاد .
* <u>h</u>onest /أنست/ أمين - مخلص honesty , الأمانة ,
  honour / أنر / شرف -تكريم-يكَّرم .

١٨

٢- ننطق sh /ش/ كما في الحالات التالية:

سمك fish , shirt,قصير , short , محل shop , يضرب , سفينة ship , يطلق / شوت / shoot
dish / طبق , wish يتمنى , shark سمكة القرش , حاد sharp , crash , rash , smash , lash,
flash, bash, shame عار - حياء , shameful فاضح- مخجل , shameless وقح - لا يعرف الحياء ,
shock / شوك / صدمة, share يشارك-سهم- حصة -نصيب .

٣- ننطق th /ذَ/ كما في الحالات التالية:

this / ذس / هذا , that ذلك , then عندئذ , than / ذان / ,
these / ذيز / هؤلاء they , هم there هناك , with مع , thus وهكذا – الأمر الذي نتج
عنه, therefore ولهذا السبب / thereupon/ لأجل ذلك / ذير أبون / father الأب ,
mother / ماذّ / الأم , brother / براذّ / الأخ weather الجو , feather / فذّ / ريشة .

٤- ننطق th /ث/ كما في الحالات التالية:

thank / ثانك / يشكر , thin / ثن / نحيف , think يعتقد - يفكر , ضرس tooth
health الصحة , depth / دبث / العمق , length / لنقث / الطول thought / ثوت /
, therapy/ ثيرابي / علاج , throne / ثرون/ عرش الملك , breath النفَس إعتقدَ - فكرة ,
throat/ ثروت/ زور الانسان , theory/ ثيوري / نظرية , theme مبحث-موضوع/ ثيم / , thick
/ ثيك / سميك- كثيف , lethal /ليثال/ مميت -قاتل , thesis/ أطروحة للحصول على درجة علمية ,
ثيسِسthreat / ثريت / تهديد, threaten يهدد .

١٩

Read the sentences : اقرأ هذه الجمل

* I think you are fair and right . إني أعتقد أنك عادل و محق..
* You have good health .
* Health is more important than wealth. *الصحة أكثر أهمية من المال.   I have a
tooth-ache ألم في الأسنان , but I think that **the**
dentist طبيب الأسنان will **scare** يروع me .
* If you care for me, I will care for you.

إذا أنت تهتم بي , فإنني سوف أهتم بك.

* If you scare me, I will scare you .

إن أرعبتني , فإنني سوف أرعبك.

* Smoking is harmful, so you should stop it.

التدخين ضار, ولهذا يجب أن تتوقف عنه

* It is bad to play with sharp knives.

من العيب أن تلعب بالسكاكين الحادة.

* We are free to show our thoughts to others.

إننا أحرار في أن نبرز أفكارنا للآخرين.

* ثامناً: ١- ننطق i /أي/ ai/ في الحالات التالية:

نايس/ظريفnice, السعر - الثمن / price/ برايس , الارز , rice , الثلج ice
drive , خمسة five الزوجة wife الحياة , life يحب / لايك / like , القمل lice / فئران mice
, الخمر wine يغوص /dive/دايف ,يسوق
die /داي / يموت , died / دايد / مات , lie يكذب -أكذوبة-يستلقي
libel /لايبل / (في المطبوعات) يفتري على-يقذف - قذف - تشهير ,
slide انزلاق slice شريحة, line خط , in line with مع منسجم ,
lime ليمون - الجير
** idle /aidl آيدل, idol /aidl /آيدل عاطل عن العمل-تافه-صنم,
* saliva / سالايفا / لعاب

٢٠

* **Read these sentences:**

*   It is bad to lie to other people.

إنه لأمر سيئ أن نكذب على الناس الآخرين.

*   If you drive too fast , you will die .
* Mice and lice are harmful , so we must kill them.

الفئران والقمل ضارة , ولهذا يجب قتلها.

*   It is not wise to drink wine.   ليس من الحكمة أن نشرب الخمر .   If you want to* win, don't drink wine.

إذا أردت أن تفوز , فلا تشرب الخمر.

٢- ننطق i /أي /ai في هذه الكلمات بسبب وجود gh مع عدم نطق gh:

, رعب fright, حق - محق / رايت / الايت / ضوء light
, عالٍ-مرتفع high ,البصر sight, طفيف slight, رحلة جوية flight
. يستقيل من/ريزاين/ resign ,يصمم/ديزاين/ design ,يوقع/ساين/ sign

توقيع signature*   الطب - دواء /ميدي سن/ medicine*, استقالة/رزقنيشن/resignation*
. إشارة – يعطي إشارة / سقنال / signal , /سقنتشر/

* The general signalled to **his army** جيشه **to start the attack.**

لبدئ الهجوم.

*Ali resigned استقال because he was getting a bad salary.
* There has been a slight rise in prices since last Friday.

هناك ارتفاع طفيف في الأسعار منذ يوم الجمعة الماضية.

٣- ننطق i /أي /ai/ في الكلمات التالية:

يعبئ الساعة-يلف wind ,يطحن grind ,أعمى blind , يجد / فايند , find / يجد
خلف behind, نوع- رقيق - لطيف / كايند / kind
. يمانع - عقل /مايند /mind , أنثى الغزال - خلفي hind

٤- ننطق i مثل e وذلك في حالة عدم وجود e أو gh أو g كما سبق:

يراهن/بت/ bet , عض / بت bit , هو him , هذا it / et
مبتل ,wet ذكاء wit, طقم-مجموعة set ,يجلس sit
جهنم ,hell تل hill ,بئر-بخير-بشكل جيد well ,سوف-وصية-إرادة will
till حتى-لغاية, tell يخبر, bill قانون مشروع-فاتورة, bell جرس, fell سقط , fill يملأ , ten عشرة , tin
. دبوس pin ,قلم حبر pen , علبة- الصفيح

يجب أن نراعي الفرق في النطق و نعرف السبب:

win يفوز , wine الخمر / bit عض, bite يعض /
hide يحجب-يخفي , hid أخفى -حجب / site – sit /

٥- ننطق ir / إير /eir/ كما ننطق كلمة fare,fair :

girl بنت , bird طائر , first أولا - الأول , birth ميلاد , third - الثالث
ثالثا shirt , قميص verb الفعل , adverse معادي- معاكس , averse to معادي ,
كاره لـ
aversion /أفيرشن/كراهية

٦- لاحظ كيفية لفظ هذه الكلمات :

Notice how these words are pronounced .

experience /إكسبيريانس/ بتجربة-يمر-تجربة-خبرة, reliant /معتمد,
appliance /جهاز/أبليانس/, defiance التحدي, reliance الاعتماد ,
self-reliant معتمد على نفسه , self-reliance الاعتماد على النفس ,
salient / سي ليانت / مهم – بارز .

Read the sentences. اقرأ هذه الجمل

*   I like the ice prices . Ice is cheap, and that is nice .

أحب أسعار الثلج . إن الثلج رخيص و هذا رائع .

*   It is mad to drink wine

من الجنون أن تشرب الخمر.

*   If you drink wine , you will die.

إذا شربت الخمر فإنك سوف تموت.

*   If you win the race , you will get a nice car .

إذا فزت بالسباق فإنك سوف تحصل على سيارة جميلة .

*   I don't mind that you drive the children there .

إني لا أمانع في أن توصل الأطفال بالسيارة إلى هناك .

*   You should learn self-reliance. يجب أن تتعلم الاعتماد على النفس.

*   You have long experience, so we can learn many things

from you. إن لديك خبرة طويلة ولهذا فإننا نستطيع أن نتعلم أشياء كثيرة منك.

* تاسعا: ١- ننطق o كما في(دو) في هذه الكلمات:

dog / دُق / كلب , fog /فق/ ضباب , hog /هق/ خنـزير , log , bog , hot حار , lot كمية ,
/هوت/ , top / توب / قمة , bottom أسفل-قاع , pork , fork , dock .

٢٣

٢- تمد إلى الأمام كما يلي :

moon / مون / قمر , soon /سون/ حالاً - قريبا , , pool بركه , ,
cool بارد- يبرّد ,hoofحافر الحصان , , tool أداة , ,mood حالة نفسية,
fool فول/ أهبل - معتوه , moody مزاجي, food طعام, boom ازدهار- رواج noon الظهر -
النهار منتصف , saloon غرفة للجلوس , salon / سالن , غرفة للضيوف .
good* /قد / الخير - ممتع - طيب , جيد , wood خشبي- خشب - غابة /ود/ wool الصوف , foot
القدم , hook صنارة , hood غطاء للرأس والرقبة - قلنسوة

٣- تنطق o من الحلق كما هو مبين في الكلمات التالية:

cold /كولد/ بارد , gold /قولد/ الذهب , hold /هولد/ يمسك ب ,
bold جسور , told أخبر , sold باع , boat قارب , coat معطف ,
goat ماعز ,bought / بوت / اشترى / caught / كوت / امسك , worn , sworn , torn, born
horn , قرن الثور - مزمار , corn الحبوب - الحنطة form شكل- يشكل, mourn يبكي - يحد على
على

٤- تنطق من تجويف الفم كما في الكلمات التالية :

boy /بوي/ ولد toy, /توي/ لعبة enjoy / إن جوي / يستمتع بـ , ,
employ يوظف , destroy / ديست روي / يدمر , toil يكد ,
oil الزيت - النفط , boil يغلي , foil يحبط , soil التربة .

٢٤

٥- تنطق ou / أوْ / آوْ كما يلي :

out / أوْت / خارج , roundabout دوار , about عن ,
found / فاوند / وجد ,round جولة - حول / house / هاوس / منـزل , mouse فأر , mouth /
. فم ماوث , south جنوب , sour حامض – يفْسِد , hour / أوار / ساعة

٦- تنطق ou مثل "o" في "port" وكذا تنطقau :

court / كورت / فناء- محكمة , four أربعة , cause يسبب - سبب / كوز / ,
pause يتوقف - haul يسحب-يجر ,
caution تحذير- حذرُ- حيطة / كوشن /, caucus اجتماع حزبي ,
precaution احترازي إجراء-احتياط , caught قبض على – أمسك ,
haughty مغرور – متكبر , haunt يتردد على- مأوى ,
haunted مسكون بالجن , exhausted اقزوستد / منهك .

٧- يتم نطق ou (أ) كما هو الحال في هذه الكلمات:

delicious /شاس ديلي/ لذيذ ,ambitious شاس أمبي / طموح ,
trouble / ترابل / مأزق - ورطة ,dangerous / خطير ,
country / كانتري / بلد , flourish / فلارش / يزدهر ,
nourish / نارش / يغذي ,rough / رَف / خشن -هائج,
honour / انار/ يكرم-تكريم-شرف, colour / كالار / لون ,
neighbour / بار ني/ الجار , vapour بخار, harbour ميناء ,
jealous غيور, jealousy غيرة .

* عاشراً: u /يو/ :

١-   تنطق "يو" في وجود "e" كما في هذه الكلمات:

use /يوز/ يستخدم , fuse /فيوز/ , refuse /رف يوز/ يرفض ,
amuse /أم يوز/ يفرح , accuse /أك يوز/ يتهم ,
pure /بيور/ صافي, cure /كيور/ علاج - يعالج,
huge /هيوج/ ضخم , reduce /رديوس/ يخفض من ,
produce ينتج .

* flute /فلوت/آلة موسيقية/ rude /رود/ وقح-فظ ,
brute /بهيم- وحش/ بروت/ , brutal /وحشي/ بروتال/ ,
brutality شراسة – /وحشية/ بروتليتي/
lettuce / ليتص / الخص , superb/سوبيرب / فاخر - فخم-راقي .

٢-   في حالة عدم وجود "e" تنطق "u" / أ / مثل : " مَ – تَ- دَ" :

bus /باس/, us , up , cup /كب/فنجان ,كأس , must/ماست/ يجب ,
rust /راست/ صدأ , cut /يقطع , study كوخ, hut كوخ, يدرس,
hurry/هاري/ يسرع , hunt يصطاد , minimum الحد الأدنى,
maximum الحد الأعلى , insult إهانة-يهين, gum اللثة-الصمغ ,
difficult/ صعب/ديفي كلت , consult يستشير, referendum استفتاء,
result/النتيجة, impulse نزوة-دافع, pulse نبض , bud برعم ,
budget ميزانية / بدجت / , duck بطة , luck حظ , sun الشمس ,
lucky /محظوظ/ لاكي / , fun مرح-لهو , gun سلاح ناري , nun راهبة ,
sum up يلخص -يوجز , gum اللثة - الصمغ sum up , حاصل الجمع- المبلغ
lull فترة هدوء – أغنية بقصد تنويم الطفل – ينوم .

٢٦

* put , pull , push , lubricate , luxury , ludicrous مثير للضحك
* lucid / لوسد / واضح .

٣- ur ←تنطق مثل /hare, mare/

curve منحنى, turn يستدير - يلف , burn /بيرن/يحرق-يحترق,
hurt يؤذي, urge حافز-باعث-يحث, urgent عاجل , surplus فائض- إضافي/ سيربلاس /, church كنيسة / تشيرتش / , burden عبئ , suburb ضاحية

** شواذ hurry / هري / سرعة- يسرع , curry وجبة ذات طعم حار

٤- تنطق au مثل / وَ / في هذه الكلمات :

language وج لانق / لغة , quality /كواليتي/ جودة / نوعية ,
persuade / بيرسويد / يُقْنِع , quantity كمية, qualify يتأهل-يؤهل, quarrel يتشاجر - شجار
- يختلف مع – مشادة كلامية .

* He quarrelled with Ali over the quality of bread.

اختلف مع علي حول جودة الخبز .

* I persuade you to learn this language.
* We care about quality and quantity. إننا نهتم بالكم والكيف.

٥- ui / ue تنطق " وي " كما في :

fluent فلي ونت / طلق اللسان , queen / كوين / ملكة ,
liquid / لك ويد / سائل , fluid سائل مائع / كويك / quick , سريع , suicide/ سوي سايد/
, انتحار, commit a suicide يرتكب عملية انتحارية

٢٧

هادئ – هدوء quiet , اختبر quizzed اختبر – لغز – اختبار- يختبر/ كويز/ quiz,
quit يترك – يرحل عن , question , equipment معدات ,
quench يخمد quell , يطفئ(لهب- عطش) ,
quest (for) البحث عن – يبحث عن , question / كويس شن / سؤال - مسألة

* quay / كي / رصيف في الميناء .

٦- تنطق "u" مثل / o / في "do"

glue / قلو / الصمغ , blue / بلو / أزرق , flu أنفلونزا ,
truce /تروس/ هدنة , brute /بروت/ وحش , brutal/بروتل/ وحشي ,
flute مزمار

٧- تنطق "sure" / جر / كما يلي :

pleasure / بلي جر / treasure كنـز , measure يقيس , closure لذة - متعة - السعادة - السرور
/كلوجر/ إغلاق.
seizure / سيجر / الحجز على-نوبة قلبية , pressure* /بريشر/ ضغط

٨- تنطق "ture" / تشار / كما في :

nature / ني تشا / الطبيعة , future / فيوتشا / المستقبل ,
fracture (اسم) كسر , lecture / لك تشا / يحاضر - محاضرة ,
picture صورة , mature / ماتشا(ر) / ناضج .

* **Read the sentences :**

* We must learn many languages . يجب أن نتعلم لغات كثيرة.
* The queen can speak this language ; she is fluent .

٢٨

* The queen was amused when she got the crown .

كانت الملكة فرحة عندما تلقت التاج.

* I want to express my ideas freely . أريد أن اعبر عن أفكاري بحرية.

* The queen will guarantee freedom of speech .

إن الملكة سوف تكفل حرية الكلام.

* He will lecture on the nature of pleasure .

سوف يحاضر عن طبيعة اللذة.

* أحد عشر: تنطق "tion" و "ssion" / شن / شن /

كما في الكلمات التالية:

station / ستيشن / مركز - محطة , علاقة relation

information معلومات / عاطفة-انفعال , emotion / إموشن

diction / دك شن / المفردات , dictionary القاموس

mission / ميشن / بعثة - مهمة , transmission البث

expression التعبير discussion / دس كشن / مناقشة, fission الانشطار

recession ركود / admission / اد ميشن / الاعتراف -قبول- إدخال ,

confession الاعتراف / passion / با شن / عاطفة.

* cushion / كاشن / وسادة , fashion / فاشن / موضة

martial / مارشال / عسكري martial law قانون الأحكام العرفية ,

court- martial محكمة عسكرية .

● تنطق sion / جن / كما في الكلمات التالية:

vision الرؤية , revision المراجعة , division القسم - القسمة ,

fusion الاندماج , cohesion / كوهيجن / تماسك .

إلا أنه في هذه الكلمات تنطق sion /شن/ :

dimension البعد-حجم, tension توتر , comprehension فهم ,
apprehension خوف-قلق-استيعاب-إلقاء القبض على.

اثنا عشر :١

- يتم نطق ال s مثل / س / في الكلمات التالية :

send / سند / يرسل , seat مقعد , sit يجلس , sin إثم , sinful إثم
same نفس الشيء , sell يبيع , so , speaks , save يدّخر-يوفر-ينقذ ,
west / وست / الغرب , waist الخصر waste يبدد - يسرف في , rest راحة mist ضباب , list
قائمة fist قبض , ransom / ران سام / فدية ,
breast/ برست / الصدر- النهد-الثدي ,
beast / بيست / وحش إنسان- حيوان ,
sack يطرد من العمل – (مدينة) ينهب – كيس ,
ransack يفتش مكاناً بطريقة همجية – ينهب مدينة

٢- تنطق s مثل / z / في "زيت" :

rise / رايز / يشرق - يرتفع , rose ارتفع - وردة , wise عاقل , dose جرعة hose, nose أنف ,
noise ضوضاء , names , legs ,
pose / بوز / يخلق -لصورة وقفة يقف -وقفة- (مشكلة) يثير ,
problems / لمز بروب / مشاكل , use يستخدم, refuse يرفض.

ثلاثة عشر: تنطق "w" مثل / وَ / في وكيل :

win / ون / يفوز , wine / واين / الخمر , well بخير , will , wife , ,
won فاز , winter الشتاء, wolf ذئب, want يريد ,
week أسبوع weak ضعيف , wing جناح , wink غمزة-يغمز , wind ريح.

**** لا تنطق w في هذه الكلمات :-

write يكتب , who من - الذي , whom , whose ,

, يصارع / ريسل / wrestle , ينتزع قسراً من wrest from

, يحطم سفينة -- حطام سفينة wreck , إنسان تعيس wretch

, التجاعيد wrinkles , العصارة (الغسالة) wringer , يعصر -يلوي wring

. رسغ اليد /رست/ wrist

تنطق "w" و لا تنطق "h" في هذه الكلمات :

, عندما - متى when , ماذا - ما / وات / what

, لماذا why , بينما while , ابيض / وايت / white

, يسن (سكيناً) whet(, القمح wheat , أين- حيث where

, يضرب بالكرباج- سوط - كرباج whip, الحوت /wail / whale

whipped ضرب بالكرباج , whetted سن ,

wherewithal / وي وذَ ل / الوسيلة الضرورية , whirl- pool دوامة ,

whirl-wind إعصار , whisper همسة-يهمس .

- **Read these sentences:**
- I want to paint the door white.
- Where are you going ?
- When is Ali leaving ?   متى سيغادر علي؟
- He whetted the knife on the stone.   سن السكين على الحجر .
- They whipped the man because he lied to them .

ضربوا الرجل بالكرباج لأنه كذب عليهم.

- I don't have the wherewithal to buy a car.

لا أملك الوسيلة اللازمة لشراء سيارة.

* أربعة عشر: x تنطق /أكس/ كما في الكلمات التالية:

box صندوق / fox فوكس / ثعلب , fax , tax ضريبة ,
fix يصلّح-يثبّت , يركّب , mix يختلط-يخلط , wax واكس / الشمع maximum الحد
. يزيد من maximize, الأعلى/ماكسيمم/

* خمسة عشر:

● ١- تنطق y مثل / يا / كما في هذه الكلمات:

yet يت / مع ذلك و - بعد , yes يس / نعم ,
yard يارد / الباردة , yellow اصفر you / يو / انت ,
young / يانق / شاب -صغير السن youth / يوث / الشباب , yolk/يوك/صفار البيض,
. يوك/ النير , year سنة, yield/ييلد/ يثمر-يستسلم

● ٢- تنطق y مثل / e / في me :
slowly / سلولي / بطيء , happy سعيد , angry غاضب ,
easy سهل , lazy كسول icy شديد البرد-قارس , greedy طماع , needyمحتاج , hungry , speedy ,
windy , rainy.

٣- تنطق y مثل "i" في ice_ :

my اماي/ لي , try اتراي/ يحاول , cry ييكي , defy يتحدى ,
sky السماء , fly يطير-يسافر جوا , deny ينكر , rely on يعتمد على. , dry -يجفف جاف-
. يجف

ملاحظة مفيدة : تهمل "y" و ننطق "أيه" في هذه الكلمات :
pay يدفع , say يقول , may , day , play .

أما في حالة عدم وجود "a" قبل "y" فإننا ننطق "y" مثل "i" :

by / باي / بواسطة , my , sky السماء , why لماذا , try يحاول , cry يبكي

ملاحظة : "uy" لا ننطق "u" و ننطق "y" مثل "i"

buy / باي / يشتري , guy / قاي / شاب .

* ستة عشر: ننطق z / زَ / كما في الكلمات التالية:

zero / زيرو / الصفر , zeal حماس , freeze يتجمد , breeze النسيم ,

haze الضباب , hazy به ضباب , raze يزيل , craze جنون , crazy مجنون ,

maze متاهة- ورطة , plaza ميدان- سوق , maize ذرة ,

seize / سيز / مسك - يقبض على - يحجز على ,

realize / ريا لايز / يدرك - يحقق (هدفاً) ,

recognize / ريكوق نايز / يعترف ب - يتعرف على .

* سبعة عشر:١- ow تنطق /آو /aw/ مثل الكلمات التالية:

crown التاج, brown بني, drown يغرق, down أسفل,

clown . , bow مقدمة السفينة-ينحني , cow بقرة , now الآن

٢- يتم نطق o مع عدم نطقw في الكلمات التالية:

grow يزرع, flow يعرف/نو/, know يتدفق-تدفق/فلو/,

low منخفض , slow بطيء, swallow يبلع, throw يرمي,

blow ضربة-يضرب-يهبglow يتوهج, low منخفض, yellow أصفر,

window نافذة, follow يطارد-يتبع, borrow يستعير يستلف-يستعير.

٣٣

ثمانية عشر: لاحظ طريقة نطق الكلمات التالية :

know نو / no / يعرف , knowledge نالدج / المعرفة ,

kneel نيل / يركع - يسجد , knot عقدة / نوت / ,

knock نوك/ يُخَبِّط , knit يطرز enthusiasm /إنذيوزيازم/ حماس

region ريجن / إقليم / religion / ريلجن / ديانة ,

imagine اماجن / يتخيل /castle كاسل/ قلعة ,

whistle ويسل / يصفر صفارة citadel سيتادل / قلعة ,

muscle ماسل / عضلة blood بلاد / الدم , flood فيضان ,

fruit فروت / ثمار - فاكهة juice جوس / عصير

* boatswain رئيس البحارة بوسن / بريك break / brake استراحة - يكسر

* vague فيق/ غامض

* bowels باؤيلز / أحشاء - أمعاء

* bowl / ball بول / وعاء ,

* mourning مورننق / حداد , morning الصباح .

* busy / bezy بيزي / مشغول , business /بزنس / عمل - شغل

prejudice /بريجيدس/ تحامل , * new نيو / /

جديد , few قليل , dew الندى ,

*pull بُل/يجر-يسحب , put يضع , push يدفع ,

* rush /رش/ يندفع-يسرع bush شجيرة ,

brush فرشاة ينظف بالفرشاة يفرش-فرشاة. crush يسحق

*debris /دي بري/ حطام- أنقاض , * debt دَيْن

/دت/ , owe /o/ لـ يدين.

* He is in debt. إن عليه دين.

* She is out of debt ليس عليها دين.

*I owe you 100 riyals. إني مدين لك بـ ١٠٠ ريال

* I owe this job to you. إني مدين بهذه الوظيفة لك.

٣٤

*ewe /يو/ نعجة , eulogy /يولجي/ ثناء-مديح ,

eunuch* /يونك/ مخصي , victual / فيتال / يزود بالتموين

indict * /إندايت/ يتهم , indictment / منت اندايت / إتهام ,

soldier /سولجَ/ جندي .

lieutenant*/نانت /لفتي الجيش في ضابط-وكيل

colonel /carenel* اكِرنل/ الجيش في ضابط

individual*/جول في/ فردي-فرد , dual /ديول/ ثنائي ,

procedure * / بروسيجر / سير-إجراءات

excuse*/يوز /إكسك عذر-يعذر , expect /بكت إكس/ يتوقع

exchange*/تشينج إكس/ تبادل-يتبادل , exercise تمرين,

explain يوضح-يفسر ,

except*/إكسبت /باستثناء , exception /إكسبشن/ استثناء ,

exempt from*/إقزمبت /من معفى-من يعفي ,

exert*/إقزيرت/ يبذل , exact مضبوط,

exaggerate*/إقزاجيريت /في يبالغ . exam /إقزام/ امتحان , example قدوة-مثال*

issue / إشيو - إسيو / يصدر -صدور- إصدار-قضية *

marijuana / وانا ماري / مخدّر عقار *

** Read these sentences:-

1- The food prices are going down, so we are happy
about that.

إن أسعار الأغذية آخذة في الهبوط ولهذا فإننا سعداء بذلك.

2- A storm blew strongly and the boat turned over.
Five people drowned .
A rescue team tried to save them, but they failed.

هبت عاصفة قوية وانقلب القارب. وغرق خمسة أشخاص. وحاول فريق إنقاذ أن ينقذهم ولكنه فشل.

3- If you read a lot, you will increase your knowledge.

إذا قرأت كثيراً فإنك سوف تزيد من معرفتك.

4- It is important to check your blood pressure from time
    to time.

من المهم أن تتأكد من ضغط دمك من وقت لآخر.

5- It is unfair to have any prejudice against members of other classes.

ليس من العدل أن يكون لدينا تحيز ضد أعضاء الطبقات الأخرى .

6- He had to leave the school, to the prejudice of his future.

اضطر لأن يترك المدرسة مما يلحق الضرر بمستقبله.

7- Women are asking for more freedom without
    prejudice to men.

النساء يطالبن بمزيد من الحرية دون ضرر يلحق بالرجال.

8- Your way of thinking prejudices me in your favour.

إن طريقة تفكيرك تجعلني أنحاز إليك.

*****

Why we learn a language.

لماذا نتعلم اللغة ؟

يتعلم الإنسان اللغة لكي يتفاهم مع غيره من الناس : فاللغة هي وسيلة التفاهم والاتصال بـين الناس . فما هو المقصود بالتفاهم ؟ أن لدى الإنسان أفكاراً ومشاعر يريد أن يوصلها إلى الغير , فلا بد له من وسيلة تمكّنه من توصيل هذه الأفكار والمشاعر إلى غيره . و الوسيلة القـادرة عـلى ذلـك هـي اللغـة , وكلما كانت الوسيلة جيدة كان التفاهم جيداً , و مـن هنـا بـات مـن الضـروري أن نتعلم اللغـة حسـب الأصول.

People learn a language to communicate with others ; language is a means of conveying one's ideas and feelings to others. If one uses sound language , communication becomes effective. This makes it necessary for us to learn the language well.

كيف نتعلم اللغة؟
How to learn a language

يبدأ الإنسان بسماع اللغة listen على شكل أصوات لها معنى وهذه الأصوات تفرض استجابة response من المستمع الذي يقوم بالكلام speak و شيئا فشيئا , يبدأ الإنسان بتكوين كلمات يرددها عند الحاجة ثم يتدّرب عن طريق الأسرة على كيفية تكوين جملة مفيدة, ثم ينتقـل الطفـل إلى المدرسـة حيث يبدأ في تعلم اللغة حسب الأصول . و في المدرسة يتعلّم الحروف و أصواتها و كيفية نطقها و يتعلم كيفية القراءة , و هذه المهارة تستغرق كثيراً من الوقت لأن مهارة القراءة هي مفتاح تعلم مهارات اللغـة الأخرى : الكتابة و المحادثة .

One starts learning any language by listening to people ,which prompts him(her) to respond by uttering meaningful words. The family environment helps the child develop his (her) language to such an extent that he becomes able to form meaningful sentences.

At a later stage, the child is sent to school , where he is taught the alphabets and how to read . This reading skill takes much time to develop , and if this skill is well learnt, it will pave the way for learning other language skills , namely speaking and writing.

It is true that one can acquire the speaking skill before the reading one, but both skills are integrated in the sense that any improvement in a skill   affects positively the other , giving the learner confidence ,which can speed up his language development.

How to command language
كـيـف نـتـقـن اللــغـة ؟

إن حلم الإنسان أن يتقن اللغة لأن ذلك يؤهله لأن يكون قادراً على التفاهم السليم مـع الغـير ، و حتـى يتحقق الحلم لا بد من الاستعداد لبذل الجهد و ممارسة اللغة التي يتم تعلمها أولا بأول ، وهنـاك أربـع مهارات وهي الاستماع listening و الحـديث speaking و القـراءة reading و الكتابـة writing . و نحن العرب نريد أن نتعلم الإنجليزية و لكن من أين نبدأ ؟ هنـاك وجهـات نظـر وأسـاليب متعـددة , و إنني من واقع التجربة وجدت أن أفضل بداية تكمن في تعلـم أصوات ا لحـروف لأن الحـرف الواحـد في الإنجليزية له أكثر من صوت واحد , و هذا يسبب ارتباكا عند المبتدئين .

إن معرفة أصوات الحرف الواحد يجعل المتعلم قادراً على نطق الكلمة بشكل سـليم . إن النطـق السـليم يساعدك على امتلاك كم كبير من المفردات التي تمكنك مـن أن تطـور لغتـك باسـتمرار . إلا أن المفردات وحدها لا تكفي إذ لا بد من   معرفة أساسيات قواعد اللغة ... أي نتعلم كيف نكوّن جملاً مفيـدة مـن هذه المفردات . و نحن نعلم أن عند الإنسان أفكاراً يريد أن ينقلها إلى غـيره , فـلا بـد لـه مـن أن يصـب هذه الأفكار في قوالب لغوية متعارف عليها عند أهل اللغة , فالإنسان لا يبتكر تراكيب لغوية بل يجـدها في الحياة وعليه أن يتعلمها حتى يستخدمها في نقل أفكاره إلى الغـير   . وهـذا يقودنا إلى كيفيـة تكـوين الجملةالإنجليزية.

It is highly important to pronounce words well because this will help the process of word retention a lot. Learners must also know how to use a word in a sentence. We provide the learner with some sentence patterns that he can imitate whenever he (she) is willing to convey an idea or opinion to others . Once the learner acquires and masters these sentence patterns, he becomes able to practise the different language skills with the minimum of errors. When the learner realizes that he has achieved something, he acquires a sense of self-confidence , which makes language learning a pleasurable experience.

The Simple English Sentence
الجملة الإنجليزية البسيطة

نحتاج إلى عدة أشياء لبناء الجملة .

To make an English sentence, we need some key constituents , namely parts of speech
.

علينا معرفة مكونات الجملة وهي ما تسمى بأجزاء الكلام.

1- The noun or pronoun : الاسم أو الضمير

Ali , Huda , book , tea , food , school , oil , English , Amman , tree شجرة , sand رمـل ,
beach شـاطئ , tourismالسياحة, lake بحيرة , health الصحة , freedom الحرية , life الحياة ,
moneyمال, death الموت , smoking التدخين , speed السرعة , diseaseمرض,reading القراءة
, pollutionالتلوث,educationالتعليم,travelالسفر.

هذه أسماء و هناك ضمائر و الضمائر مثل الأسماء تماما :

Ali = he, (she - her هي) , (he - him هو) , (you أنت- أنتما - انتم you) , (I - me أنا)
Mona = she , (it = book , car) (we - us نحن), (they - them هم), boys -cars = they,
that ذلك .

2- The adjective : الصفة تصف الاسم

good طيب - جيد , bad سيئ , mad مجنون , sad حزين ,
glad فرحان , happy سعيد , ill مريض , well بخير , nice لطيف ,
polite مؤدب , tall طويل , short قصير , fat سمين ,
angry غضبان , hungry جوعان , late متأخر , busy مشغول ,
free حر- فاضي , hot حار , cold بارد , lazy كسول ,

friendly ودود , careful منتبه , careless مهمل , tidy منظم ,
مصيب - على حق right وسخ, dirty غير منظم, untidy
wrong غلطان , important مهم , useful مفيد ,
necessary ضروري , dangerous خطير , easy سهل ,
difficult صعب , new جديد , old - كبير في السن - قديم ,
young شاب , fresh طازج , harmful ضار , harmless غير ضار , comfortable مريح ,
interesting مشوق-ممتع , interested مهتم ,
holy مقدس , possible ممكن /بوسي بول/ ,
impossible/امبوسيبول / مستحيل , hard صعب . - متشدد-صلب ,
flexible/فلكسي بول/ مرن , boring ممل ,
disappointing/دس أبويتنق / مخيب للآمال , legal شرعي- قانوني /لي قال/ illegal غير / ال لي قال/
shameful مخزي - مخجل . قانوني ,

3- The verb الفعل وله أربعة أشكال :

eat يأكل , drink يشرب , learn يتعلم , speak يتكلم , read يقرأ , write يكتب , visit يزور ,
sit يجلس , save يدخر - ينقذ , waste يبذد - يبدد , help يساعد , feed يغذي , use يستخدم , give يعطي , take يأخذ , make يصنع , drive يسوق , ride يقود , kill يقتل , fill يملئ ,
misuse يسيء استخدام , need يحتاج , spoil يفسد , destroy يدمر ,
benefit from يستفيد من , suffer from يعاني من , lose يخسر, improve يُحسّن- يتحسن ,
change يغيره-يتغير , spoil يُفسد , deny ينكر , ignore يتجاهل , fight يقاتل- يناضل - يحارب ,
fight for يناضل من أجل solve يحل , mix with يختلط مع , reduce يقلل من , accept يقبل
promote يروج لـ , cause يسبب

4- The Adverb الظرف :

A- The Adverb of Place ظرف المكان :

in the car في السيارة , at school في المدرسة , next to بجوار ,
on the wall على الحائط , under the tree تحت الشجرة , behindخلف
in front of the bank أمام البنك , at the top of .... في قمة ,
at the bottom of ... في قاع , across the sea عبر البحر ,
between London and Amman بين لندن وعمان .

B- The Adverb of Time ظرف الزمان :

at six o'clock في الساعة , in the morning في الصباح , in the afternoon
عصرا , in the evening في المساء , at noon ظهراً , at dawn فجراً ,
at night ليلا , at sun-rise عند شروق الشمس ,
at sun-set عند غروب الشمس , at lunch-time في وقت الغداء ,
on Monday في يوم الاثنين , in April في شهر أبريل , in 1998 ,
now الآن yesterday أمس , tomorrow غداً , next Friday يوم
الجمعة القادم , in the year 1980 .

C- The Adverb of Manner ظرف الحال :

slowly ببطيء , carefully بحذر , sadly بحزن , happily بسعادة
angrily بغضب , fast بسرعة , well بشكل جيد ,
luckily لحسن الحظ , madly بطريقة جنونية , easily بسهولة , early مبكراً
badly بشكل سيئ , late متأخراً , sharply بشكل حاد , sharply بحدة .

دعنا نؤجل الحديث عن الظرف بأنواعه إلى مرحلة لاحقة و دعنا نركز على كيفية استخدام الاسم و الصفة و الفعل في تكوين الجملة .

In English , there are two major types of sentence:

يوجد في اللغة الإنجليزية نموذجان للجملة أو شكلان هما :

1- Noun اسم ⟶ Verb فعل ⟶ Adjective صفة

I	am	nice .
Ali (he)	is	nice .
Mona (she)	is	nice .
The car (it)	is	nice .
You	are	nice
We	are	nice . نحن ظرفاء.
They	are	nice. إنهم ظرفاء.

نلاحظ أن بداية الجملة اسم ثم فعل ينسجم معه ثم صفة لهذا الاسم والصفة تصلح للمفرد والجمع والمثنى والمذكر والمؤنث.

* تأمل هذه الجمل :

I am **a student**.   Ali is **a student**.   We are **students**.

* The word " student " is a noun acting as a complement.

نلاحظ أن الاسم student جاء في موقع صفة للفاعل.
وإذا أردنا أن نتحدث عن اسم فلا بد من وضع الفعل المناسب ثم نختار صفة مناسبة .

وحتى نتقن هذا الشكل من الجمل علينا أن نستبدل الصفة بصفة أخرى بدلا من nice . نجد أنه يمكننا أن نكوّن على الأقل ٧ جمل باستخدام الصفة الواحدة , ويجب في بداية التدريب أن نبقي على الاسم و الفعل دون تغيير بل نغير الصفة فقط.

حاول أن تقرأ الجملة وأن تفهم معناها و مع التكرار ستجد أنك اتقنت التراكيب و حاول أن تستخدم صفة جديدة لتكون جملاً غياً وهذا يعطينا ثقة بالنفس لأنه أصبح لدينا إحساس بأننا حققنا شيئاً الأمر الذي يزيل حاجز الرهبة و الخوف و يزرع بدلا منه الإحساس بالقدرة على الإنجاز .

أما النموذج - الشكل الثاني للجملة فهو :

Noun(object)اسم (مفعول به)	Verb فعل	اسم (فاعل) -2 Noun (subject)
food a lot.	need	We
food a lot	use	We
the mobile phone	misuse	We
trees.	benefit from	We
pollution.	suffer from	We
pollution.	don't need	We
freedom. نحارب من اجل	should fight for	We
smoking.	should fight	We

* **We should know that a verb has four forms.**
  Let us start with the first verb-form.

*يجب أن نلاحظ أن الفعل له أربعة أشكال . دعنا نستخدم الشكل الأول للفعل .

* I   visit   Ali.   إني أزور علياً .
* Ali (he) **visits** me .   إن علياً يزورني .
* Mona (she) **visits** Noura.
* I   **don't visit** Nasser.   إني لا أزور ناصراً .
* Ali **doesn't visit** me.
* I (He- She) **will visit** you .   إني (إنه -إنها) سوف أزورك.

٤٣

* I (He –She) **can visit** you.	إني أستطيع أن أزورك .
* I (He- She) **can't visit** you .	إني لا أستطيع أن أزورك.
* You (He- She) **could visit** Ali .	بإمكانك أن تزور علياً.
* We **must visit** Ali.	يجب أن نزور علياً.
* You **should visit** Ali .	يجب عليكم أن تزوروا علياً.
* I **want to visit** Ali .	أريد أن أزور علياً.
* I **want you to visit** Ali.	أريدك أن تزور عليا.

نلاحظ أننا استخدمنا الفعل visit أولاً بمفرده ثم مع أفعال مساعده لكي تعطي أفكاراً عديدة.

* Try to make similar sentences replacing a verb with another. You will find that you have produced a variety of sentences that express different ideas. The more sentences you produce , the better you master the sentence structures.

● حاول أن تصنع جملاً مماثلة باستبدال الفعل visit بفعل أخر . كرر العملية مع أفعال أخرى وستجد أنك أصبحت قادراً على أن تصنع جملاً تعبر عن أفكارك . وأحب أن أسمي الأفعال المساعدة مثل should -must -can – will بالمقويات إذ أنها تكون بمثابة مقوٍ له.

* I learn English .

* Ali learns French .

* You don't learn French .

* She doesn't learn English .

* He will learn English .

* She can learn English ; it is easy .

* She can't learn French ; it is too difficult .

* We must learn English ; it is important

* We should learn English ; it is necessary.

* I want to learn Arabic ; it is necessary .

تأمل كل جملة و ستجد أن كل واحدة تعبر عن فكرة , و نلاحظ أن الفعل له دور محوري في تكوين الجملة و نلاحظ قيمة المقويات الخاصة بالفعل مثل will , can , must ...

ننصح دائماً بقراءة الجملة بصوت عـال و فهم المعنى و ضرورة إتقـان شكل   الجملـة والتدريب على تكوين جمل مماثلة بإتباع الطريقة السابقة .

حاول أن تكوّن مزيداً من الجمل باستخدام فعل جديد في كل مـرة و ستجد مـدى التحسـن الذي حدث و هذا يشجع على مواصلة الممارسة .   مع التكرار ستجد انك قد حفظت هذه الجمـل ... و القوالب غيبا بحيث إذا رغبت مستقبلا أن توصل فكرة أن تصب هذه الفكرة في قالب مـن هـذه القوالب . يجب أن نعلم بأن الفعل الواحد له أربعة أشكال أو صيغ و كل شـكل لـه وظيفـة معينـة .. وفي الأمثلة السابقة , استخدمنا الشكل الأول للفعل وحصلنا على كم كبير من الجمل المفيدة   لاحظنـا كيـف تـم اسـتخدام الشكل الأول للفعل و كيف تـم تقويـة الفعل بمقويات بسـيطة. و مكننا الآن أن ننتقل إلى اسـتخدام مقويات أخرى للفعل في الشكل الأول وهذه المقويات مفيدة جدا و تفيدنا في الكتابة والمحادثة على حـد سواء

The following is another way of using the first form of   " visit" with other auxiliary verbs to express new ideas.

* **I asked** Ali to visit me .   أنا طلبت من علي أن يزورني.
* He agreed to visit me .   إنه وافق على أن يزورني.
* He promised to visit me .   إنه وعد بان يزورني.
* He refused to visit me .   إنه رفض أن يزورني.
* **I advise you to** visit Ali .   إني أنصحك بان تزور علياً.
* I advise you not to visit this man.

إني أنصحك بأن لا تزور هذا الرجل .
* I intend to visit Ali .   إني أنوي أن أزور علياً.

يمكنك أن تركّب جملاً مماثلة و ذلك باستخدام فعل غيره وسوف تحصل على نفس شكل الجمل و لكن هذه الجمل تعطي معاني مختلفة.. الشكل واحد والمعنى مختلف تماما مثل الكأس .... تستطيع أن تصب فيه ماءً أو شاياً أو حليباً أو قهوة .

We can use adjectives to enhance the verb

يمكننا أن نستخدم صفات لتقوية الفعل بهدف الترغيب فيه كما يلي.

* **It is important to** visit Ali .   من المهم أن تزور علياً .
* **It is necessary to** visit Ali .   من الضروري أن تزور علياً .
* **It is useful to** visit Ali .   من المفيد أن تزور علياً .
* **It is nice to** visit Ali .   من الجميل أن تزور عليا.
* **It is good to** visit Ali .   من الخير أن تزور علياً .
* **It is right to** visit Ali .   من الصواب أن تزور عليا .
* **It is fair to** visit Ali .   من العدل أن تزور علياً.
* **It is easy to** visit Ali .   من السهل أن تزور علياً.
* **It is possible to** do that.   من الممكن أن تفعل ذلك.

أما المقويات التالية فهي للتنفير من الفعل:

* **It is unfair to** visit this man .   ليس من العدل أن تزور هذا الرجل.
* **It is wrong to** visit Ali .   من الخطأ أن تزور علياً.
* **It is mad to** visit Ali .   من الجنون أن تزور علياً .
* **It is bad to** visit Ali .   من السوء أن تزور عليا.
* **It is dangerous to** visit Ali .   من الخطر أن تزور علياً.
* **It is difficult to** visit Ali .   من الصعب أن تزور عليا.
* **It is impossible to** do that.   من المستحيل أن تفعل ذلك.
* **It is shameful to** do that.   من العيب أن تفعل ذلك.

* نجد أننا استخدمنا الصفات مقويات للفعل و حصلنا على جمل تؤدي معاني قوية وهذا يفيدنا في الكتابة والمحادثة . حاول أن تستخدم نفس التراكيب مع تغيير الفعل . المهم أن تتدرب بنفسك وستجد أن لغتك بدأت تتطور . كل ما

عليك هو إتباع التراكيب السابقة ومع التكرار يمكنك أن تستخدمها مستقبلاً بطريقة تلقائية.

Try to make similar sentences replacing a verb with another . It is through practice that you can improve your English , and you will be able to use this language easily.

Here is another way of enhancing the verb.
هناك طريق أخرى لتقوية الفعل:

* If you visit Ali , you will benefit a lot .

إن تزر علياً فانك سوف تستفيد كثيراً.

* If you visit Ali , you will learn good things.

* If you don't visit Ali , you will suffer a lot .
إذا لم تزر عليا فانك سوف تعاني كثيراً.

* If you don't visit Ali , you will **lose** a lot . تخسر
* If you see this bad film, you will learn bad things.

* حاول أن تستخدم فعلاً غير   visit , وسوف تحصل على جمل قوية في الشكل والمعنى
نلاحظ مما سبق أننا استطعنا أن نركب جملاً عديدة باستخدام الشكل الأول للفعل ولا بـد مـن إتقـان هـذه التراكيب جيداً لأن هذه التراكيب تشبه الوعاء الذي نصبُّ فيه أفكارنا التي نريد أن ننقلها إلى الغير .
وسنعود إلى مزيد من التمارين على الشكل الأول للفعل فيما بعد .

قلنا أن هناك نموذجان للجملة في الإنجليزية.

1- Ali is nice .

2- I like Ali.

* I can visit you .

* I want to buy a car .
و يمكننا أن نجمع بين النموذجين.

* I like Ali . He is nice .

  I like Ali **because** he is nice .   لأن

* I am free . I can visit you .

* I am free , **so** I can visit you .   و لهذا

* I can't visit you . I am too busy.   إني مشغول جداً.

* I can't visit you **because** I am too busy.

* I am too busy , **so** I can't visit you .

إن هناك أفكارا متصلة ببعضها و هذا يفرض علينا أن نجمع بين جملتين أو أكثر و هناك كلمات تربط
بين الجمل مثل because أو so أو if (إذا - أن) .

* I must stay at home **because** I am ill .

* I must stay at home because I feel ill .

* I should visit Ali because he is ill .

* I should visit Ali because I want to tell him something.

* You can learn English because it is easy .

* I need English a lot , **so** I should learn it .

* **If** you learn English , you will benefit a lot .

* **If** you don't learn English , you will suffer a lot.

نجد اتحاداً بين جملتين و الاتحاد أصبح ممكناً بفضل أدوات الربط. ادرس هذه الجمل وحاول أن تعمل
جملاً مماثلة و تأمل المعنى دائماً.

* عندما تواجه كلمة يجب أن تعرف هل هذه الكلمة اسم أو صفة أو فعل لأن هذه المعرفة تكفل لك
استخدام الكلمة في جملة سليمة و إذا راجعنا نموذجي الجملة فسوف نجد موقع الاسم و الفعل و
الصفة في الجملة .

قلنا أن للفعل ٤ أشكال . و لقد قمنا باستخدام الشكل الأول في تكوين جمل عديدة علينا تقليدها . و
الآن علينا أن ننتقل إلى الشكل الثاني للفعل .

The Second Verb-form الشكل الثاني للفعل

This form is used to show things that happened in the past.

نستخدم هذا الشكل عندما نتحدث عن شيء حدث في الماضي .

* I **visited** Ali **yesterday** .   إني زرت عليا يوم أمس.
* I didn't visit Hani last night .   إني لم أزر هاني ليلة البارحة.
* Ali **went** to the bookshop yesterday .

ذهب علي إلى المكتبة يوم أمس .

* Mona didn't go to the party yesterday .

لم تذهب منى إلى الحفلة يوم أمس .

* Did Ali visit you yesterday ?   هل زارك علي أمس؟
* When did you visit Ali ?
* I was late yesterday.
* They were at home an hour ago.   * كانوا في البيت قبل ساعة
* Where was Ali an hour ago ?   أين كان علي قبل ساعة ؟

ملاحظة : بعد أداة النفي didn'tومعناها "لم" يجب أن يكون الفعل في الشكل الأول.
نستخدم did عندما نريد عمل سؤال عن شيء حدث في الماضي ويأتي الفعل في الشكل الأول كما في المثال السابق .
* حاول أن تستخدم أفعالاً أخرى متبعا" نفس النموذج السابق .
* وسنعود إلى الشكل الثاني للفعل بمزيد من التمارين فيما بعد.

٤٩

The Third Verb- Form الشكل الثالث للفعل

تأمل هذه الأمثلة :

*   I have visited Ali twice since last Friday .

لقد زرت علياً مرتين منذ يوم الجمعة الماضية .

*   He has given me some information.

لقد أعطاني بعض المعلومات .

* <u>ملاحظة</u> : نلاحظ بأننا استخدمنا have أو has كمقوٍّ للفعل في الشكل الثالث وهذا أمر لا بد منه .
و يجب أن نلاحظ بان الشكل الثالث مع have أو has يعبر عن نوع من الماضي   و لكن الحدث
له آثار لا تزال باقية حتى الآن .

*   I have built a villa at this area.

لقد بنيت فيلا في هذه ا لمنطقة . البناء تم في الماضي و لكنه لا يزال قائما.

*   She has written a letter to Mona .
* Ali has phoned twice since the morning .
* It has not rained for years.   الدنيا لم تمطر منذ سنوات.
* I have not seen Ali yet.   أني لم أرى علياً بعد.

* <u>ملاحظة</u> : نستخدم has في حالة وجود :
Ali (he) , Mona (she) , It (the car - the book)

أما have مع باقي الأسماء و الضمائر مثل I , you , we , they
* ننصح بتكوين جمل مماثلة باستخدام أفعال أخرى في الشكل الثالث.
و نستخدم أيضا الشكل الثالث للفعل مع had و في هذا الحالة نعبر عن شيء حدث في زمن الماضي
البعيد . و لكي يكون هذا واضحاً لا بد من استخدام فعل ثان يعبر عن الماضي .

*Examples :

● Ali **told** me that he **had sold** his car .

أخبرني علي بأنه قد باع سيارته . هناك حـدثان .. فعـلان .. و هـما "أخبر" و "باع" و كلاهـما حـدثا في الماضي .. و لكنهما لم يحدثا معاً في نفس الوقت .. بل أن أحدها "باع" حدث قبل "أخبر" . نلاحظ أن فعلاً في الشكل الثاني وأخر في الشكل الثالث يجتمعان معاً لتكوين جملـة مركبـة تعبــر عـن حدثين وقعا في الماضي.

● Mona **told** Huda that she **had phoned** Noura .

Ali **said** that he **had invited** everybody to the party .

******

The Third Verb-form and the Passive :

الشكل الثالث للفعل والمبني للمجهول :

يستخدم الشكل الثالث للفعل في تكوين جمل في صيغة المبني للمجهول في وجود أحد أشكال فعـل be و هي :

(be) → 1-   am , is , are   2- was , were   3- been
         4- being

The passive form is characterized by three basic things.

1-   The object is placed at the beginning of the sentence.

يتم وضع المفعول به في بداية الجملة .

2-   A suitable form of verb " to be " is used.

استخدام شكل مناسب من الفعل   " to be ".

3- We change the main verb of the given sentence into the third form.

يتم تغيير الفعل الأساسي في الجملة إلى الشكل الثالث.

Study these examples :

* The car **will be repaired** soon .   السيارة سوف تُصلح قريباً.
* The car **can be repaired** .   إن السيارة يمكن أن تُصلح.
* The car **must be repaired** .   إن السيارة يجب أن تُصلح.
* The car **is repaired** every month.   إن السيارة تُصلح كل شهر.
* The car **was repaired** yesterday.   صُلحت السيارة يوم أمس .
* The car **has been repaired** .   لقد صُلحت السيارة.
* The cars **have been repaired** .   لقد صُلحت السيارات.
* The car **is being repaired** .   يجري تصليح السيارة.
* The cars **are being repaired** .   يجري إصلاح السيارات .

أدرس الأمثلة جيداً و سوف تجد أن شروط المبني للمجهول الثلاثة قد تحققت .
جرب فعلاً آخر و عليك أن تختار اسماً مناسباً تضعه بدلاً من the car في بداية الجملة وهـذا الاسـم لا
يفعل الفعل بل الفعل واقع عليه أي أن هذا الاسم يكون مستقبلاً لا مرسلاً للفعل .
و سوف نعطي مزيداً من التمارين على المبني للمجهول فيما بعد .

The Fourth Verb- Form الشكل الرابع للفعل

نحصل على الشكل الرابع بإضافة ing- إلى مصدر الفعل .

playing , going , reading , speaking , listening , writing , driving, sitting, getting , running , die , dying , lie , lying .

* **How to use it** كيف يتم استخدامه :

1- This verb-form is used together with " **am , is , are** " to form the present continuous tense which describes an action that is taking place at this moment. But this only applies to motion verbs.

يتم استخدام هذا الشكل لتكوين زمن المضارع المستمر الذي يصف حدثاً يحدث في هذه اللحظة بشرط أن يكون فعل الجملة متحركاً .

run يركض speak يتكلم / walk يمشي / wash يغسل /

هذه أفعال فيها حركة ظاهرة للعيان ولهذا يمكننا أن نستخدمها للتعبير عـن حـدث مسـتمر الآن .

* **Examples** أمثلة :
   * I **am reading** a book now .
   * Ali **is reading** a book now .
   * It **is raining** now .
   * We **are reading** English now .
   * They **are reading** English now .

يمكنك أن تعمل جملاً أخرى مماثلة باستخدام أفعال أخرى , و سوف نعطي المزيد من التمارين لاحقاً .

2- This verb-form is used together with " **was , were** " to form the past continuous tense which describes an action that was happening at a certain moment in the past.

يستخدم الشكل الرابع لتكوين زمن الماضي المستمر الذي يصف حدثاً كان مستمراً في لحظة معينة في الماضي لكن في وجود   was " أو " were .

Examples :

* I **was reading** a book .   كنت اقرأ كتاباً.
* They **were playing** football. كانوا يلعبون كرة القدم.
                     4   2
* I **was reading** a book *when* you **phoned** .

كنت أقرأ كتاباً عندما اتصلت .

            2   4
* Ali phoned *while* بينما I was writing a letter .

اتصل علي بينما كنت أكتب رسالةً.

اصنع جملا مماثلة و افهم المعنى .. فكر في فعلين أحدها تضعه في الشكل الرابع والآخر في الشكل الثاني مستخدما (while) (بينما) أو when عندما   لربط الجملتين و سوف نعطي مزيداً من التمارين لاحقاً .

3- The 4th verb-form is used to show our disapproval of something that continuously takes place.

يتم استخدام الشكل الرابع للتعبير عن استنكارنا لشيء يتكرر باستمرار .

Study these sentences to see how the above idea is expressed.

ادرس هذه الجمل لكي ترى كيف تم التعبير عن الفكرة السابقة .

* He is always reading.   .إنه دائماً يقرأ

* She is always sleeping .   .إنها دائماً تنام

* You are always coming late.   .إنك دائماً تأتي متأخراً

4- The 4ᵗʰ verb-form is used together with " have been أو

has been " to form the present perfect continuous tense

which describes an action that started in the past , but is still going on.

يستخدم هذا الشكل لتكوين زمن المضارع التام المستمر الذي يصف حدثاً بدأ في الماضي ولكنه لا يزال
مستمراً حتى هذه اللحظة بشرط وجود :

a-   since   أو   for)   . (مفتاحي هذا الزمن

b-   have been   أو   has been .

c-   فعل متحرك :   go , drive , watch , swim .

Examples :

* I **have been reading** this book **since last Friday.**

. إنني أقرأ هذا الكتاب منذ يوم الجمعة الماضية

* Ali **has been reading** this book **for three days** .

كوّن جملاً مماثلة باستبدال الفعل بفعل آخر . و سوف نعطي مزيداً من الأمثلة والتمارين المعززة فيما
. بعد

5- The 4th verb-form is used as a noun. يستخدم الشكل الرابع كاسم

Examples :

*   I like reading .   أنا أحب القراءة.
*   Reading is important.   القراءة مهمة.
*   Ali is good <u>at</u> reading.
*   I like your way of reading.   إني أحب طريقتك في القراء.
*   I thank you for helping me.   إني أشكرك على مساعدتك لي.
*   They are serious about fighting crime.

وبما أن الفعل له دور محوري في تعلم اللغة ، نرى من الضروري أن نزود دارس اللغة بقائمة مـن الأفعـال الشائعة التي يجب أن يتم حفظها واستخدامها في جمل مماثلة لتلك الجمـل التـي سـبق أن شـاهدناها . وننصح باستخدام أشكال الفعل الواحد في جمل عديدة مقلدين النماذج التي سبق أن ذكرناها .

Since the verb plays a pivotal role in learning the language , it is useful to supply learners with a list of key verbs . Learners are advised to use each form in making sentences similar to the above ones.

A list of Common verbs — قائمة بأفعال شائعة

	1	2	3	4
يسمح لـ	allow	allowed	allowed	allowing
يزعج	annoy	annoyed	annoyed	annoying
يقبل	accept	accepted	accepted	accepting
يوافق	agree	agreed	agreed	Agreeing
يتفق مع	agree with	agreed with	agreed with	agreeing with
يختلف في الرأي	disagree	disagreed	disagreed	disagreeing
يختلف مع	disagree with	disagreed with	disagreed with	disagreeing with
يختلف عن	differ from	differed from	differed from	differing from
يهاجم	attack	attacked	attacked	attacking
يتجنب	avoid	avoided	avoided	avoiding
يدافع عن	defend	defended	defended	defending
يطلب من	ask ..for	asked for	asked...for	asking ..for
يجيب على	answer	answered	answered	answering
يعبر عن	express	expressed	expressed	expressing
يعبر (طريق)	cross	crossed	crossed	crossing
يجمع	collect	collected	collected	collecting
يصحح	correct	corrected	corrected	correcting
يحمي	protect	protected	protected	protecting
يفسر	explain	explained	explained	explaining
يعامل - يعالج	Treat	treated	treated	treating
يهزم	defeat	defeated	defeated	defeating
يدهن	Paint	painted	painted	painting
يصلح	repair	repaired	Repaired	repairing
يصلح	mend	mended	mended	mending
يحني يطعج	Bend	bent	bent	bending
يفشل	fail	failed	failed	failing
ينجح	succeed	succeeded	succeeded	succeeding
يملئ	fill	filled	filled	filling
يقتل	kill	killed	killed	killing
يسيء إلى	offend	offended	offended	offending
يسيء إلى	wrong	wronged	wronged	wronging

يعلق-يؤجل	suspend	suspended	suspended	suspending
يشك في	suspect	suspected	suspected	suspecting
يشك في	doubt	doubted	doubted	doubting
يمكث	stay	stayed	stayed	staying
يصلي	pray	prayed	prayed	praying
يلعب	play	played	played	playing
يساند/يؤيد	support	supported	supported	supporting
يؤجر -يستأجر	rent = hire	rented= hired	rented= hired	renting=hiring
يشاهد	watch	watched	watched	watching
يغسل	wash	washed	washed	washing
يتمنى	wish	wished	wished	wishing
يصطاد	fish	fished	fished	fishing
يؤكد	confirm	confirmed	confirmed	confirming
يؤكد لـ	assure	assured	assured	assuring
يمنع	prevent	prevented	prevented	preventing
يموت	die	died	died	dying
يكذب	Lie	lied	lied	lying
يربط	tie	tied	tied	tying
يطيع - يتقيد بـ	obey	obeyed	obeyed	obeying
يعترض على	object to	objected to	objected to	objecting to
يتبع - يتابع- يفهم	follow	followed	followed	following
يصبغ	dye	dyed	dyed	dyeing
يبدأ	start	started	started	starting
ينتهي	finish	finished	finished	finishing
يعاقب	punish	punished	punished	punishing
يلتحق ب	join	joined	joined	joining
يوقع	sign	signed	signed	signing
يصمم	design	designed	designed	designing
يستقيل من	resign	resigned	resigned	resigning
يعرض للخطر	endanger	endangered	endangered	endangering
يزدهر	flourish	flourished	flourished	flourishing
يهلك / يبلى	perish	perished	perished	perishing
يتعلم / يحفظ	learn	learned	learned	learning
يكسب	earn	earned	earned	earning
يكسب / يكتسب	gain	gained	gained	gaining
يبوح ب/ يفشي	disclose	disclosed	disclosed	disclosing

يفرض	impose	imposed	imposed	imposing
يفسد	spoil	spoiled / spoilt	spoiled / spoilt	spoiling
يحرق- يحترق	burn	burned / burnt	burned / burnt	burning
يلف - يستدير	turn	turned	turned	turning
يرفض	turn down	turned down	turned down	turning
يقفل أضواء/ أجهزة	turn off	turned off	turned off	turning off
يفــتح أضـــواء / أجهزة	turn on	turned on	turned on	turning on
يعود - يعيد	return	returned	returned	returning
يفتح - يفتتح	open	opened	opened	opening
يغلق	close	closed	closed	closing
يؤذي	hurt	hurt	hurt	hurting
يقطع	cut	cut	cut	cutting
يضع	put	put	Put	putting
يضرب	hit	hit	hit	hitting
يكلف	cost	cost	cost	costing
يقرأ	read	read	read	reading
يضع	set	set	set	setting
يكذب	lie	lied	lied	lying
يرقد – يستلقي	lie	lay	lain	lying
يضع	lay	laid	laid	laying
يسبب	cause	caused	caused	causing
يرفض	reject	rejected	rejected	rejecting
يرفض	refuse	refused	refused	refusing
يستخدم	use	used	used	using
يحرك- يتحرك	move	moved	moved	moving
يزيل	remove	removed	removed	removing
يلوم	blame	blamed	blamed	blaming
يعتذر	apologise	apologised	apologised	apologising
يُتلف	damage	damaged	damaged	damaging
يوفر - يدخر يقتصد في	save	saved	saved	saving
يبدد	waste	wasted	wasted	wasting
ينقلب	overturn	overturned	overturned	overturning
ينصح	advise	advised	advised	advising
يراجع	revise	revised	revised	revising
يستحق	deserve	deserved	deserved	deserving

يلاحظ	observe	observed	observed	observing
يخدم	serve	served	served	serving
يصل	arrive	arrived	arrived	arriving
يتجاهل	ignore	ignored	ignored	ignoring
يحاول-يحاكم	try	tried	tried	trying
يبكي	cry	cried	cried	crying
ينكر	deny	denied	denied	denying
يتحدى	defy	defied	defied	defying
يرد على	reply	replied	replied	replying
يوقف	stop	stopped	stopped	stopping
يطرد	expel	expelled	expelled	expelling
يلغي	cancel	cancelled	cancelled	cancelling
يسافر	travel	travelled	travelled	traveling
يتشاجر	quarrel	quarrelled	quarrelled	quarrelling
يحمل	carry	carried	carried	carrying
يتزوج	marry	married	married	marrying
يسرع	hurry	hurried	hurried	hurrying
يدرس	study	studied	studied	studying
يدفن	bury	buried	buried	burying
يرضي-يشبع	satisfy	satisfied	satisfied	satisfying
يؤهل - يتأهل	qualify	qualified	qualified	qualifying
يشغل - يحتل	occupy	occupied	occupied	occupying
يحتفل ب	celebrate	celebrated	celebrated	celebrating
يزيد من	increase	increased	increased	increasing
يخفض من	decrease	decreased	decreased	decreasing
يزود - يمد	provide	provided	provided	providing
يستمتع ب	enjoy	enjoyed	enjoyed	enjoying
يدمر	ruin	ruined	ruined	ruining
ينظف	clean	cleaned	cleaned	cleaning
يحل	solve	solved	solved	solving
يخلق	create	created	created	creating
يسحب	pull	pulled	pulled	pulling
يدفع	push	pushed	pushed	pushing
يندفع	rush	rushed	rushed	rushing
يسحق	crush	crushed	crushed	crushing
يتحطم	crash	crashed	crashed	crashing
يهدم	demolish	demolished	demolished	demolishing

ينشر	publish	published	published	publishing
يختفي	vanish	vanished	vanished	vanishing
يظهر	appear	appeared	appeared	appearing
يختفي	disappear	disappeared	disappeared	disappearing
يبين- يعرض	show	showed	shown	showing
يجذب	attract	attracted	attracted	attracting
يروق لـ	appeal to	appealed to	appealed to	appealing to
يقفز	jump	jumped	jumped	jumping
يلوث	pollute	polluted	polluted	polluting
يصدق	believe	believed	believed	believing
يخفف من معاناة	relieve	relieved	relieved	relieving
يستقبل	receive	received	received	receiving
يخدع	deceive	deceived	deceived	deceiving
يتصور	conceive	conceived	conceived	conceiving
يركز	concentrate	concentrated	concentrated	concentrating
يساهم في	contribute to	contributed to	contributed to	contributing to
يشارك	participate	participated	participated	participating
يبدل	change	changed	changed	changing
يتبادل	exchange	exchanged	exchanged	exchanging
يتقاضى-يتهم يشحن	charge	charged	charged	charging
يتهم بـ	accuse of	accused of	accused of	accusing of
يفرح- يمتع	amuse	amused	amused	amusing
يشگل	constitute	constituted	constituted	constituting
يتذكر	remember	remembered	remembered	remembering
يذكر	remind of	reminded of	reminded of	reminding of
يتصل بـ _يسمي	call	called	called	calling
يتصل بـ	phone	phoned	phoned	phoning
يشم – له رائحة	smell	smelled/ smelt	smelled/smelt	smelling
يذوق – له طعم	taste	tasted	tasted	tasting
يسمع – يسمع بـ	hear (of)	heard	heard	hearing
يتصنت على	overhear	overheard	overheard	overhearing
يستعد/يعد	prepare	prepared	prepared	preparing
يقرر	decide	decided	decided	deciding
ينظر في- يعتبر	consider	considered	considered	considering
يعتبر	regard	regarded	regarded	regarding

يتحمل - يحمل	bear	bore	born	bearing
يلد – تنجب	bear	bore	borne	bearing
يعض	bite	bit	bitten	biting
يخفـي-يختبـئ-يحجب	hide	hid	hidden	hiding
يأتي	come	came	come	coming
يصبح	become	became	become	becoming
يتغلب على	overcome	overcame	overcome	overcoming
يكتب	write	wrote	written	writing
يسوق	drive	drove	driven	driving
يركب (دراجة)	ride	rode	ridden	riding
يؤدي إلى	lead to	led to	led to	leading to
يضلل	mislead	misled	misled	misleading
يجلس	sit	sat	sat	sitting
يقف	stand	stood	stood	standing
يتفهم- يفهم	understand	understood	understood	understanding
يسئ فهم	misunderstand	misunderstood	misunderstood	misunderstanding
يفوز	win	won	won	winning
يخسر	lose	lost	lost	losing
يجد	find	found	found	finding
يحفظ	keep	kept	kept	keeping
ينام	sleep	slept	slept	sleeping
يشعر	feel	felt	felt	feeling
يزحف	creep	crept	crept	creeping
يعني	mean	meant	meant	meaning
يرى	see	saw	seen	seeing
يجري- يدير	run	ran	run	running
يترك- يغادر	leave	left	left	leaving
يذهب	go	went	gone	going
يحصل على	get	got	got	getting
ينسى	forget	forgot	forgotten	forgetting
يبني	build	built	built	building
يرسل	send	sent	sent	sending
يقضي- ينفق	spend	spent	spent	spending
يقرض	lend	lent	lent	lending
يقترض	borrow	borrowed	borrowed	borrowing
يغذي	feed	fed	fed	feeding

يقابل	meet	met	met	meeting
يحتاج	need	needed	needed	needing
ينزف	bleed	bled	bled	bleeding
يبيع	sell	sold	sold	selling
يخبر	tell	told	told	telling
يرتفع-تشرق-ينهض	rise	rose	risen	rising
يرفـــع – يـــربي – يجمع تبرعات-يثير	raise	raised	raised	raising
يسقط -يهبط	fall	fell	fallen	falling
يخفض	reduce	reduced	reduced	reducing
يعرف	know	knew	known	knowing
يرمي	throw	threw	thrown	throwing
ينمو – يزرع	grow	grew	grown	growing
يطيح ب	overthrow	overthrew	overthrown	overthrowing
يسحب- يرسم	draw	drew	drawn	drawing
يسحب-ينسحب	withdraw	withdrew	withdrawn	withdrawing
يمسـك ب-يستولي على	seize	seized	seized	seizing
يمسك ب	hold to	held to	held to	holding
ينطبق على	apply to	applied	applied	applying
يتقدم بطلب ل	apply for	applied for	applied for	applying for
يطير-يسافر	fly	flew	flown	flying
يشتري	buy	bought	bought	buying
يُحضر- يجلب	bring	brought	brought	bringing
يعتقد-يفكر	think	thought	thought	thinking
يقاوم – يحارب	fight	fought	fought	fighting
يمسك	catch	caught	caught	catching
يدرّس	teach	taught	taught	teaching
يختار	choose	chose	chosen	choosing
يختار	select	selected	selected	selecting
يرعب	scare	scared	scared	scaring
يدفع	pay	paid	paid	paying
يقول	say	said	said	saying
يأخذ	take	took	taken	taking

تقلـع (الطـائرة) يخلع	take off	took off	taken off	taking off
يتجاوز	overtake	overtook	overtaken	overtaking
يعتني بـ	take care of	took care of	taken care of	taking care of
يعطي	give	gave	given	giving
يسعى إلى	seek	sought	sought	seeking
يعفو عن – يصفح	forgive	forgave	forgiven	forgiving
يستسلم	give in	gave in	given in	giving in
يتخلى عن	give up	gave up	given up	giving up
يكسر	break	broke	broken	breaking
يخرق القانون	break law	broke law	broken law	breaking ......
يتعطـل(السـيارة)- ينهار	break down	broke down	broken down	breaking down
يتكلم	speak	spoke	spoken	speaking
يسرق	steal	stole	stolen	stealing
يملك	have (has)	had	had	having
يعمل- يقوم ب	do	did	done	doing
يكون	be(am - is- are)	was (were)	been	being
يشرب	drink	drank	drunk	drinking
يتصل ب	ring	rang	rung	ringing
يغني	sing	sang	sung	singing
يغرق	sink	sank	sunk	sinking
يصدر رائحة كريهة	stink of	stunk	stunk	Stinking
يلدغ – يؤلم	sting	stung	stung	stinging
يضرب – يعجب – يعثر على(نفط)	strike	struck	struck	striking
يعصر– يلـوي – ينتزع - يؤلم	wring	wrung	wrung	wringing
يسبح	swim	swam	swum	swimming
يبدأ	begin	began	begun	beginning
يأكل	eat	ate	eaten	eating
يصنع	make	made	made	making
يعكس	reflect	reflected	reflected	reflecting
يمتص	absorb	absorbed	absorbed	absorbing

يحترم	respect	respected	respected	respecting
يتوقع	expect	expected	expected	expecting
يهين	insult	insulted	insulted	insulting
يقود إلى	result in	resulted in	resulted in	resulting in
ينتج عن-يتأتى من	result from	resulted from	resulted from	resulting from
يشاور	consult	consulted	consulted	consulting
يثبت –يبرهن	prove	proved	proven	proving
يدحض	disprove	disproved	disproved	disproving
يصادق على	approve	approved	approved	approving
يحبذ-يستحسن	approve of	approved of	approved of	approving of
يستهجن –يذم	disapprove of	disapproved	disapproved	disapproving
يحسّن/ يتحسّنْ ن	improve	improved	Improved	improving
يطـــور- ينمــي – يتطوّر	develop	developed	developed	developing
يراقب-يتحكم في	control	controlled	controlled	controlling
يسترد-يجدد	restore	restored	restored	restoring
يستبدل	replace	replaced	replaced	replacing
يقاوم	resist	resisted	resisted	resisting
يصر على	insist on	insisted	insisted	insisting
يتكون من	consist of	consisted of	consisted of	consisting of
يحتوي على	contain	contained	contained	containing
تشـــتمل عـــلى- يضمن	include	included	included	including
يوصي ب	recommend	recommended	recommended	recommending
يسترجع	recall	recalled	recalled	recalling
يعترف ب	recognize	recognized	recognized	recognizing
يلتقط - ينتقي	pick	picked	picked	picking
يتنزه	picnic	picnicked	picnicked	picnicking
يصاب بذعر	panic	panicked	panicked	panicking
يرعب	frighten	frightened	frightened	frightening

collude with يتواطأ مع	/	collaborate with يتعاون مع - يتواطأ مع
collide with يصطدم بـ - يصدم	/	starve يتضور جوعاً
repeat يكرر	/	exceed يتجاوز
detain يعتقل	/	assess يقيّم
exaggerate يبالغ في	/	retain يحتفظ بـ
contaminate يلوث	/	evaluate يقيّم
devaluate يخفض من قيمة	/	abstain from يمتنع عن
exterminate يستأصل - يبيد	/	attain يحصل على
analyse يحلل	/	reconcile يوفق
compare يقارن	/	compromise يتوصل إلى حل وسط
contradict يناقض	/	procrastinate يسوّف
conclude يختتم - يبرم	/	mediate يتوسط
abort يحبط	/	mastermind يكون العقل المدبر لـ
intercept يعترض (طريق)	/	pioneer يكون رائداً لـ
intercede with يتشفع لدى	/	invest يستثمر
protest يحتج	/	withhold يحجز / يحبس
detest يكره	/	withstand يقاوم / يصمد
define يعرّف	/	pretend يتظاهر بـ (يدّعي)
recede يتراجع	/	testify to يشهد على
discover يكتشف	/	explore يستكشف
escalate يصعّد	/	adapt to يتكيف مع
adopt يتبنى	/	consider ينظر في / يعتبر
comply with يُخضع , يعرض , يستسلم submit	/	يتقيد بـ يذعن , يستسلم
adhere to يتمسك بـ	/	subscribe يساهم / يتبرع
dominate يهيمن / يسود	/	prevail يسود

condemn = denounce ينددبـ - يستنكر	/	slander يفتري على
flatter يتملق	/	betray يخون
recover يسترد-يتماثل للشفاء	/	lay – يضع – laid – laid
lie يستلقي – lay استلقى - lain	/	lie يكذب - lied كذب
exclude يستبعد-يستثني	/	assassinate يغتال

The first verb-form الشكل الأول من الفعل

a- The present simple tense.

* The first verb-form is used in several ways.

* يستخدم الشكل الأول للفعل بأساليب شتى.

1- We can use the first verb-form to form

   the present simple tense.

بإمكاننا أن نستخدم الشكل الأول للفعل لتكوين زمن المضارع البسيط .

* We use this tense to express facts or things we generally

   do at the present time ... things are not necessarily done

   at the moment of speaking.

* We use the present simple tense with these adverbs of

   frequency :

أ- يستخدم الشكل الأول للتعبير عن حقيقة أو عادة في زمن الحاضر

Present Simple Tense وغالباً ما يتم استخدام مؤشرات زمنية تفرض استخدام الشكل الأول وهذه

الإشارات هي :

sometimes **عادةً** usually **غالبا** , often **دائماً** always, **أحيانا**

every day (week , month) .... **كل** , scarcely **نادرا- قلما**

seldom **نادرا** , rarely , generally **عموماً**

وأرى أن نطلق على هذه الإشارات الزمنية " مفاتيح زمن الحاضر". حاول أن تعمل

جملاً مماثلة للجمل التالية للتعبير عن الإثبات والنفي والسؤال.

● Study these sentence to see where to place the above adverbs.

ادرس الجمل التالية لكي تري أين يتم وضع المفاتيح السابقة.

   1- I *visit* Ali **every** Monday .

2- Ali **always** *visits* me .

3- I **often** *visit* Nasser.

4- Ali **sometimes** *visits* me

5 – We **rarely** *visit* Ali .

6- Ali is always ready to help me.

7- We are always willing to do something.

8- We are **still** willing to come.

9- I **no longer** mix with this person.

I do not mix with him any more. (any longer)

Negation النفــي :

1- I **do not visit** Ali . (I **don't visit** Ali.)

2- Ali **does not visit** me. (Ali **doesn't visit** me.)

She does not help anybody.

This tree does not bear any fruit.

3- I **am not** ready to come.

Ali **is not** happy about that. (isn't)

There **are not** any mistakes. (aren't)

ملاحظة : الفعل يكتسب "s " كما في الجملة الثانية فقط في حالة الإثبات.. لماذا ؟ إذا كان الاسم الـذي يسبق الفعل اسم شخص مثل "علي " أو " منى " أو " الكتاب " أو " he " أو " she " أو "it ".

ملاحظة: في حالة عدم وجود مفتاح تعبر الجملة عـن عـادة أو حقيقـة وفي هـذه الحالـة لا بـد مـن استخدام الفعل في الشكل الأول كما يمكن أن نستخدم أي شكل صحيح للفعل.

أمثلة أخرى :

1- I usually (walk) *walk* to school.

نلاحظ وجود "المفتاح " [usually] ... لذا فأننا يجب أن نضع الفعل الذي بين القوسين في الشـكل الأول

2- Ali always (walk) _walks_ to school.

المفتاح "always" ... لذا يجب أن نضع الفعل في الشكل الأول مع مراعاة إضافة الـ "s" إليه مراعـاة لـ "Ali" .

3- It (rain) _rains_ a lot in London.

المفتاح "حقيقة" .. لذا نضع الفعل في الشكل الأول و لا بد من إضافة الـ "s" إليه مراعاة لـ "It" .

Notice that these verbs take " –es" :

(I go . / Ali goes.)   (I mix. / He mixes.)

(I wash . / Ali washes .)   (I pass. / He passes.)

(You teach . / She teaches . (I buzz . / He buzzes.)

(I study . / He studies . ⟶ (carry – cry – deny)

(I play/ He plays⟶ (pay يدفع, enjoy, destroy يدمر, employ يوظف)

** **When asking a question, we use " do , does ":**

1- a: Do you speak English ?   هـل تتكـلم الإنـجـليـزية ؟

   b : Yes , I do. (أو) No , I don't .

2- a : Does Ali accept it ?   هـل علي يقبل هـذا ؟

   b : Yes , he does. (No , he doesn't .)

3- What do you like ?

   Where do you go ?

   When does Mona come ?

   Why does Ali use the Internet ?

● For **emphasis** we use " **do or does** " before the verb .

من أجل التأكيد على أمر ما فإننا نستخدم do أو does قبل الفعل في الشكل الأول .

1- We **do** love peace .

2- Mona **does** speak good English.

3- They **do** need food and medicines.

4- It **does** rain a lot in this country.

- We usually use " do or does " to avoid repetition.

في العادة نستخدم do أو does لتفادي التكرار . •

1- Ali always **comes** late as I **do**.   إن علياً يأتي دائماً متأخراً.
   (do = come)

2- I **do not smoke** , but Ali **does**. أنا لا أدخن , ولكن علياً يفعل .
   (does = smokes).

3- My brothers **go** to bed early. So **do** I . (do = go)

إن إخوتي يذهبون للنوم مبكرين , وكذلك أفعل هذا.

4- I **play** football. So **do** my brothers. (do = play)

5- I **speak** good English. So **does** my sister. (does = speaks)

6- Ali **does not smoke** . **Neither does** Nasser.

علي لا يدخن , و كذلك ناصر لا يفعل ذلك .

7- Ali **does not smoke** . **Neither do** I .

8- I **do not smoke** . **Neither does** Ali.

*****

* **Choose the correct verb- form:**

1- Ali (come- comes) by car , but we (come – comes)
   by bus.

2- Mona always (tell – tells) us interesting stories.

3- I (not – don't – doesn't) have any problem.

4- Ali (don't – doesn't) need any money.

5- Do you (need- needs) any money ?

6- Does Ali (speak- speaks) English ?

7- A: (Is – Do – Does) Ali like music ?

   B: Yes, he (do – does- is) .

8- (Is – Do- Does) free ?

9- A: (Are- Do – Does) you free ?

   B: Yes, I (do- are – am).

10- A: (Do – Does – Are) you have any questions ?

   B: No, I (don't- aren't- am not).

11-   Nasser likes milk as I (does – do – done) .

12-   I don't know French , but Ali (do – does- did).

13-   Ali has a small car . So (does – do) I .

14-   Mona (not – do not – does not) come by car. Neither (I do -   did I - do I
).

15- Ali does not travel a lot , but we (don't – do – does).

*****

** **Note : be →   am , is , are .**

لاحظ الفعل السابق إذ لا بد أن يتغير إلى واحد من الأشكال الثلاثة حسب الاسم.

   * I am   busy. Ali (Mona – The car) is under the tree.

     The boys are busy.

   * There is a book on the table.

* There are some books in the bag.

** I **have** أمتلك a new car , but Ali **has** يمتلك an old one. You **have** تتناول
   lunch at home , but Mona **has** lunch at school.

Correct the verbs in brackets :

1- I (eat) ....   too much meat, but Ali (eat) ....
   a little of it.

2- You (drive) .... too fast. That (be) ....
   dangerous.

3- Ali (drive) ....slowly. That (be) .... nice.

4- She usually (allow) .... me to go out.

5- Food (give)............................ people energy.

6- The sun (rise) .... in the East.

7- Qatar (produce) ....oil and (sell) ....it to other
   countries.

8- They often (go) ....fishing alone on Fridays.

9- Ali always (do) ....his homework here.

10- She (teach)...............me English , and her way
    (appeal)............ to me.

11- He (study) ....hard because he (want)
    ....to succeed.

٧٢

12- I (have) ....a Japanese car.

13- Ali (have) ....a problem with his teacher.

14- I (be) ....happy with my wife.

15- Ali (be) ....a doctor at Hamad General Hospital.

16- Mona (be)............. a nice person.

17- We (be) ....busy at the moment.

18- Cairo (be) ....the capital of Egypt.

19- The sun (be)..............the main source of energy.

20- I (not smoke) ....because smoking (be) ....bad
    for health.

21- You (not allow) .... your sister to go out.

22- I (not accept) ....that.

23- Ali (not accept) .... that .

24- Mona (not believe) .... you .

25- I (not offend) ....anybody.

26- Ali (be)...........polite; he (not offend) ....
    anybody.

27- I (deny)...................................that.

28- Mona (deny) .... that.

29- I (not drink)...................wine . A Muslim (not do)
    ....that.

30- Muslims (not eat)................................pork.

31- Do you (like) .... that?

32- Does Ali (pray) .... in the mosque ?

33- Where do you (go)..................... in the afternoon?

34- When does Ali (come) .... here?

35- How do they (come) .... here ?

36- ....(be) Ali a pilot ?

37- Where ....(be) you now ?

38- How ....(be) your father ?

39- Ali (not, be)............. happy about that.

40- We (not have) .... any problem with you.

41- Ali (not be) .... busy at the moment.

42- We (not be) .... willing راغبون to go fishing with you.

43- I (not be) .... ready to do anything I (not like) ....

44- Stolen waters (be) .... sweet , and bread eaten in
    secret (be) .... pleasant. (A proverb حكمة)

45 – In much wisdom (be) …….. much grief , and whoever

(increase) …………….. knowledge increases sorrow.

في كثرة الحكمة يكمن الكثير من الشقاء , ومن يسعى إلى زيادة المعرفة فإنه يسعى إلى زيادة

46- Work (consist) الشقاء.

………… of whatever a body is obliged

to do. Play (consist) ……….. of whatever a body is not

obliged to do .

العمل هو كل شيء يكون الشخص ملزماً أن يؤديه. أما اللعب فهو كل شيء يكون الشخص غير ملزم أن

يؤديه.

47 – Ignorance الجهل (be) ………… bliss . السعادة في الجهل.

Wisdom الحكمة (be) ……….. folly حماقة- غباء .

- **Choose the correct verb-form :**

1-   Ali (like – likes – liking) music a lot.

2-   I (not go- doesn't go- don't go) fishing on Fridays.

3-   Ali and Hamad (comes – come – coming) on time.

4-   The weather (get – gets- got) hot in summer.

5-   Where (do – does- doing) you go in the evening ?

6-   How (does- do – done) Ali come here ?

7-   Where (is- are – was) you now ?

8-   (Do – Does – Is) Mona know that ?

9-   We (do – are – does) help others .

10-   The problem (are – does – is) easy to solve.

* **Find what is wrong and correct it: أوجد ما هو خطأ ثم صوبه**

1- I am not offend anybody.

…………………………………………….

2- He not believe you .

………………………………………….

3- I not like that .

………………………………………….

٧٤

4- She don't like that .

....

5- Ali speak good English . ...

....

6- Mona visit me on Friday .

....

7- I is busy . ...

8- Books is important . ...

9- Food are necessary . ...

10- Water important . ...

11- We are need water a lot . ...

12- Ali need water, too . ...

13- I not need money . ...

14- Mona need money to buy a book . ...

15-   Huda not need much money . ...

16-   He teach me Arabic ....

17-   You is nice . ...

18-   Qatar not is in Africa. ....

19-   Ali and Mona is learning Arabic . ...

The First verb- form with auxiliaries:

الشكل الأول للفعل مع أفعال مساعدة

The first verb- form can come with these auxiliaries to express a variety of ideas.

can (can't) / could تفيد القدرة / will (won't) - would / must يجب / shall –
should يجب shouldn't / may - might ربما , / ought to ينبغي أن / had better =
should / would rather يفضّل / need = must = have to /

وهذه تسمى أفعال ناقصة لأن لكل منها شكلين-أي إنـها ليست كاملة التصريف . وغالباً شكل الماضي لا
يدل على الماضي.

* must = (have to / has to لا بد , had to اضطر)

Examples أمثلة :

* I **can** do something .   إني أستطيع أن اعمل شيئا.
* You **can** do something. (قدرة و نصيحة) انك تستطيع أن تفعل شيئاً
* You **could** stay there.   بإمكانك أن تقيم هناك (اقتراح)
* He **will** leave tomorrow .   (المستقبل)
* I **will** show you how to do it. (وعد) سأريك كيف تعمل هذا.
* **Will** you wait for me , please ?   (طلب مؤدب)
* I **would like to** go fishing.   (رغبة)
* I **wouldn't** do it this way .   (عدم استحسان)
* You **must** do something.   (واجب)
* We **have to** accept that.   نحن مضطرون لا ن نقبل ذلك.
* I **had to** leave.   اضطررت لأن أغادر.
* He **might** tell you .   انه قد يخبرك.

* We **ought to** solve this problem. ينبغي علينا أن نحل هذه المشكلة.
* The weather is too cold.You **should** put on your sweater.
* You **had better** buy a small car. You **had better not** buy this big car.
  You'd better do something else.
* I **would rather** walk **than** drive to school.
  إني أفضّل أن أمشي عن أن أركب السيارة إلى المدرسة.
  I would rather not drive to school.
  إني لا أفضّل أن أركب السيارة إلى المدرسة.
* You need to do something better.
  You must do something better.
  He needn't do that.
  He doesn't need to do that.
* I have all my friends come my party.
  إني أحمل جميع أصدقائي على أن يأتوا إلى الحفلة.
* Ali got me to do that.
  إن عليّاً حملني(دفعني – أجبرني) على أن أفعل ذلك.
* **Find what is wrong and write the correct sentence:**

1-He may allows you . ………………………………………………

2-She could paints her room white ; she like this colour.

  ……………………………………………

3-Can you answering this question? …………………………………………

4-She cannot did anything. ……………………………………………..

5-We has to explain that. ………………………………………………

6-You ought tell your father . ……………………………………………

7-I would not rather cancel my booking.

……………………………………………

8-We should learning English.   ……………………………………………

9-She would rather to travels soon.   ……………………………………………

10-You has to hurry.   ……………………………………………

* Give the missing verb:

1- Ali has to …………………………… Hani.

2- We should …………………..food to <u>the victims</u>.الضحايا

3- She could …………………..what she likes.

4-   I had better …………… that.

5- They ought to ……………………… the exam.

6- She can ……………………a small car.

7- You'd better ……………… it on your own.

8- We shouldn't ……………… money from banks   .

2-   These verbs are followed by infinitives.

الأفعال التالية يتبعها أفعال في المصدر

In the following sentences , the word " to " is not a
preposition , so it is followed by a verb in the first form.
ليست حرف جر في الأمثلة التالية لأنها تسبق فعل شكل أول.**to**

*   I want to say that.   أريد أن أقول ذلك.
*   He asked me to stay.   طلب مني أن أبقى .

* I agreed to come.   وافقت على أن أحضر .
* He promised to come.   وعد بأن يحضر.
* She refused to give me a book.
* It is easy to do that.
* It is necessary to learn English .

لكن لاحظ في الأمثلة التالية ... تجد أن "to" حرف جر و بالتالي لا يأتي بعدها فعـل شـكل أول بـل فعـل شكل رابع .

* In the following sentences, the word " to " acts as a preposition , so it is followed by a noun or by the fourth form of a verb acting as a noun.

* We are close to solving this problem.

نحن قريبون من حل هذه المشكلة.

* I am used to eating meat. (used to : adj.) (صفة) معتاد على
* We are used to walking.   (صفة) نحن معتادون على المشي.
* They got used to walking across the desert.

اعتادوا على المشي عبر الصحراء

** I used to eat meat. (used to: verb)

(فعل) : اعتدت أن أكل اللحم (عادة في الماضي)

* We should contribute to solving the traffic problem.

يجب علينا أن نساهم في حل مشكلة المرور (السير)

4- The first verb-form and the future   الشكل الأول للفعل والمستقبل

الشكل الأول مع المقوي will يعبر عن زمن المستقبل و هناك مفاتيح ترشدنا إلى   و هي :

The first verb-form with " will " helps express the future time in the presence of these clues :

tomorrow ,   **soon /** قريبا **next week /** الأسبوع القادم **/**غداً
I hope that / آمل بأن **I think that /** اعتقد بان **if /** إذا-لو-إن

I am sure that أنا متأكد من أن , in a few days في غضون أيام قليلة ,
in ... weeks في غضون أسابيع .

للتعبير عن المستقبل هناك ثلاث طرق :

* There are three ways of expressing the future :

1- I **will** come with you.

*(هنا نتحدث عن قرار تم اتخاذه في هذه اللحظة استجابة لأمر ما).

I think Ali will come to the meeting.

* (هنا نتحدث عن توقعات .)

I will help you if I can.

*(هنا نتحدث عن وعد استجابة لطلب من شخص لديه مشكلة ما).

2- I am going to buy a new car next month.

We are going to buy a new car next year.

Ali is going to join this college.

في هذه الأمثلة نتحدث عن قرارات سبق أن تم اتخاذها ونحن بصدد تنفيذها ولكن تنفيذها لا
يتطلب الكثير من الإجراءات.

3- We **are moving** to a new house next Friday.

I **am leaving** for London tomorrow.

Ali **is seeing** his boss this afternoon.

إن علياً سيقابل رئيسه عصر اليوم.
هنا نتحدث عن قرار تم اتخاذه ولكن تنفيذه يتطلب القيام بسلسلة طويلة من الترتيبات.

Correct the verbs in brackets:

1- I (leave) .... tomorrow.

2- They (open) ....a new branch soon .

3- I am sure that Ali (win) .... the rally .

4- I hope that you (give) ....me the necessary information .

5- She (move) .... to a new flat next month .

6- They (finish) .... in two weeks.

٨٠

7- If you smoke , you (destroy) .... your health.

8- If Ali (come) .... , I will tell him.

9- I will come to the party if I (have) .... time.

10- Hamad will buy one if he (have) .... money.

11- Hamad can join our university if he (get) .... high marks.

12- I think Ali (pass) .... all his exams.

13- Don't worry ! I (show) .... you how to do that.

10-The house is too old. I think they (remove) ....it

as soon as possible.

5- The first verb-form and the Imperative form صيغـة الأمر

* يتم الحصول على هذه الصيغة باستخدام الشكل الأول للفعل كما في هذه الأمثلة:

1- **Stop it** ! قف!كف عن هذا! **Tell me** why you are crying .

أخبرني لماذا تبكي .

2- Go out ! أخرج Leave me alone.   اتركني لوحدي !

3- Walk as far as the bank. Turn right at the bank.   4-إعطاء إرشادات Read the

message well .   (إعطاء نصيحة)

5- Be careful ! كن حذراً Don't play with matches.

لا تلعب بثقاب الكبريت

6- Don't be silly! Don't say such a thing ! لا تقل مثل هذا الشيء

7- Don't be too selfish ! لا تكن أنانياً بدرجة كبيرة.

8- Don't accept this offer ! لا تقبل هذا العرض.

It's unfair. إنه غيـر عادل.

9- Never go sailing alone ! لا تبحر بمفردك.

10- **Always keep** medicine away from children. أُما

احفظ الدواء بعيداً عن الأطفال.

** " Do " and " make " :

We use " do ' with abstractions .   نستخدمها مع المجردات

1- Ali is doing good business.
2- I will do my best.   سوف أبذل قصارى جهدي .
3- This book will do you a lot of good.
4- Don't take this medicine. It can do you harm.
5- You can do me justice.   يمكنك أن تنصفني .
6- You can do me a favour.   يمكنك أن تصنع لي معروفاً .
7- Everybody has to do his duty.

We use " make " with concrete things .

نستخدمها مع المجسدات

1- We are making good profits.
2- Let's make a bargain . = Let's agree.
3- She wants to make a cake .
4- You always make mistakes.
5- We want to make a fire .
            (noise , war , peace , a statement بيان)
6- You should make an attempt.
  (a decision قرار , an end to , an offer عرض , a promise وعد)

* **Correct the mistakes in these sentences :**
  1- Mona comes always late. ....
  2- You had better to apply . ...
  3- I want doing something else. ....
  4- You can make me a favour. ....
  5- She is moving to a flat every day. ....
  6- I asked Ali helping me . ...

7- I will rather buy a small car. ....

8- You should are polite . ...

9- She not is friendly. ....

10- You needn't to go alone. ....

The second verb-form الشكل الثاني للفعل

زمن الماضي البسيط The Past Simple Tense

We use the second verb-form when talking about the past in the presence of these clues :

هو التصريف أو الصيغة الثانية للفعل و يتم استخدامه عندما نريد أن نتحدث عن شيء وقع في الماضي . وهناك إشارات أو مفاتيح clues خاصة بهذا الشكل و هي :

yesterday يوم أمس , last Friday يوم الجمعة الفائت , in 1980

, قبـل ثـلاث أيـام ago.... , 3 days ago قبـل ثـلاث أيـام , الأسـبوع المـاضي last week

this morning هذا الصباح , the other day, one day في يوم من الأيام

* Examples أمثلة :

  - I (visit) **visited** Ali last Monday .
  - She (tell) **told** Mona yesterday .
  - I (not visit) **didn't visit** Ali yesterday .
  - **Did** you **visit** Ali yesterday ?
  - When **did you visit** Hamad ?

* Correct the verbs in brackets :

1- She (phone) ....an hour ago .

2- He (receive) .... his salary yesterday .

3- I (not see) .... any of my friends yesterday .

4- Ali (be) ...... ill yesterday , so he (stay) ....at home .

٨٣

5- They (be).......... late this morning , so the teacher   (get angry)
.... and (refuse)............... to (let) .... them in .

6- I (write)............. this letter last night , and I intend to (post).......... it today .

7- I (see) .... Mona last Monday and (tell) ....her about my wedding party .

8- She (buy) .... a new ring yesterday .

9- We (begin) ....to (build) .... the road in 1995 .

10-My father (leave) .... for London this morning.

11- Did you (see) .... Ali this morning ?

- **We use " did not (didn't) " to show negation .**

نستخدم did not   لتدل على النفي في الماضي. 1- I **did not**

see Hamad yesterday.

2- Mona **did not tell** me about her prize.

3- Some people **did not bring** food .

4- It **did not rain** last night.

- **We use " did " to emphasize something or to replace a verb in the second form.**

* نستخدم " did" للتأكيد على أن الأمر وقع , ولتحل محل فعل في الشكل الثاني لتجنب التكرار.

1-   Ali **did come** on time yesterday. (Emphasis تأكيد)

2-   I did not come late , but Ali **did.** → (did = came late)

3-   Mona **saw** the film , but Sarah **did not.** → (did not = did not see .)

4-   I **came** walking to school . So **did** Ali.

أنا جئت إلى المدرسة ماشياً. وكذلك فعل علي.

5-   Mona **did not come** on time. Neither **did** I .

منى لم تأتي في الموعد ولا أنا فعلت ذلك .

● The second verb-form is used with " if " to show that what we are talking about is impossible to happen , and has nothing to do with the past tense.

* يتم استخدام الشكل الثاني للفعل لكي نوضح بأن الأمر الذي نتحدث عنه مستحيل حدوثه ولا علاقة له بالماضي :

Examples :

1- If it **rained** , I **would stop** driving

إن أمطرت فسوف أتوقف عن السياقة.

* تعليق : إنني أفترض شيئاً أعرف أنه يستحيل حدوثه في هذا الوقت.

2- If Ali **had** time , **he'd come**. (would come)

3- If you **played** , we **might win** the match.

إن لعبت فإننا قد نكسب المباراة.

* إننا نفترض أمراً نشك في حدوثه لأننا لا نتوقع من الشخص المذكور أن يلعب المباراة.

4- If I **were** you , I **wouldn't go**.   لو كنت مكانك لما أذهب.

* **Use the right verb-forms :**

    1- If he came on time , he (see) ....

    2- If she (know) ....that , she would not give it to you.

    3- He might change his mind if you (break) ....your promise.

    4- If I (be) .... Ali , I wouldn't buy that car. It's too old.

    5- If it snowed in Qatar, we (not travel)..........abroad.

  6- If he (have) .... time, he might do it.

* **Choose the correct verb-form :**

1- Ali (go- goes- went) to the park yesterday.

2- I will (buy- buys- bought) a new car for you soon.

3- Did you (see – saw) the doctor this morning ?

4- We didn't (do – did) anything last night.

5- They (meet – met) some farmers yesterday.

6- In 1980 ,we (have-has-had) some problems with the villagers.القرويين

7- He (is – was – were) late for school this morning.

8- She (wasn't- doesn't – didn't) busy when you phoned an hour ago.

9- They did not (said – say – saying) anything.

10-   Ali does not   (have - has – had) any idea about this matter.

* **Correct the mistakes in these sentences:**

1- She give me the report yesterday. ……………………..

2- They did not came on time. …………………………

3-   He is tired yesterday.   ………………………….

4-   She does not go out yesterday. ………………………

5-   I meet Hamad an hour ago . …………………………..

6-   We   build the mosque in 1980. ……………………..

7-   Does Ali phone this morning ? …………………….

8-   Where did you found it ?   …………………………

9-   How the accident happen ?   ……………………………

10- There was some boys an hour ago. …………………….

* **We can use the past form of a verb to talk about things**
  we used to do .

يمكننا أن نستخدم صيغة الماضي للفعل للحديث عن أشياء كنا نعتاد القيام بها.

1-   I played football when I was young.

2-   She drank too much coffee when she was at school.

3-   I used to walk to school , but now I do not do it any more.

4-   4-She used to travel a lot , but now she never leaves her city.

5-   5-They **used to** ride camels , but now they drive cars.

فعل مساعد L

6- We **were** *used to* swimming in deep water.

كنا معتادون على السباحة في المياه العميقة.   صفة L

7- She **got used to** running .   تعودت على الجري.

٨٦

** Note: "used to " is an auxiliary followed by the first verb

form. If it comes with verb " to be " or " get ", it is followed by a gerund .

" used to "فعل مساعد بعدها فعل شكل أول. أما إذا جاءت كصفة يتبعـها فعل شكل رابع (اسم)

The third verb-formالشكل الثالث للفعل

The third verb- form is used in a variety of ways .

هو التصريف الثالث للفعل و له عدة استخدامات كما سبق أن رأينا .

يستخدم هذا الشكل في وجود المقوي have أو has للتعبير عن شيء حدث في الماضي و لا تزال آثاره قائمة .

Present Perfect Tense) زمن المضارع التام)

1-   We use this verb-form together with " **have**" or " **has**" to talk about an action that started in the past , but it still has a bearing on the present.

We can say that **the present perfect tense** is a bridge linking the past the present.

* **Examples : أمثلة :**

*	I have seen Ali.	لقد رأيت (قابلت) عليا .
*	You **have started** the car.	لقد شغلت السيارة .
*	He **has told** me everything.	لقد اخبرني بكل شيء.
*	She **has sold** her car.	لقد باعت سيارتها.

و لكن هناك clues مفاتيح ترشدها إلى هذا النوع من الجمل باستخدام الشكل الثالث و هي :

* **Clues to the present perfect tense :** مفاتيح الشكل الثالث

just توه , already بالفعل yet , بعد , ever , never أبداً , since منذ , for منذ , recently = في الآونة الأخيرة , so far حتى الآن lately

تمارين Exercises

1   3

1- I (just finish) ***have just finished.***

The clue is " just ", so we do two things : use an auxiliary
(have or has) and the 3rd form of the given .

[هنا المفتاح " just " , ولهذا نستخدم فعلاً مساعداً إما have أو has ثم نضع الفعل المعطى لنا في الشكل الثالث .]

2- I (not phone) ....Ali yet . إني لم اتصل بـ علي بعد

3- It (not rain) .... for years.

4- She (not leave) ....the country since 1990.

5- I (be) .... free for days.

6- He (already buy) .... the blue car.

7- She (not find) .... the answer so far.

8- I (recently speak) ....to Ali.

9- The weather (be) ....cloudy for days.

10- This is the best film I (ever see) ....

11- I (never eat) .... pork.

12- She (never see) .... a better film.

13- I (never drive) .... a more comfortable car.

14- She (not find) .... her ring yet.

15- We (already send................... aid to the homeless .

16- I (just tell) .... my father about the new timetable.

17- There (be) ....too many cars on the roads lately.

18- There (be) ....too much snow for days.

19- Have you (write) .... the report?

20- Has Mona (give) ....you a copy of her book?

21- What have they (do) ....?

* Correct the mistakes in these sentences :

1- I have be busy for days.   ....
2- She has gone to a theatre yesterday. ....
3- I did not saw Ali yesterday.   ....
5- We have did that this morning.   ....
6- Mona have got what said.   ....
7- They not have found the answer. ....
8- Mona not call her friends yet.   ....
9- I forget to bring my book yesterday. ....
10- Ali has forget his book .   ...

Note : " have , has " as auxiliaries are used o replace a verb in the third form .

• Have / has كأفعال مساعدة تستخدم لتحل محل فعل في الشكل الثالث لتفادي التكرار.

1- My friends have gone to the circus , but I **haven't**.
   (**haven't** = haven't gone)
2- Noura has not finished , but Huda **has**.
   (**has** = has finished)
3- I have accepted the offer , but Ali **hasn't**.
   (**hasn't** = hasn't accepted)

The future Perfect Tense زمن المستقبل التام

يستخدم هذا الزمن عندما نتحدث عن فعل سيكون قد تم إنجازه في وقت ما من المستقبل .

2- We use this tense when talking about an action that will have been completed at a future moment.

* By this time tomorrow I **will have arrived** in London.

في هذا الوقت من يوم غدٍ سأكون قد وصلت إلى لندن .

* By five o'clock this evening I **will have done** my homework.

بحلول الساعة الخامسة من هذا المساء سأكون قد أديت وظيفتي .

* By six o'clock tomorrow morning we will have left the
   city of Doha.

سنكون قد غادرنا مدينة الدوحة بحلول الساعة السادسة من صباح غدٍ.

The Past Perfect Tense
زمن الماضي التام

3- We use **the third verb-form** together with " **had** " when talking about **an
action** that took place **in the remote past.**

- يأتي الشكل الثالث للفعل مع   had ويعبر عن شيء حدث في الماضي البعيد ... ومكن فهم ذلك من
هذه الأمثلة .

* **Examples** أمـثلة :

       2   3

* Ali **told** me that he **had sold** his red car.

الفعلان في الماضي ، ولكن أحدها حدث قبـل الآخر . الفعـل في الجملـة الثانيـة وهـو البيـع حـدث أولا ،
والفعل في الجملة الأولي وهو " أخبر " حدث بعد ذلك بمعنى انه مكن أن يجتمع فعلان ، أحـدها شـكل
ثاني والآخر شكل ثالث مع المقوي had.
نأخذ أمثلة أخرى .

      2   3

* Ali told me that Mona had taken his book.

    2   3

* Mona said that Ali had gone out.

نلاحظ أن حدثاً(شيئا) حدث قبل الآخر ولمزيد من التوضيح مكننا أن نستخدم مفاتيح خاصة بهذه
الحالة .يمكن أن نقول:

    2   3

Ali told me *after* Mona had taken his book.

      3   2

Mona had taken the book *before* Ali told me.

after / before ← clues مفاتيح هذه الحالة هي (قبل before و. بعدafter)

* Correct the verbs in brackets :

1- Earlier today, Ali (leave) *had left* before you (come) *came* .

لحل هذه السؤال ... نسأل ... من الذي حدث أولاً ؟ ... طبعاً المغادرة (leave) ولهذا نقوم بوضع هذا الفعل في الشكل الثالث مع (had) ، أما (come) نضعه في الشكل الثاني لأنه حدث بعد ذلك.

2- Earlier today , Mona (phone) …………. after she (do)

………………. her homework.

3- Last Friday , I (visit) …………… my boss before I (go)

……….to the park.

4- Ali (take)…… the book last night after you (leave) …………..

5- I (pay) …………………. the bill before they disconnected the telephone.

6- They had connected the telephone before you (arrive)………

7- Ali said that he (lend) ……………… his uncle some money.

8- They told me that they (not do) …………… the homework.

9- She had seen everybody off before (talk) …………. to me.

10- We left after (see) ……….. the manager.

* نلاحظ في ٩ و ١٠. جاء بعدها الفعل مباشرة ولهذا نضع الفعل في الشكل الرابع before وafter

* Complete these sentences:

1-Ali had washed the car before ……………………………….
2- We had gone to the zoo before ………………………….
3- Mona arrived after ………………………………………….
4- I did my homework after ……………………………………...
5-They had started the game before …………………………

* **These clauses are correct :**
    1- We went home after we finished.
    2- She did the homework before she watched the film.
    3- We got everything ready before we set off on the trip.

* **Find the mistake and correct it :**

1- They have finished before I arrived. ....
2- She leave after she had seen the manager. ....
3- I had write the letter before calling you. ....
4- Ali said that he has found his book. ....
5- My father has sent the money before he left for London.

    ....

6- She had got the money after she finished. ....
7- We prepared everything before the guests had arrived.

    ………………………………………….................

* **Choose the right verb- form :**

    1- We have (go –went- gone) there many times before.
    2- She hasn't (do- did- done) the homework yet.
    3- Have they (see- seen- saw) the new boss yet?
    4- Ali had (taken- took- take) the medicine **before leaving**.
    5- What has (happen – happens – happened) to Ali ?

* **Put " after " or " before" in the right place:**
1- .... I got the licence, I had practised a lot .
2- .... I had cooked the meal, I went out .
3-They left .... they had had the lunch.
4-She had left .... you phoned.
5-They found it .... they had looked everywhere.

- This verb-form " **had seen** " and the like is used with " **If** " to express a condition and the result of that condition.

Had seen وما شابها تستخدم للتعبير عن شرط وجواب هذا الشرط .

Examples :

1- If I **had seen** Hamad, I **would have told** him.

لو أنني رأيت حمداً لأخبرته

Comment : This sentence shows that I did not see Hamad , and consequently , I did not tell him.

* التعليق : تبين هذه الجملة أنني لم أقابل حمداً ولم أخبره .

2- If it **had not rained** , I **would have travelled**.

لو أن الدنيا لم تمطر لكان سافرت.

Comment : This sentence shows that it rained , and because of that I did not travel.

* التعليق : تبين هذه الجملة أن الدنيا أمطرت ولهذا السبب أنا لم أسافر.

3- If you **had studied** well , you **would not have failed**.

لو أنك درست جيداً لما رسبت .

- **Correct the verbs in brackets :**

1- If she had done that , she (not get) ....into trouble.

2- If it (not rain) ...., we would have come.

3- I might have cancelled the project if they (have) ....doubts about it.

4- If I had money , I (lend) ....you some of it.

5- If I had had enough money, I (lend) ....
you some of it.

How to blame others. ؟ كيف نلوم الآخرين

4- We use **the third verb-form** together with " **should have** " or
" **could have**" to blame somebody for failing to do something
expected of him (her).

الشكل الثالث في الجمل التالية يساعد على توصيل فكرة اللـوم والتـوبيخ . فعنـدما نريـد أن نلـوم
شخصا على تقصير منه أو على خطأ قام به .. ماذا نقول له ؟

* You **should have told** me.   كان يجب أن تخبرني.

هنا نلوم شخصاً لأنه أخطأ .... إذ أنه لم يخبرني .

We blame a person for not having told me.

نأخذ مزيداً من الأمثلة . مع ملاحظة أننا نستخدم الفعل في الشكل الثالث مسبوقاً بـ
could have أو should   have

* He **should have studied** well.   كان يجب عليه أن يدرس جيداً .
* She **could have phoned** the police.

كان في مقدورها أن تتصل بالشرطة.

* They should have taken him to hospital.

كان يجب عليهم أن يأخذوه إلى المستشفى.

* You could have done something .

كان بمقدورك أن تفعل شيئا.

* He needn't have gone alone .   لم يكن بـحاجة لأن يذهب بـمفرده.
  * **Correct the verbs in brackets:**

    1-That was wrong of you. You (check) ....the car .
2- What she did was wrong. She (not buy) ....
    a green car.
3-He failed the English test. He (follow)...................
    Ali's instructions.

٩٤

4-He came late for school. He (not stay) ....
up late last night .

5- You did the wrong thing. You shouldn't have (take)
.... it without asking your doctor.

**5- We use the third verb-form to explain an action that took
place in the past.**

الشكل الثالث يساعد في تفسير حدث وقع في الماضي.

أمثلة:

1- Ali must have bought a car.   لا بد وأن علياً قد أشترى سيارة.

تفسير الموقف : شاهدت علياً يقود سيارةً وفسّرت ذلك بأنه اشترى سيارة ". أنا متأكد من هذا
التفسير"

Comment : Ali is driving a car . I give an explanation showing certainty .

2- Mona must have passed.   لا بد وأن منى قد نجحت.

3- Huda must have joined the university.

لا بد وان هدى قد التحقت بالجامعة.

4- She might have taken everything.

ربما أنها كانت قد أخذت كل شيء . "أنا غير متأكد من هذا التفسير"

I am not certain of that."

5- The father might have killed his son.

ربما أن الأب كان قد قتل أبنه.

6- A storm could have damaged the trees.

أن عاصفة يمكن أن تكون قد دمرت الأشجار.

* أما إذا أردنا أن نفسّر حدث يقع أمامنا الآن , فإننا نستخدم هذه التراكيب :

* If we explain an action that is taking place at the moment,
we can use these structures.

-   Ali hasn't called for days.

    He must be busy.   لا بد وأنه مشغول.

    He must be sick.   لا بد وأنه مريض.

    He must be studying for the exams. لا بد وأنه يدرس للامتحانات

     Here you are giving an explanation you are sure of :

     في الأمثلة السابقة إننا قدمنا تفسيرات متأكدون منها.

* But if you are giving an explanation you are not sure of ,   you can say:

-   **I haven't seen Ali for days.**

    He may be sick.   ربما يكون مريضاً.

    He might be busy.   ربما يكون مشغولاً.

    He may be studying for the exams.   ربـما أنه يدرس للامتحانات.

     * What do you say to comment on what you see ?

     1-   Mona is glad .

     ....

     2-   Huda is sad .

     ....

     3-   Ali didn't come to school yesterday.

     ....

     4-   Mona came to school, but she was ill.

     ....

     5-   You found the door of your house broken.

     ....

The Passive Voice

صيغة المبني للمجهول

6- We use **the third verb-form** together " any form of " **to be** "
to obtain the **passive voice**.

- يدخل الشكل الثالث للفعل في تكوين المبني للمجهول passive كما سبق أن قلنا .

- We have to differentiate between the active voice and the
passive voice.

To make the passive voice clear , let us give examples in
Arabic.

لا بد أن نُفرّق بين المبني للمعلوم و المبني للمجهول.
نأخذ أمثلة باللغة العربية .

كَسَرَ عليٌّ البابَ (مبني للمعلوم - الفاعل معلوم)

تكتب منى الدرس (مبني للمعلوم - الفاعل معلوم)

كُسِرَ البابُ (مبني للمجهول - الفاعل غير معروف)

يُكتب الدرسُ (مبني للمجهول - الفاعل غير معروف)

* لاحظ عند التحويل من مبني للمعلوم إلى مبني للمجهول أننا شطبنا الفاعل و تم تغيير في نطق
الفعل و في الإنجليزية يحدث شيء مشابه لذلك .

أمثلة :

مبني للمعلوم Active. ➜	Passive. مبني للمجهول
Ali will clean the car . ➜	The car will be cleaned .
Ali cleans the car ➜	The car is cleaned .
Ali cleaned the car . ➜	The car was cleaned .
Ali has cleaned the car ➜	The car has been cleaned .
Ali is cleaning the car ➜	The car is being cleaned .

● When changing the active verb into the passive , we do the following :

1- We divide the sentence into three main parts : subject , verb and object.
نحدد مكونات الجملة : الفاعل – الفعل – المفعول به .

2- We omit the subject , putting the object at the beginning of the new sentence.
نحذف الفاعل ونضع المفعول به في بداية الجملة الجديدة.

3- We use a form of verb " be " suitable for the main verb of the given sentence.
نستخدم شكلاً من be يكون من نفس شكل فعل الجملة المعطاة.

4- We change the main verb into its third form.
نحول الفعل الرئيسي إلى شكله الثالث .

5- We keep the auxiliaries as they are unless changes are necessary.
نبقي على الأفعال المساعدة كما هي ما لم تكون هناك ضرورة لتغييرها إلى شكل أخر .

* Say if these sentences are active or passive :

1- Ali has kept the food there . (   ) .
2- The food must be covered . (   ) .
3- The food must be fresh . (   ) .
4- The boy must be dreaming . (   ) .
5- The problem must be solved . (   ).
6- The problem will be solved soon. (   ).
7- The cars have been repaired . (   ).
8- The bill has been paid . (   ).
9- Ali has been busy for days . (   ).
10- The car is washed daily . (   ).
11- Ali is washing the car. (   ).

لا بد من معرفة أشكال فعل "be":

	1	2	3	4
be →	am, is, are, →	was, were →	been →	being

ملاحظة :   نستخدم "be" إذا كان الفعل المعطى لنا شكل أول مع مقو.

ملاحظة : يجب أن نقطع الجملة إلى أجزاء ثلاثة: الفاعل-الفعل-المفعول به.

1   Ali **can wash** the car . (active)

The car **can be washed** .   (passive)

لقد حققنا شروط passive و علينا أن نتبع نفس الطريقة عند التحويل من active إلى passive .

2- Ali **must tell** Hani about the accident.

Hani **must be told** about the accident .

في (١٠٢) نجد أن الفعلان wash و tell في الشكل الأول ومع كل واحد مقوٍّ هو can و must ولهذا لا بد من استخدام be في المبني للمجهول.

3- I **wash** the car every day .

الفعل شكل أول بدون مقوٍّ ولهذا نستخدم هنا "am" "is" "are"

The car **is washed** every day.

4-   Ali **washed** the car yesterday.

هنا الفعل شكل ثانٍ ولهذا لا بد من استخدام الشكل الثاني من be   The

car **was washed** yesterday.

5- Ali **has washed** the car.

هنا الفعل شكل ثالث. لماذا؟ .. ولهذا نستخدم be في الشكل الثالث.

The car **has** been washed.

6- Ali has washed the cars .

The cars **have been washed**. (لماذا ؟)

7 - Ali **is planting** some trees in the garden.

هنا الفعل شكل رابع ولهذا نستخدم be في الشكل الرابع.

Some trees **are being planted** in the garden.

* **Change from active into passive:**

1- They are studying the problem.

   The problem ………………………………………

2- Ali is making the tea.

   The tea ………………………....……………… by Ali.

3- <u>Nasser</u> is managing <u>the company</u>.

The company ....by ....

4- <u>We</u> <u>import</u> <u>cars</u> from Japan.............................

5- They should send <u>tents</u> to <u>the homeless</u> .

Tents ....

The homeless ....

6- We can protect <u>the environment</u> .

The environment ....

7- They sell <u>meat</u> at good prices.

Meat ....

8- We will do something to help the poor.

Something .... She broke my pen

yesterday.

My pen ....

10- She hid the money somewhere.

....

11- You should hide the money.

....

12- He has wasted my money.

....

13- He has removed all the obstacles. (العقبات)

All the obstacles ....

14- I have prepared the report.

....

15- You must pay <u>the bill</u> there.

....

16- He pays <u>the telephone bills</u> here.

....

17- He had paid all the water bills. (كل فواتير المياه)

....

18- The police are doing everything to fight crime.

....

19- Ali is watering the trees now.

....

20- We ought to solve the problem.

....

21- He has **made** me leave the country.

I ....**to** leave the country .

22- You must **let** the grass grow.

The grass ....**to** grow .

*ملاحظات مفيدة تتعلق بـ passive :

1- Mona prepares all the meals.
    All the meals are prepared by Mona .

إن جميع الوجبات يتم إعدادها بواسطة منى
*هنا يستحسن وضع فاعل الفعل مسبوقا ب by.
و لكن هذا ليس ضروريا في جميع الحالات وإنما المعنى هو الذي يفرض ذلك.

2- The police control traffic.

....

3- `Mrs. Nasser is studying our case.

....

4-We can say that Ali is right. (نبدأ الجملة الجديدة بـ it ')

It can .... that Ali is right.

5- People say that the king will step down.

....

6- People have confirmed that two people were killed.

   ....

7-   They have agreed to build more houses.

   It ....

8-   Many people confirmed that Ali would win the race.

   It ....

9- People hope that the problem will soon disappear.

   It ....

10-People have decided to complain about the new traffic system. It

....

قلنا أن أحد شروط passive هو أحد أشكال be ولكن في بعض الحـالات يمكـن اسـتبدال be بـ get أو
have

مثال:

* Five people were killed .   قتل خمسة أشخاص.
  Five people got killed.

* **Study these sentences:**

1-   I **will get my car repaired**.   سوف أصلح سيارتي .
2-   You can **get your house painted**.   يمكنك أن تدهن منـزلك.
3-   I **got my hair cut**.   إني قصصت شعري.

* في حقيقة الأمر أنا لم أقص شعري بنفسي ولكن أنا دفعت لشخص آخر و قام بقص شعري مقابل ذلك.
* في هذه الجمل "الفاعل في بداية الجملة "ليس هو الفاعل الحقيقي بل انه "استأجر شخصاً آخر ليقدّم له
الخدمة.
لا حظ الفرق بين هاتين الجملتين:
1-   I change the oil.   (أنا أبدل الزيت.(أنا الفاعل الحقيقي

2-   I get the oil changed.

      I have the oil changed.   أنا أبدل الزيت . (أنا لست الفاعل الحقيقي.)

*   **Similar examples :**

1- I **had** *my blood pressure* **examined**. كنت قد فحصت ضغط دمي.

        فعل شكل ثالث ┗ اسم ┗ شكل من ┗ have

2-   I will **get** *my blood* **tested**.   سوف أفحص دمي.

3-   She has *her tooth* pulled . (لقد خلع لها ضرسها.)لقد خلعت ضرسها.

4-   You can have *your trees* **watered**.   يمكنك أن تسقي أشجارك.

5-   We got *the problem* solved ٦. (لقد حلت لنا المشكلة.) لقد حللنا المشكلة.- We

should have *trees* planted everywhere.

        يجب أن نزرع الأشجار في كل مكان (يجب أن تزرع لنا الأشجار في كل مكان).

*   **Correct the mistakes in these sentences :**

1-   A car hit yesterday morning a lorry , and fifteen people killed.

    ....

2- The problem has not solved yet.

    ....

3- Everybody was pleasing because the exams were easy .

    ....

4- Bread and cake make here.

    ....

5- Several houses demolished by the Israeli army.

    ....

6- Last night the Israeli army kill three children in this area .

    ....

7-   That was wrong of you. You shouldn't have buy that car.

    ....

8- We have decide to widen the roads , so these buildings must remove.

………………………………………………..………………

9- Mona not arrived so far .

………………………………………………………………

10- We are happy because our salaries raised.

………………………………………………………………

* Tick (√) or (**X**) in front of each sentence :

1- A man has been kill in the accident.   (   )

2- The storm pulled most of the trees . (   )

3- Some of the houses fell down .   (   )

4- Some of the old houses were damaged . (   )

5- The thief caught and taken to prison.   (   )

6- The money spent on silly things.   (   )

7- The Internet is being use badly by some people. (   )

8- My father is takes me to school every day.   (   )

9- The children are driven to school before six o'clock. (   )

10- We are happy because our salaries have been raised.(   )

7- The Third Verb- Form as an Adjective
الشكل الثالث كصفة

Study these examples   : ادرس هذه الأمثلة

● I am **worried** about my sister ; she has some health problems.

إني قلق على أختي . إن لديها بعض المشاكل الصحية.

* **Ali is pleased with his exam results.**

إن علياً راضٍ عن نتائج امتحاناته .

* We are satisfied with your progress.   إننا راضون عن تقدمك .

* I am tired and bored. إني متعبٌ ومتملٍ.

* The coach was shocked and disappointed.

كان المدرب مصدوماً و خائب الأمل.

* We are annoyed and embarrassed. إننا منزعجون ومحرجون.

* نلاحظ من هذه الأمثلة أن الشكل الثالث يقوم بدور الصفة .

● It is important to recognize the third verb-form when acting as a verb.

يجب التعرف على الشكل الثالث عندما يقوم بدور الفعل.

* The good news has pleased me a lot.

إن الخبر الطيب قد أسعدني كثيراً.

* That film has bored me . ذلك الفيلم ملني .

* The players did not play well , so they have disappointed the fans.

اللاعبون لم يلعبوا بشكل جيدٍ , ولهذا فإنهم خيبوا أمل المشجعين.

الشكل الرابع للفعل The fourth Verb-Form

هو عبارة عن الفعل الأصلي مضافا إليه ـing مع مراعاة ما يلي:

* go ⟶ going
  play ⟶ playing
* sit ⟶ sitting   beg ⟶ begging يتوسل
  win ⟶ winning   bet ⟶ betting يراهن
  cut ⟶ cutting   rob ⟶ robbing يسرق
  put ⟶ putting   drag ⟶ dragging يسحب
  refer ⟶ referring   trap ⟶ trapping يوقع في فخ/ يحبس
* write ⟶ writing

drive ⟶ driving		leave ⟶	leaving يغادر
come ⟶ coming		remove ⟶	removing يزيل
* see ⟶ seeing		* die موت ⟶	dying
flee يهرب ⟶ fleeing		lie يكذب ⟶	lying

The Present Continuous Tense زمن المضارع المستمر

يتم استخدام الشكل الرابع للحـديث عـن شيء يحـدث الآن بشرط وجـود المقويات   am, is , are وأن
يكون الفعل موحياً بالحركة.

1- We use the fourth verb –form together with (am / is / are) to express an
action that is happening at this moment rovided that the verb is that of motion.

- **Clues to the present continuous tense**
مفاتيح المضارع المستمر

now   الآن , at the moment في هذه اللحظة , Listen ! استمع   at present في
انظر   ! Look , حالياً , currently , الوقت الحالي

* **Examples** أمثلة :

1-   I **am going** home *now* .

2-   Ali **is studying** English *at the moment* .

3-   *Look*! They **are climbing** the tree .

* These are examples of motion verbs :

walk , play, read , watch , discuss يناقش) be + busy,
noisy مزعج, nice, polite, worried قلق , confused مرتبك ,
fair عادل , helpful متعاون , friendly ودود, careful حذر ,
troublesome مثير للمشاكل, bad- tempered حاد المزاج, funny مضحك

** Verb " to be " is a motion verb if followed by an
   adjective demonstrating a concrete action.

(to be / verb) -----------⟶ .... ↓

يكون فعلاً متحركاً إذا جاء معه صفة تنطوي على سلوك مجسدٍ كما هو مبين في القائمة السابقة .

أما إذا جاء مع صفات لا تدل على حركة , فانه لا يجوز وضعه في الشكل الرابع
كفعل ومن هذه :

wrong , early , well , late, ill , happy, sad , angry, poor ,
rich, right .

The above adjectives do not imply a concrete action , so we
cannot use the fourth form of verb " to be " .

* Correct the verbs in brackets :

1- We (build) *are building* a new road now .

هنا المفتاح "now" و الفعل "build" (يبني) فعل يدل على حركة ولهذا نقوم بوضع هذا الفعل في الشكل الرابع مع
وضع المقوي المناسب.

2-   Ali and Mona (do) .... nothing at the moment .

3- My father (watch) ....a TV film at the moment .

4- At present, I (read) .... an article on pollution .

5- Look! A cat (chase) ....a mouse .

6- Listen ! A man (knock) ....at the door .

7- The boys (swim) .... now .

8- Look ! Ali (push) ....the table.

9- We (paint) .... the front door now.

10-Mona (wash) .... the dishes now.

11-Ali , unlike his brothers, (be) .... tidy these days .

١٠٧

12- We (be) .... glad that they (be) .... friendly

these days.

13- You (be) .... wrong . I think Ali and Hamad (be)

.... helpful and careful these days.

14- Ali (be) .... ill these days. He (be) .... in hospital.

Many friends (visit) .... him.

15- Hamad (be)......... late today . There (be) .... too much traffic.

* يجب أن نلاحظ بان الفعل المتحرك "يوحي بالحركة" فقط هـو الـذي يـتم اسـتخدامه عـلى النحـو
السابق .

* Only motion verbs are used to form the present continuous .

* Ali is walking to school now.   (√)

* Mona is liking tea.   (X)

* They are wanting you now.   (X)

* I am understanding you .   (X)

* We are learning English now .   (√)

* I like tea .   (√)

* I want you now .   (√)

* Ali wants milk now .   (√)

* We think that you are right .   (√)

* Mona is ill at the moment.   (√)

* Hamad is being busy at the moment.   (√)

مشغول/ هذه صفة سلوك توحي بحركة.

* Ali is being ill at the moment.   (X)

مريض/ هذه صفة لا توحي بحركة.

Correct the verbs :

1- Ali (have) .... lunch now .

2- I (have) ....a car at present .

3- We (believe) .... that Ali is the best of all .

4- Right now, we (believe)…………. that the company should improve our

working conditions .

5-   Now , I (want) …………. to tell you something .

6- Listen ! I (think) …………. that the problem is not too difficult to solve.

7- Now , I (think) ……….. of how we can find a way out of this bad situation.

8- Ali and Hamad (be) ………….. in London now.

9- At the moment, Ali (have) ……….. no idea of what the meeting will discuss.

10- Now, they (have) ………… a great holiday in Europe.

11- …………. Ali (study) ………………. now ?

12- What …………… you (do) …………… now ?

13-Ali (be) ………. noisy these days. I don't know what to do.

14- The boys (be) ……………….. confused مرتبكون these days.

We have to do something.

15- Mona (be) …………. late . I don't know why.

16- I think they (have) ………….. a problem with the

neighbours these days.

17- I (see) …………….. some birds in the sky.

18- My father (see) ……… his secretary at the moment.

19- My mother (taste) ……………… the soup now.

She likes soup that (taste) …………… delicious.

20- My sister (smell) ………………….. a flower now.

I think the flower (smell) ……………. nice.

2-The Fourth verb-form with " always " shows disapproval.

ثانيـاً: الشكل الرابع في وجود المفتاح "always" و في وجـود المقويـات am, is , are يعـبر عن التذمر و عدم الرضا من شيء تكرر كثيرا و أصبح سببا لتذمرنا.

أمثلة :

*   You are always talking .
*   She is always writing .
*   They are always calling at night .

لاحظ الجمل التالية :

*   You always come on time .
*   She always calls me at mid-night .
*   They always visit me on Friday .

هذه الجمل الثلاثة لا تعبر عن عدم الرضا بل تقرر أشياء لا تسبب لنا إزعاجاً . بل تخبرنـا عـن واقـع يـتم عادةً :

أمثلة :

1- You (always smoke) _always smoke_ here .

هنا نعبر عن حالة التدخين دون تذمر.

2- You (always smoke) _are always smoking_ here.

هنا نتحدث عن التدخين ونبدي تذمرا.

3 – The Fourth Verb-form and the future tense
الشكل الرابع والمستقبل

ثالثـاً: الشكل الرابع مع المقويات am , is , are . يعبر عن زمن المستقبل . إننا ننوي أن نقوم بشيء في المستقبل و الآن اتخذنا الإجراءات و قمنا بالترتيبات المؤدية لتنفيذ العمـل ..مثـل الـزواج ... لـه قرار و مقدمات و ترتيبات تسبق عملية الزواج الفعلي .

1- I **am leaving for** London tomorrow .

2- Ali **is getting married** next Monday .

3- They **are having** an exam next Saturday .

* Correct the verbs :

1- Ali (move) .... to a new house next month.

2- We (have) .... a party tomorrow .

3- Huda (get married) .... next Friday .

4- I (visit) .... Ali tomorrow .

5- They (open) .... the bank branch next week .

4- The Future Continuous Tense   : زمن المستقبل المستمر

We use this tense when talking about an action that will be taking place at a particular moment in the future.

يتم استخدام هذا الزمن للحديث عن حدثٍ سيكون مستمراً في الحدوث في لحظة ما من زمن المستقبل. فنحن لا نتحدث عن كل المستقبل بل عن جزء منه.

How to form it : كيفية تكوينه :

We use the 4th verb form of a motion verb together with " will be (shall be) ."

Examples :

1- At five o'clock tomorrow morning , I **will be leaving for** Doha.

2- We **shall be building** more houses next April.

3- All the students **will be taking** exams at 8 o'clock tomorrow morning.

4- People **will be celebrating** the Eid during the next week.

إن الناس سيكونون منشغلين بالاحتفال بالعيد خلال الأسبوع القادم.I shall be

furnishing my new house by next May.

سأكون منشغلاً بتأثيث بيتي الجديد بحلول مايو القادم.

* We can say :

I **will be busy furnishing** my new house .

They will be busy planting more trees.

You must be dreaming. (لا بد وإنك تحلم / تعبيراً عن عدم التصديق)

You must be joking . لا بد وإنك تمزح .

5- The Past Continuous Tense زمن الماضي المستمر

رابعـاً: الشكل الرابع مع المقويات   was   أو   were   يعبر عن حدث كان مستمراً في لحظة مـا مـن زمـن
الماضي .

1- I was playing football at five o'clock .

2- They were having breakfast at five o'clock .

مفاتيح هذه الحالة : بينما while , أو بينما as , أو عندما when

4   2

3- I was playing football *when* you called .

4- You called *when* I was playing_ football .

5- You called *while* I was washing .

6- *While* we were studying_ English , Ali came in .

بينما كنا ندرس إنجليزي , دخل علي .

ملاحظة: في وجود while أو when يوجد فعلان.. أحدها شكل ثانٍ والآخر شكل رابع مع was أو
were .

ملاحظة: الفعل في الشكل الرابع كان يحدث قبل وقوع الفعل في الشكل الثاني.

 * Put "while" or "when" :

1- .... you phoned , Ali was sleeping .

2- ....I was reading , Mona came in crying .

3- Ali left .... we were listening to music .

4- We went out .... it was raining .

5- .... I was driving home, a cat ran across the road .

* Join every two sentences using " when " or " while ' :

* لكي تكون عملية الربط ناجحة , علينا أن نتذكر القاعدة المتعلقة بـهذا الأمر.
و لا بد من التنبيه إلى أن الفعل الذي يحدث في الأول , يتم وضعه في الشكل الرابع.

1- I saw Ali . He drove home.

(هذا غير ممكن. إننا بحاجة إلى إحداث تغيير)

When I saw Ali , he was driving home .

(هذا الفعل كان مستمراً قبل مشاهدتي لعلي drove)

(ولكي نضعه في الشكل الرابع لا بد من إعادته إلى شكله الأول ثم نضيف إليه ing-)

2- It rained . She went out. ....

3- They watched TV. They heard a knock .

....

4- The president gave a speech . A man fired at him.

....

5- He took the test . He felt dizzy.

....

* Correct the verbs:

1- A car (hit) .... a child while he (cross)......... the road .

2- When Ali (arrive) ...., we (sit) .... under the tree .

3- Hamad (break) ...... a cup while we (have) ...... lunch.

4- We (have) .... a problem while we (drive)...... home .

5- Ali (write) ....a letter when I came in.

ملاحظة : يمكن أن يتم حذف الاسم و المقوي , إذا كان نفس الاسم في الجملتين .

1- Ali felt ill while driving home .

علي هو الذي شعر بالمرض . و علي هو الذي كان يسوق السـيارة متوجهـا إلى البيت .هنـا يجـوز حـذف الاسم و المقوي اللذين بعد while و when .

2- I saw a snake while walking in the farm .

3- Ali screamed when touching the wire .

4- Mona ran away on seeing the dog . فرت منى عند رؤيتها الكلب

5-Ali fell down while running. سقط علي على الأرض بينما كان يجري.

* **Correct the mistakes in these sentences :**

1- Ali is read a newspaper in the garden.

....

2- We are watching TV every day.

....

3- It snowing , so we have cancel the trip.

....

4- He is having lunch when I called.

....

5- I saw them while they waiting for you .

....

6- We shall be do something else by next Sunday.

....

7- I do not believe it. He must dreaming.

....

8 - It is raining when we arrived.

....

9- Ali was reading a book while we arrived.

....

10- The boys play at the moment.

....

11- She is knowing Noura well.

....

12- The soup is tasting delicious.

....

13- We fighting for freedom.

....

14- The farmer works in the farm at the moment.

....

15- They asking for help .

....

6- The Present Perfect Continuous Tense

زمن المضارع التام المستمر

This tense shows that an action started in the past and is still
going on.

خامســاً: الشكل الرابع مع المقويات have been أو has been يعبر عن حدث وقع في الماضي و استمر
في الحدوث حتى هذه اللحظة ... بمعنى أن هذا النوع من الجملة يربط الماضي بالحاضر .

Clues to this tense : " since / for " مفاتيح هذا الزمن

ملاحظة :

since Friday , since last Monday , since yesterday , since 1995, since last year , since
April, since last April , since 3 o'clock .

بعد since يأتي اسم الزمن ...اسم ساعة (الساعة الثالثة) أو اسم يـوم، أو اسـم شـهر، أو اسـم سـنة. أي
زمن يحدد بداية القيام بالفعل (نقطة البداية) .

" since " is followed by a time indicator showing the start of the action.

أما for فيأتي بعدها طول مدة الفعل ... طول مدة البناء أو طول مدة الدراسة .

" for " is followed by a time indicator showing the length of the action.

for 3 days , for a day , for hours , for 3 hours , for weeks,   for a week ,   for years ,
for a year , for 5 years , for a long time منذ وقت طويل- لوقت طويل .

* Examples أمثلة :

1- Ali has been studying English *since 1995* (سنة البداية).

2-   We have been studying English *for 4 years* .

(طول مدة الدراسة) إن علياً يدرس إنجليزي منذ ٤ سنوات.

3- I **have been living** here since 1990 .

4- Mona **has been playing** there for hours_.

5- We **have been waiting**   here since 5 o'clock.

* Put "since" or "for" :

1- It has been raining .... the morning .

2- It has been snowing .... days .

3- I have been waiting ....ten minutes now .

4- She has been swimming .... 1995 .

5- We **have been talking** .... you **left** .

6- My brothers haven't gone out .... the last three day.

7- She hasn't visited me .... last April.

8- These boys have been sitting here .... 5 o'clock.

9- I have wanted to get a new car .... a long time.

10- Mona has been busy .... hours.

* **Study these sentences to see the difference.**

   1- I have been walking here for hours . (√)
      I have sat there for hours .   (√)
   2- I have been knowing Ali for years .   (X)
   3- Ali has been wanting a car since 1995 (X)

   *   Only verbs showing concrete motion are used in the
       continuous forms . With " since " and " for " , stative
       verbs are used in the forms shown in these sentences.

الأفعال التي تدل على حركة ظاهرة هي التي يتم استخدامها في صيغة الاستمرار (الشكل الرابع).
ولهذا في وجود since أو for مع فعل خالٍ من الحركة أو فعل يدل حركة محدودة يتم استخدام
صيغة المضارع التام .

*   I **have known** Ali for years . (√)
*   Ali **has wanted** a car since 1995 . (√)
* My father **has been** busy for days.
* I **have not seen** Ali since last Friday.

* It **hasn't rained** for years.

* She **has eaten five apples** since the morning.

أكلت خمس تفاحات منذ الصباح.(عملية الأكل تدل على حركة مقيدة بخمس تفاحات)

* I **have written three letters** since lunch-time.

* I **have been writing letters** for years. (الكتابة هنا حركة مطلقة.)

* **Put the verbs in brackets in the right forms:**

1- It (snow) .... for days .

2- She (cry) .... since five o'clock .

3- They (shout) .... for hours .

4- Ali (learn) .... English since he **came** to Qatar (تربط فعل

(لا بد من ملاحظة أن since شكل ٤ وفعل شكل ثانٍ

5- I (write) ....since you (go) .... out .

6- They (walk) .... for days .

7- I (not walk) .... for days .

8- I (write) .... five sentences since the morning .

9- I (write) .... letters since the morning .

10- He (be) ....busy for days .

11- He (borrow) .... money from banks
    since 1990 .

12- He (borrow) .... five million dollars from
    banks since 1990 .

13- I (be) .... busy since you (leave) ....

14- I (know) .... this man for years.

15- He (make) .... five mistakes since you left.

16- He (make) .... mistakes since he took over.

ملاحظة هامة : since إذا جاء بعدها مؤشر زمني فيكون معناها "منذ" . أما إذا جاءت تربط بين جملتين فيكون معناها "لأن" أو "بما أن" .

* Since (= because) you come late, I have to expel you .

بـما أنك تأتي متأخراً , فإنني مضطر لأن أطردك .

* Since he is impolite, we cannot invite him .

بـما أنه غير مؤدب , فإننا لا نستطيع أن ندعوه .

١١٧

11- I play football <u>for two hours</u> every day. (لمدة ساعتين)

12- I will (can- have to- want to) play <u>for two hours</u>.

13- I played <u>for two hours</u> yesterday.

14- I have played <u>for two hours.</u> (لقد لعبت لمدة ساعتين)

15- I have waited *for two hours.* (لقد انتظرت لساعتين)

* **Join every two sentences using " since " :**

1- She has been cooking . She finished the washing-up.

   ....

2- I study . I got up at 5 o'clock.

   (لا بد من إحداث تغييرات. و لا بد من معرفة الفعل الذي حدث أولاً.)

   ....

3- They repaired the fault . They arrived.

   ....

4- I did not receive any letter from him. He left the city.

   ....

5- She is pregnant حامل . She got married last May.

   ....

* **Find the error and correct it   أوجـد الخـطـأ وصححـه**

1- We are waiting for hours. ....

2- It has been rain for days. ....

3- Ali hasn't phoned since two weeks. ....

4- I have been reading since three hours ....

5- Mona has been cooking for 8 o'clock. ....

6- We have been doing this job since years. ....

7- Ali has been ill for last Monday. ....

8- He has been calling since a long time. ....

9- The boys have been talking since the class start. ....

10- She was shopping since 6 o'clock ....

7- The Past Perfect Continuous Tense
زمن الماضي التام المستمر

This tense shows that an action started in the past and was still going on.

يبين هذا الزمن أن حدثاً بدأ في الماضي وكان لا يزال مستمراً .

Examples :

         2   4

1- Ali told me that he had been studying since 5 o'clock.

2- The players said that they had been training for hours.

3- People complained that they had been suffering for years.

اشتكى الناس من أنهم يعانون منذ سنوات .

* Put the verbs in the correct forms :

1- The farmer said that he (work) .... on the farm for years.

2- Noura told her brother that she (paint) .... since he came home .

3- Some people believed that Ali (wait)...................... for a long time.

4- The firemen explained that they (fight) .... the fire since they reached the place.

5- My father said that he (read) .... a newspaper for half an hour.

* Correct the mistakes in these sentences :

1- We have looking for it since the morning.

....

2- Ali has been at home since two hours.

....

3- I have been wanting to see Ali for a long time.

....

4- She has drank two cups of tea for 4 o'clock.

....

5- Ali said that he have been teaching his son since he came back.

....

١١٩

8-The Fourth Verb – form without auxiliaries : The Gerund. الشكل
الرابع بدون مقويات

A- The 4th verb form without an auxiliary is **a gerund** functioning
as a noun .

الشكل الرابع بدون مقويات يكون اسماً.

* I hate smoking .   إني أكره التدخين.
* You can improve your reading and writing .

يمكنك أن تحسّن قراءتك وكتابتك.

* Collecting stamps is an interesting hobby.   جمع الطوابع هواية مـمتعة
* Cheating is forbidden .   الغش محرم.
* I enjoy looking at the blue sky.

إني أستمتع بالنظر إلى السماء الزرقاوية.

في الجمل السابقة نجد أن الشكل الرابع للفعل احتل مكان الاسم في الجملة .

B- **The gerund functions as an adjective** .

الشكل الرابع يعمل عمل الصفة

1-Ali is interested in the study of **climbing** plants .

إن علياً مهتم بدراسة النباتات المتسلقة .   2-We don't

إننا لا نقلق من المياه الجارية.   worry about **running** water.

3- I have done my **reading** task .

4- The **developing** countries should overcome their
borrowing problem .

إن البلدان النامية يجب أن تتغلب على مشكلتها المتعلقة بالاقتراض .

5- Some **oil-producing** countries don't stick to the quota
   system.

بعض الأقطار المنتجة للنفط لا تتقيد بنظام الحصص .

6- The result is encouraging .   النتيجة مشجعة.

7- The story is disappointing and insulting.

القصة مخيبة للآمال و مهينة .

8- We need interesting and exciting films.

إننا نحتاج إلى أفلام ممتعة ومثيرة.

9- We do not need boring films.   إننا لا نحتاج إلى أفلام مملة.

10- We are expecting to get amazing results.

إننا نتوقع أن نحصل على نتائج مذهلة.

11- He is asking for convincing evidence.   إنه يطلب دليلاً مقنعاً .

He is still not convinced.   إنه لا يزال غير مقتنع - 12 - I saw a man

crying. → (يبكي - وتصف الرجل)

13-   We heard some people **shouting.** → (يصرخون-وتصف الناس)

C- The **gerund** follows **a preposition**.

الشكل الرابع يأتي بعد حروف الجر

1- You should change your way of thinking .

يجب أن تغير طريقتك بالتفكير.

2- Your way of writing appeals to me a lot .

إن طريقتك بالكتابة تروق لي كثيراً .

3-We are worried about having more deaths .

إننا قلقون من كون لدينا مزيدا من الوفيات .

4-You are responsible for running the company.

أنت مسئول عن إدارة الشركة .

5-You are good at solving problems.   أنت جيد في حل المشاكل.

6-We are tired of watching non-Arabic films .

إننا متعبون من مشاهدة أفلام غير عربية.

7-You should read the question carefully before answering it

8- I will tell you on receiving my salary.

9- We are committed to making peace .   (هنا حرف جر to)

نحن ملتزمون بصنع السلام .

10- We can improve traffic by using traffic-lights.

إننا نستطيع أن نحسّن المرور بواسطة استخدام إشارات ضوئية.

11- The problem can be solved **through improving** salaries.

المشكلة يمكن أن تُحل من خلال تحسين الرواتب .

12 - They are still far from reaching an agreement.

إنـهم لا يزالون بعيدون عن التوصل إلى اتفاق.

13- I am against teenagers driving cars.

إنني ضد قيادة المراهقين للسيارات.

● In general, if a verb is followed by an infinitive , we use the word " to " . Here it is not a preposition.

1- I want *to tell* you the truth.

مقوٍ للفعل الذي يليه. └

2- She asked me *to help* her.

3- They refused *to sign* the contract.

إنـهم رفضوا أن يوقعوا على العقد.

4- He forgot *to bring* money.

5- We tried *to see* the manager.   حاولنا أن نقابل المدير .

من الأمثلة السابقة نلاحظ وجود فعل مقوٍ لفعل آخر بينهـم to وهي
ليست حرف جر.

وهناك صفات تكون مقويات للفعل وتنطبق عليها الحالة نفسـها.

1- It is good *to do* that.

2- It is important *to use* the seatbelt.

3- It is easy *to learn* English.

4- It is fair *to give* women their rights.

من العدل أن نعطي النساء حقوقهن.

5- It is shameful *to degrade* people.   من الخجل أن نحتقر الناس.

6 - We are   هناك صفات كثيرة تؤدي نفس الوظيفة .

willing *to come*.   نحن راغبون في الحضور .

I am happy to say that.

We are proud to do that.   إننا فخورون بأن نفعل ذلك.

**In some cases "to" is a preposition followed by a gerund .

It is through practice that we can avoid confusion .

في بعض الحالات تكون to حرف جر يتبعها فعل شكل رابع.
وعن طريق الممارسة نستطيع أن نتجنب الخلط.

1- We **object to** building a church here.

إننا نعترض على بناء كنيسة هنا.

2- This will **lead to** having problems with the police.

يؤدي إلى

3- We **look forward to** seeing you.   نتطلع إلى

4- We **are used to** doing such a thing.   معتاد على

5- They **are close to** making a decision.

إنهم قريبون من اتخاذ قرار.

* Correct the verbs in brackets :

1- I like (swim) .... and (travel) ....

2- Mona is good at (cook) .... and (paint) ....

3- She thanked me for (give) .... her some useful information .

4- We should insist on (have) .... a hospital built here .

5- I look forward to (see) .... you as soon as possible.

6- I asked Ali to (see) .... his doctor .

7- She used to (eat) ......a lot , but now she no longer does .

8- Don't worry about that. They are used to (climb) ....high mountains

.

9- There is another way to (do) .... that .

10- I can show you another way of (do) .... that.

11- You should tell your mother before (go) .... out   It is nice to (do)

.... that.

12- It is fair to (help) .... the needy .

13- It is easy to (learn) ....English .

14- (learn) .... English has become a necessity

15- I prefer (read) ....**to** (write) ....

* **Correct the mistakes in these sentences :**
    1- It is wrong to smoking here.
    ....

    2- We are happy to taking you .
    ....

    3- She is used to drink cold water.
    ....

    4- He is the first one to leaving .
    ....

    5- She was the last one to arrived.
    ....

    6- We are close to finished the job.
    ....

    7- I am for discuss the problem in public.
    ....

    8- I object to have any problem with neighbours.
    ....

    9- I refused to coming to the party.
    ....

    10- We have to changing our way of do things.
    ....

* Correct the verbs:

المطلوب وضع الفعل في الشكل المناسب ,ويحدد هذا أمران :

١-وجود مفاتيح الشكل .

٢- وجود مقويات الشكل .

1- Look ! Ali (run) ....

2- I (see) .... Mona while she (go) .... home.

3- Ali (be) ....in London ,where he is (study) .... English . He (finish) ...... next summer. He(get) .... there four years ago, and (join)......London university.

4- She (study) .... English since 1990.

5- I (teach) .... for 30 years , but I (not be) .... fed up.

6- He (not eat) .... anything for days.

7- That is (alarm) .... I (be) .... worried .

8- They (be) ....busy since last Friday .

9- I (watch) ....T.V since you (leave) ....

10- Ali always (pay) .... the telephone bills .

11- Ali usually (go) ....fishing on Fridays .

12- I (not meet) .... Ali yesterday ; he (be) .... too busy.

13-   Nasser (not live) ....here ; he (live) .... somewhere else .

14-   She (find) .... it an hour ago. She was (please)......

15- She (be) .... nervous last night , so nobody dared (talk) .... to her.

16-   I (just get) .... Ali's letter .

17- He (take) .... it before you (come) ....in.

18 -She (be)........... ill for days . I am really (worry)..........

19 - I hate (swim) ....

20- You can (do) .... it .

21- I am against your way of (think) ....

22- You are for (build) .... a school here .

23- You should (eat) .... healthy food .

24- He has not (find) .... it yet.

25-We are (wait) .... for Ali.

26-It has been (rain) .... for hours .

27-The car has been (wash) ....

28-Ali has been (wash) .... the car since 4 o'clock.

29-You are always (do) .... such unpleasant things .

30-He should have (go) .... somewhere else .

31-It is necessary to (respect) ....others . If you respect

   people , they (respect) ....

32-We have got some (encourage) ....news.

33-The new project has (displease) .... many people.

34-Your performance أدائك is (disappoint) ....

35-I sometimes (come)...... by bus, but Ali (come) ....
   by car.

36- Look! They (come). .... We should stop (work)
   ...., and go to (meet) .... them . It (be) ....
   nice to welcome the people who (come) .... to
   visit you .

37- Ali (come) .... late yesterday, so I (get) ....
   angry with him .

38- She (not come) .... yet. I (not know) ....

what (do) ....

39 -I am (write) .... to Ali. I (not write) ....

to him for months. I hate (write) .... letters.

40-The hospital was (build) .... in 1992 and

opened last year .

41-Ali was (build) .... a wall when I came to see him . 42-You

(spend)........... too much money . That (be).......

wrong .

43-I spend some time (read)...............newspapers and

magazines

44-He has(spend) .... all his money; he must have

(go)......... mad .

* Put these words into the correct order :

ضع الكلمات في الترتيب السليم:

1- at / I / English / school / will / learn /

....

2- can't / French / speak / I /

....

3- Arabic/ be / the afternoon /during / they / learning / will /

....

4- is / to / easy / learn / it / Arabic /

....

5- must / this / you / carefully / road / cross /

....

6- will / it / he / before / finish / noon /

....

7- just / the / he / report / has / finished /

....

8- were / when / they / washing / arrived / you /

....

9- difficult / is / this / too / question /

....

10- my / lost / I / passport / have .

....

11- don't / where / I / to / know / look for / it /

....

12- waiting / been / here / have / since / I / o'clock / three /

....

13- can't/ the/ car / buy/ I / it/ too/ because / is /expensive /

....

14- been / sick / has / for / days / five / he /

....

15- buy / a / I / want / car / to / new /

....

16-don't / traffic problems / have / any / we / because / are / roads / wide / our /

....
....

17-reduce / we / accidents / the / of / number / can /

....

18-fluently / proud / Ali / of / am / I / because / speaks / he /
English /

....

19-dangerous / is / to / it /madly / drive /

....

20- endanger / if / that / you / will / you / do / others /

....

21- important / read / is / to / it / books / provide / us / because / with / information / they / useful /

....

....

22- been / for / Ali / working / has / 10 years / company / with / this /

....

....

16- can / you / car / your / repaired / there / have /

....

....

17- are / prices / so / are /rising/complaining يشتكون /we/

....

....

20- have to / taxes ضرائب / we / pay / high /

....

....

21- is / everywhere / spreading ينتشر / corruption الفساد /

....

....

22- should / something / do / we / people /

to relieve يخفف من معاناة /

....

....

الأفعال المساعدة The Auxiliaries

1- **Primary auxiliaries** : أفعال مساعدة أولية

a- have (has) / had / had / having .

** A lexical verb with 4 forms فعل له أربعة أشكال وله معنى.
1- I have five boys and three girls. عندي ٥ أولاد و ٣ بنات.
2- I had lunch at one o'clock yesterday.

تناولت طعام الغداء في الواحدة يوم أمس.

3 We are having a party tomorrow.
4 I hope that you will have the job.
5 I have just had my lunch. ٦- **She has not** لقد تناولت غدائي للتو .
had her lunch yet.
7- Do you have any complaint ? ٨- هل لديك أية شكوى؟ **Does Hassan**
have new ideas ?

** A functional verb used to form the perfective
فعل مساعد في تكوين زمن المضارع أو الماضي التام .
1- I **have washed** the car.
2- Ali **has found** his book.
3- She **had phoned** before she came.
4- We **have been playing** since the morning.
5- By this time tomorrow, I **shall have finished** the report.

b- (to be) ⟶ am, is , are / was , were / been / being/

** A lexical verb having 4 forms :

1- I **am satisfied** with the result. إني راضٍ عن النتيجة.

2- They **are interested** in the job.   إنهم مهتمون بالوظيفة.

3- Ali **was busy** yesterday, and I think he **will be busy** tomorrow.

4- We **have been busy** for many days.

5- Ali **is being nice** these days.

** **A functional verb used to form the progressive.**

1- Ali **is washing** the car at the moment.

2- Ali **was sleeping** when you phoned.

3- Ali **has been playing** football since 1996.

4- We **have been talking** for hours.

5- Mona said that she **had been asking for** aid for months.

It is a functional verb used to form the passive
* يدخل في تكوين المبني للمجهول

1 - The car **is checked** every day.

2- All the old houses **must be removed.**

جميع البيوت القديمة يجب أن تُزال.

4-   The old houses were removed .

أزيلت البيت القديمة.(تمت إزالة البيوت القديمة).

5-   Some of the old houses have been removed.

6-   Many of the old houses are being removed.

إن كثيراً من البيوت القديمة تجري إزالتها.

C- do   did   done   doing

*A lexical verb with four forms: فعل له معنى وله أربعة أشكال

1- I always **do** my homework before I **do** anything else.

إنني دائماً أودي وظيفتي قبل أن أعمل أي شيء أخر.

2- You **can do** that easily.   إنك تستطيع أن تفعل ذلك بسهولة.

3- We **should do** what is right.   يجب أن نفعل ما هو صحيح.

4- He **did** me a favour.   إنه صنع لي معروفاً.

5- She **has done** the wrong thing.   إنها فعلت الشيء الخاطئ.

6- He **is doing** his duty at the moment.   إنه يؤدي واجبه الآن.

** **A functional verb**   فعل مســـاعد

1- I **do not** (**don't**) **like** tea.   إني لا أحب الشاي.

2- She **does not do** anything at night.   إنها لا تفعل شيئاً في الليل.

3- He **did not tell** anybody.   إنه لم يخبر أي شخص.

4- **Do** you **agree** with me ?   هـل تتفق معي في الرأي؟

5- **Does** Ali **accept** this idea ?   هـل يقبل علي بالفكرة؟

6- Where **do** you **go** in the evening?   أين تذهب في المساء؟

7- When **does** Ali **call** ?   متى يتصل علي؟

8- **Did** you **see** the film ?   هـل شاهدت الفيلم ؟   9- Why **did**

your father **cancel** the trip?   لماذا ألغى والدك الرحلة؟

** **We notice that we only use verb " to do " as an auxiliary in the first and second forms . In this case we use these two forms to make a verb negative or to make a question.**

يجب أن نلاحظ بأن الفعل المذكور أعلاه يتم استخدامه كفعل مساعد فقط في شكله الأول والثاني. وفي هذه الحالة يتم استخدامه في النفي وفي تكوين سؤال شريطة وجود فعل أخر في الشكل الأول.

2- **Defective Auxiliaries:**أفعال مساعدة ناقصة/ سبق التعرض لها

Each has two forms , one for the present and the other for the past.

But the past form sometimes has nothing to do with the past tense.

كل فعل منها له شكلين, أحدها للمضارع والأخر للماضي, ولكن صيغة الماضي لا تفيد الماضي أحياناً.

can يستطيع / may قد- ربما / must يجب / shall / will سوف /
could استطاع / would / should يجب/ ought to أن ينبغي/ might

1- I can do everything. You cannot carry this box ; it is too heavy.
   (القدرة)

2- Can you carry this box for me ,please ?
   (طلب بأدب polite request)

3- I could go everywhere when I was young.
   (القدرة في الماضي)

4- You could use my car.   بإمكانك أن تستخدم سيارتي (اقتراح)

5- He could come if he is free.   قد يأتي إذا كان حرا(بلا عمل)

6- He may (might) come if he is free.   (الاحتمال)

7- Shall I turn the radio off ?   (اقتراح)

8- We should drive slowly to avoid accidents (يجب-نصيحة)

9- We must defend our country if attacked.   (واجب)
   يجب أن ندافع عن بلادنا إذا هوجمت.

10- We ought to respect others.   ينبغي أن نحترم الآخرين.

11- You need study well= You need to study well.
    = You must study well.

12- You needn't come on Friday.   لست بحاجة لأن تأتي يوم الجمعة.
    You mustn't come on Friday.
    Need I tell the boss ? = Must I tell the boss ?
    (Yes, you need./ No, you needn't.)

** We need fresh water. (نحتاج) This road needs rebuilding.

You need to do something.

You don't need to go by car. = You needn't go by car.

** I daren't say that.   إني لا أجرؤ أن أقول ذلك.

How dare you say that ?

I don't dare to say that.

He daren't say that. = He doesn't dare (to) say such a thing.

إنه لا يجرؤ أن يقول مثل هذا الشيء.

* **Underline the auxiliaries in these sentences :**

1- We <u>can</u> come at six o'clock.

2- She has finished and left.

3- They are waiting at the gate.

4- Did you get one ?

5- She is doing nothing at the moment.

6- They had left before they could see the boss.

7- You needn't come before lunch.

8- You don't have to say something like that.

9- We daren't do anything.

10- You had better cancel the trip.

* **Underline the main verbs in these sentences :**

1- I have <u>received</u> a lot of letters from my fans.

2- I have cheese , honey and bread for breakfast.

3- She has got a headache .

4- She has long , fair hair.

5- You don't drink milk.

6- She does what she can.

7- We are having a party.

8- He did me a favour and left.

9- They were abroad when their father died.

10- They were talking when I came in.

Transitive Verbs الأفعال المتعدية

* These verbs take a direct object هذه أفعال تأخذ مفعولاً به مباشراً

1- I **need** some more information.
2- We **accept** this idea.
3- We must **donate** money.   نتبرع بـ
4- They **have cancelled** the trip.
5- We **called off** the meeting.   ألغينا الاجتماع
6- I **advise** you to eat less food.
7- Smoking can **affect** health badly.   يؤثر في
8- Ali **has confirmed** that he is coming to the party.   أكد
9- She **has denied** the rumour.   لقد أنكرت الإشاعة.
10- We **cannot feed** this wild animal.

* وبناءً على ذلك بإمكاننا أن نضعها في صيغة المبني للمجهول.
* The trip was cancelled.   ألغيت الرحلة.
* Some of the old houses have been restored.

بعض البيوت القديمة قد تم ترميمها.

Intransitive Verbs أفعال غير لازمة

*   **These verbs do not take an object.**   هذه أفعال لا تأخذ مفعولاً.

1- You **laugh** a lot.   إنك تضحك كثيرا.
2- They can sail today .
3- They are crying.   إنهم يبكون.
4- The oil price will rise .   إن سعر النفط سوف يرتفع.
5- The oil prices are falling.   إن أسعار النفط آخذة في الهبوط.

6- The sun soon vanished .   سرعان ما أن اختفت الشمس.

7- They arrived an hour ago.   وصلوا قبل ساعة.

8- The old house collapsed suddenly   انهار البيت القديم فجأة.   9-The plane has just taken off.   أقلعت الطائرة للتو.   10- Our economy is flourishing .   إن اقتصادنا يزدهر.

** وهناك أفعال أخرى غير لازمة نذكر منها :

blow (الرياح) تهب / happen = occur يحدث-يقع / appear يظهر /

creep يزحف / dive يغوص / become يصبح / sleep ينام / die يموت /

stand يقف / sit يجلس / rain تمطر / give in يستسلم / seem يبدو /

travel يسافر / succeed ينجح / snow تثلج / work يعمل /

escape يهرب – ينجو / survive يبقى حياً

* **The intransitive verbs cannot be used in the passive form.** الأفعال غير اللازمة لا يمكن أن توضع في صيغة المبني للمجهول .

Transitive and non-transitive verbs

wake up يوقظ- يستيقظ	/	take ff (الملابس)يخلع -(الطائرة)تقلع	
drop يرمي- يخفض- ينخفض	/	increase يزيد من- يرفع-يزداد-يرتفع	
decrease يخفض من- ينخفض	/	melt يذوب-يذوّب	
stabilize تستقر-تهدأ-يهدّأ	/	worsen يزداد سوءاً-يزيد سوءاً	
improve يتحسن- يحسّن	/	freeze يجمّد- يتجمد	
explode يفجّر- ينفجر	/	run يجري- يدير	
rush يندفع- يأخذ على عجل	/	harden يتصلب-يتشدد- يصلّب	
soften يليّن- يلين- يطرّي	/	break يكسر-ينكسر	
change يغير-يتغير	/	withdraw ينسحب- يسحب	
hide يختبئ- يخبئ	/	shine يشع- يُلمّع	

١٣٦

- **Study these sentences to see differences between transitive and intransitive verbs.**

  1- I **wake up** at 6 o'clock.

  2- You can **wake me up** at this time.

  3- The plane **took off** at 7 o'clock.

  4- One has to **take off** his shoes before entering the mosque.

  5- Prices are **increasing** .   الأسعار ترتفع.

  6- They **increase** prices from time to time.   ....إنهم يرفعون

  7- His English is **improving** amazingly .   تتحسن

  8- You have to **improve** your English.   .... عليك أن تحسّن

  9- The sun is **shining** .   الشمس مشرقة.

  10- I have to **shine** the car.   يلمّع

* **Underline the main verb and write if it is transitive or intransitive :**

1- We see a lot of things.   <u>Transitive</u>

2- The sun rises earlier in Doha.   ....

3- I collect stamps of different countries. ....

4- She always comes late for lunch. ....

5- He is dreaming at the moment.   ....

6- They sell old cars .   ...

7- My father often reads newspapers . ...

8- Ali has damaged my camera.   ....

9- The camera broke into pieces.   ....

10- He broke the glass into pieces.   ....

11- We can decompose this compound. ....

12 - The food has decomposed , so we cannot eat it. ....

13- The street is too narrow ; we need to broaden it. ......

14- His business has broadened a lot. ....

15- I wanted Ali to come , but he declined. ....

16- Can you decline the word " happy " ? ....

17- It darkened after sunset.   ....

18- I think you have to darken the paint . ...

19- His health is decaying ; he cannot do anything..........

20- Sweets can decay teeth. Don't eat too many of them.
....

21- He is worrying about his father's decaying health..............

22- His ill- health is worrying me a lot.   ....

23- Nothing has improved ; things are worsening   24-   Ice has worsened the problem.   25-   We have set our targets.
....

26-   You can sit in this armchair.   ....

27-   You could sweeten this tea by adding sugar to it. ....

28-   Life has changed a lot.   ....

29-   You can change your way of thinking.   ....

30-   The number of accidents has dropped sharply. ....

31-   He dropped the bottle and ran away.   ....

Types of the sentence- pattern
أنماط شكل الجملة

1-   Noun + be + subject complement. (SC صفة للفاعل)

Ali is *polite.* (Adjective)

The girl is *famous for her great art.*   الفتاة مشهورة بفنها الرائع.
(Adjective phrase)

2-   Noun + be + Subject complement (Noun Phrase NP).

Ali is <u>a student</u>. **He is** <u>Hamad's brother</u>. **He is** <u>the manager of his father's company</u>.

.الكلمات التي تحتها خط عبارة عن أسماء وظيفتها صفة للفاعل.

3-Noun + be + Subject complement SC (Adverbial Phrase)

Mona was **at home** an hour ago.

We have been **abroad** since 1998.

They are **under a tree.**

4-Noun + linking verb + Subject complement (Adjective)

You **look** *tired.*　　　　يبدو أنك متعب.

　They **have become** *boring.*　　لقد أصبحوا مملين .

　She **appears** *happy.*

The food **tastes** *delicious.*

The song **sounds** *nice.*

هذه الأفعال تقبل بعدها صفات .

5-Noun + LV + SC (NP).

Ali **has become** *the new man*

6-Noun + Intransitive verb .

The little boys **arrived** on time.

My father **laughed** a lot.

She **cried** when *she* **failed** .

7-Noun + Transitive Verb + Object.

They **played** *football* and **sang** *songs.*

They **spent** *a good time.*

هذه أفعال يتبعها مفعول به واحد.

8- Noun + Transitive Verb + two objects.

　I **gave** Ali a present.

　She **bought** me a nice coat.

They **have sent** them food.

* الكلمات التي تحتها خط عبارة عن أسماء تقوم بدور المفعول به.ونلاحظ أن هناك مفعولان في كل جملة, واحد منها مفعول مباشر والآخر مفعول به غير مباشر.

9- Noun + Transitive Verb + Object + Object complement .

　I **consider** you responsible for the accident.

　　　　　↓　　　　　　↓

Object (مفعول به)　OC (صفة للمفعول به)

We **consider** you to be responsible.

The new road **has made** traffic a great pleasure.

* إن الطريق الجديد قد جعل حركة المرور متعة كبيرة .

Affixation

صياغة كلمات جديدة بإضافة حروف إلى الكلمة الأم

An affix is a group of letters added to the beginning
or end of the base word , producing a new one.
Affixes make the derivation of new words an endless ,
continuous process . There are two kinds of affixes :
prefixes and suffixes.

هناك نوعان من الحروف المضافة بغية تكوين كلمات جديدة.

1- A prefix زيادة بادئة is a group of letters added to beginning of the base
word , giving a totally new word.

Ab - = opposite وتعني النقيض : normal طبيعي / abnormal
Exceptions استثناءات : abhor , abolish , abreast ,
abate .

ab- في هذه الكلمات ليس إضافة بل جزء من الكلمة ولهذا يجب الحذر.

ante- = before = pre , antedate يسبق التاريخ- يؤرخ بتاريخ سابق,
antemeridian قبل الظهر , anteroom غرفة انتظار ,
antecedent سابقة =precedent .
prewar period فترة ما قبل الحرب ,
pre-lunch break فسحة ما قبل الغداء
preschool learning التعلم في فترة ما قبل المدرسة
postnatal problems مشاكل ما بعد الميلاد ,
postwar era عصر ما بعد الحرب ,
preemption حق الشفعة - حق الأولوية في الشراء
preemptive متسم بالمبادرة - وقائي , perform.
Exceptions استثناءات :
predict يتنبأ بـ , prejudice تحيز -تحامل- إجحاف ,
prepare يُعد - يستعد , postpone يؤجل
postage رسوم البريد , postman.

١٤٠

anti- = against مناهض : **anti**slavery مناهض للرق – محاربة الرق ,
antibiotic مضاد حيوي , antibody جسم مضاد,
antiseptic مطهّر – مانع للعفن , antisocial معادٍ للمجتمع,
anticlockwise ضد عقارب الساعة ,
antifreeze مادة كيميائية لمنع التجمد , anti-Semitism معاداة السامية
Exceptions : antique شيء قديم وثمين , anticipate يتوقع ,
antiquity , antiquities آثار .

auto- = self ذاتي : **auto**mobile عربة – مركبة ,
automatic ذاتي الحركة , autonomy حكم ذاتي ,
autograph مخطوطة أصلية بخط الكاتب – يوقع بخط يده ,

be- bedevil يضايق , bedaub = besmear يوسخ ,
belittle يقلل من شأن , befriend يصادق , behead يقطع رأس
bedeck = decorate يزين , besiege يحاصر .
Exceptions : bed , beat , best , beast , bewilder يربك- يحير

bi - = twice , double ثنائي : **bi**lingual متعلق لغتين ,
bicycle دراجة من عجلتين , biannual مرتين كل سنة – مرة كل سنتين
biweekly meeting اجتماع مرة كل أسبوعين

contra- against ضد : **contra**ception منع الحمل ,
contraceptives حبوب منع الحمل ,
contraceptive means وسائل لمنع الحمل , contract ينكمش ,
contradict يناقض , contraband goods سلع محظورة .

counter- = opposite : **counter**attack هجوم مضاد ,
counterpart ند – نظير , counteract يعمل ضد ,
counteraction عمل مضاد

de- = not : demoralize يُفسد – يحطم معنويات ,
derail ينحرف عن المسار ,
يخفض من قيمة (العملة) devaluate , يقلل من السكان depopulate
ينزّل من درجة demote , يعزل depose , يشوه سمعة defame
ينزع سلاح – يجعل ... منزوعة السلاح/ غير عسكري demilitarize ,
يخفّض من – يهبط – هبوط decrease , يفك الشفرة decode
يزيل اللون decolourize

Exceptions : despot مستبد , depot مستودع , deliver ,
يصور. depict , صفقة deal , عيب defect

dis- = opposite : disappear يختفي , disapprove يستهجن ,
dislike يكره , disagree with يختلف مع , dissatisfied غير راضٍ
dismantle يفكك , discourage يثبط العزيمة ,
displeased مستاء , disbelieve يكذّب , discontent ناقم ,
discomfort عناء- تعب , disorder فوضى , disobey يعصى .
disappoint يخيب الأمل , display يعرض , disclose يفشي .

Exceptions : distance المسافة , disgust اشمئزاز ,
distort يشوه , distill (الماء) يقطّر ,
disaster دي زاس تا / كارثة ,
disciple / دي سايبل / أحد أتباع (أنصار) ,
discipline / دسيب لن / الانضباطس

-en : endanger يعرّض للخطر , enlist يجنّد , enable مكّن ,
ensure يتأكد , entitle .. to يعطي الحق في , enact يجيز قانوناً ,
encircle يحيط , enrage يغضب , enlarge يكبّر -يوسع ,
endear يحبب – يعزز , entomb يقبر encourage يشجع ,

Exceptions : entrance مدخل = entry , envelope مغلف ,
enclave , entire , enterprise مشروع , energy ,
enemy عدو , entity كيان- هوية .

-ex =former السابق(used before human nouns…people still living)
ex-president الرئيس السابق , ex-friend , ex-classmate ,
ex-teacher, ex-wife , ex-husband , ex-king , exhale يزفر ,
export تصدير – يصدّر , expatriate أجنبي , expel يطرد ,
extinct منقرض , exterminate يبيد – يستأصل ,
exile النفي – يُبعد – ينفي expire ينتهي , external خارجي ,
the late kingالملك الراحل.

extra- = over : extraordinary غير عادي

homo- = same : homogeneous متجانس , homogenize يجعله متجانساً   homograph
كلمة مجانسة أي كلمة تشبه أخرى في الإملاء وتختلف عنها في المعنى أو النطق
homonym = 1- homograph , 2-
كلمة تشبه أخرى إملاءً ولفظاً وتختلف عنها من حيث المعنى

hyper- = over : hypersensitive مفرط في الحساسية ,
hypertensive لديه ضغط عالٍ , hyperactive نشيط جداً ,
hyperbole المبالغة , hyperbolic ميال للمبالغة
hypercritical شديد الانتقاد , hypermarket سوبر ماركت ضخم
Opposite : hypo - : hyposensitive قليل الحساسية ,
hypocritical قليل الانتقاد
hypochondria القلق على الصحة hypocrisy النفاق
hypocrite منافق

١٤٣

ic - = of n ⟶ adj.: symbolic رمزي , realistic واقعي, heroic
optimistic متفائل , energetic ملئ بالحيوية
scientific علمي .
Exceptions : logic منطق , magic السحر, fantastic رائع .

-il : illegal غير قانوني , illegible لا يمكن قرأته
illegitimate غير شرعي , illogical غير منطقي
illiberal معادٍ لحرية التعبير – غير كريم
illiterate (لا يعرف القراءة والكتابة) أمي ,
Exceptions : illumination إنارة – تنوير , illusion وهم
illustrate يوضح .

im = not : impatient غير كامل- به نقيصة , imperfect غير صبور ,
impersonal غير شخصي , impractical غير عملي,
improper غير لائق , implausible غير معقول , impotent ضعيف
impure غير نقي , immoral لا أخلاقي , immature غير ناضج
Exceptions : improve يحسّن , impress يترك انطباعاً حسناً على
import يستورد – مغزى , impact تأثير – أثر ,
imitate يقلد , imperative ملح – ضروري ,
imminent وشيك .

-in = not : inaccurate غير دقيق , incompetent غير جدير ,
inefficient غير كفء, ineligible لا يصلح , incorrect غير صحيح ,
incorrigible لا يمكن إصلاحه , incomplete غير كامل ,
inseparable لا يمكن فصله , inconceivable لا يمكن تصوره,
incurable لا يمكن علاجه , infallible معصوم من الخطأ ,
infeasible غير ممكن / غير مجدٍ , indecisive غير حاسم ,

infirm غير حازم , intolerant غير متسامح ,

,غير مباشر indirect , inelegant غير أنيق , ineffective غير فعّال

, inhuman غير إنساني , inedible لا يمكن أكله , input مدخلات

insane مجنون , intake.

Exceptions : internal داخلي , innate فطري , interested مهتم ,

inherit يرث , industry صناعة , indicate يؤشر ,

indict يتـهم, intimate, indignant at ناقم على – ساخط

inevitable حتمي , integral متمم – مكمل ,

intelligent ذكي .

infra- = under : **infra**-red rays الأشعة تحت الحمراء ,

infrastructure البنية التحتية

infra-human دون البشر , infra –standard دون المستوى

ir - = not : **ir**regular غير نظامي , irresponsible غير مسئول,

irreligious غير ديني , irresistible لا يمكن مقاومته ,

irrational غير عقلاني- غير رشيد , irreversible لا يمكن الرجوع عنه

irrelevant to لا صلة له بـ .

mis- = badly : **mis**treat يسيء معاملة , **mis**understand يسيء فهم ,

misspell يخطئ في الإملاء , misinterpret يسيء تفسير ,

mislead يضلل , misprint خطأ مطبعي ,

misprision إهمال – تستر على جريمة – تحريض – احتقار ,

misread يخطئ في القراءة , misquote يخطئ في الاقتباس ,

mispronounce يخطئ في النطق , mistake غلطة .

mono- = one : **mono**poly احتكار , monopolist المحتكر ,
monologue حوار أحادي , monotone نغمة واحدة ,
monotheism التوحيد , monotony رتابة – ملل ,
monoplane طائرة أحادية السطح , monogamy الزواج بواحدة .

multi- = many : **multi-** coloured متعدد الألوان,
multi- national متعدد الجنسيات,
multi-partite متعدد الأطراف , multi-storey متعدد الطوابق,
multi-form متعدد الأشكال, multiply يضرب .

non- = not : **non**-aggression عدم اعتداء , non-aligned غير منحاز ,
nonsense لا معنى له , non-alignment عدم انحياز ,
non-chalant غير مبالٍ , non-interference عدم التدخل .

omni- = all : **omni**potent القادر على كل شيء ,
omniscient عالم بكل شيء , omnivorous يأكل كل شيء ,
omnipresent الموجود في كل مكان .

quasi - = same : **quasi**- scientific ideas أفكار شبه علمية,
quasi- educated شبه متعلم , quasi- liberal شبه متحرر ,
quasi- conservative شبه محافظ .

semi- = half , same : **semi**-annual نصف سنوي , semicircle نصف دائرة ,
semiautomatic نصف أتوماتيك, semi-civilized شبه متحضر ,
semi-centenary نصف قرني – الذكرى السنوية الخمسون ,
semi-conductor شبه موصل للحرارة, semi-colon (;) أحد علامات التنقيط,
semi-final شبه نهائي – المباراة شبه النهائية, semi-finished شبه منجز,
semi-official شبه رسمي , semi-skilled شبه ماهر .

self - = oneself , itself : self- abuse امتهان الذات ,

self-absorbed منغمس في التفكير , self- acquired مكتسب ذاتيا,

self-action عمل ذاتي (كون نفسه بنفسه) a self-made man رجل عصامي

self- affected = self-conceited معجب بنفسه - مغرور,

self-assertion الحرص على توكيد الذات ولفت الأنظار إليه ,

self-centred منطوي على نفسه, self-control التحكم الذاتي ,

self-confident واثق من نفسه self-confidence الثقة بالنفس,

self-deceit خداع الذات self-defence الدفاع عن النفس, self-love حب الذات,

self-determination تقرير المصير self-exile المنفي الاختياري,

self-expression التعبير عن الذات, self-rule حكم ذاتي ,

poly= many : polyatomic متعدد الذرات متعدد ,

polygamy تعدد الزوجات,

polygamist متزوج من أكثر من واحدة ,

polymath شخص بارع في فروع المعرفة المتعددة

polyglot شخص بارع في عدة لغات – خاص بلغات متعددة,

polystyrene مادة البلوسترين polysyllable كلمة من عدة مقاطع,

polytechnic معهد عالي يقدم تدريباً على حرف ماهرة كثيرة

pro- = for : pro- Arab issues مؤيد – مناصر للقضايا العربية ,

pro- French culture مناصر للثقافة الفرنسية ,

pro- French مؤيد لما هو فرنسي , pronoun ضمير (محل الاسم)

propel يحرّك , promote يُرقي , prolong يطيل .

re- = again : rewrite , regain يسترجع , replay ,

reconsider يعيد النظر في , rebuild , reconstruct يعيد أعمار ,

redial يعيد الاتصال , reinstate يعيد شخصاً إلى منصبه,

reinsure يؤمن من جديد , react يتفاعل , reaction ردة الفعل

recall يتذكر- يستدعي , refund مال معاد – يعيد مالاً.

sub- = below , under : **sub**marine غواصة , subzero تحت الصفر , مساعد محرر subeditor , لجنة فرعية (دنيا) subcommittee , مساعد – شركة تابعة subsidiary , دون سرعة الصوت subsonic , شبه القارة subtitle عنوان فرعي.

tri- = three : **tri**partite ثلاثي = trilateral , triangle مثلث , دراجة من ثلاثة عجلات tricycle

ultra = beyond فوق : **ultra**sonic فوق سرعة الصوت , ultra-violet الفوق بنفسجي .

un- = not : **un**able غير قادر , unlimited غير محدود , لا يمكن الوثوق به unreliable , غير محتمل unlikely , غير معقول unreasonable , لا يمكن تصديقه unbelievable , غير ودي unfriendly , غير حنون unkind , لم يرى من قبل unseen , مجهول unknown , غير متعاون unhelpful , غير لائق unfit , غير مهم unimportant , غير مرحب به unwelcome , يفك unpack , يفرد unfold , يفك untie , غير ناضج unripe , غير مملوء unfilled

under- = below : **under**charge يتقاضى أجراً بسيطاً , undercoat دهان أساس, underclothes =underwear ملابس داخلية undercover سري , undercurrent اتجاه خفي للرأي , under-developed متخلف , underestimate يقلل من شأن , طالب جامعي لم يتخرج بعد undergraduate , تحت الأرض – قطار الأنفاق underground , underline = , يفهم – يتفهم understand , يبين أهمية underscore

uni- = one : **uni**lateral من جانب واحد , uniform زي موحد ,
universal كوني , unit وحدة , unity الوحدة , unify يوحد ,
unification توحيد, union اتحاد , reunion لم الشمل ,
unique فريد .

vice = for : vice – president نائب الرئيس , vice- consul نائب القنصل
vice- regent نائب الوصي على العرش , viceroy نائب الملك .

2- **A suffix is a group of letters added to the end of a base word , giving a new word.**

suffix: هو مجموعة من الحروف تضاف إلى نهاية الكلمة لتكوين كلمة جديدة .

* **Suffixes Added to Verbs** لواحق مضافة إلى أفعال :

- **s** : plays , visits , enjoys , carry ⟶ carries , goes ,
teaches , washes , passes , relaxes . - **ed** : played , visited
, carried , passed , stopped , referred ,
talked .

- **en** : been , seen , eaten , taken , given , broken , stolen ,
spoken , fallen , risen , driven , hidden , ridden .

- **ing** : sailing , eating , walking , talking , enjoying , carrying
holding ,
write / writing , move / moving , have / having ,
swim / swimming , cut / cutting , plan / planning

- **er** : reader , player , exporter , dealer , speaker , driver ,
trader , carry ⟶ carrier , swim ⟶ swimmer ,
travel / traveller , designer.

- or : sailor , inventor مخترع, collector الجابي , operator ,
collaborator المتواطئ , liberator المحرر , actor ممثل ,
mediate يتوسط / mediator وسيط ,
donate يتبرع بـ / donor متبرع .

-ion : v ⟶ n collection جمع - مجموعة , protection حماية ,
prevention منع-وقاية , suggestion اقتراح, promotion ترقية
defection ردة , inspection تفتيش , perfection الكمال ,
expression التعبير, intention النية .

-ive : v ⟶ adj active , collective , productive , protective ,
preventive وقائي , expressive معبّر , repressive قمعي .

- ation : v ⟶ n inform يبلّغ- يُعلم / information معلومات ,
found يؤسس / foundation أساس - مؤسسة ,
demonstrate يتظاهر - يبين / demonstration مظاهرة-تبيان ,
prepare يُعد- يستعد / preparation استعداد – إعداد ,
examine بفحص- يمتحن / examination فحص-امتحان,
nationalize يؤمم – يوطن / nationalization تأميم – توطين ,
immunize يحصن / immunization تحصين,
realize يحقق / realization بلوغ-تحقيق ,
investigate يحقق في / investigation التحقيق .
- ment : v ⟶ n treatment علاج- معاملة , employment توظيف,
recruitment توظيف – تجنيد, assessment تقييم ,
improvement تحسين- تحسين .

- al : $v \longrightarrow n$ refuse يرفض / refusal الرفض , remove يزيل /
removal إزالة , deny ينكر / denial إنكار,
try يحاكم – يحاول / trial محاكمة – محاولة,
dismissal العزل – الطرد , withdrawal الانسحاب .

- ance : $v \longrightarrow n$ attendance الدوام , assistance المساعدة ,
clearance إخلاء طرف- مخالصة – المقاصة , appearance بروز - مظهر ,
defy يتحدى / defiance التحدي, rely يعتمد / reliance الاعتماد
endure يتحمل/ endurance التحمل, avoid يتجنب /
تجنب avoidance

-ant : $v \longrightarrow n$ assist يساعد / assistant مساعد , observe يراقب /
. مراقب observant

- able : $v \longrightarrow adj$ agreeable معقول , reasonable مناسب- مقبول ,
acceptable ممكن قبوله , believable يمكن تصديقه ,
rely / reliable ممكن الوثوق به , محبوب likable
bearable / يتحمل ممكن تحمله bear

- ence : $v \longrightarrow n$ precede يسبق / precedence الأسبقية ,
defence/ الدفاع pretence ادعاء /يتظاهر pretend ,defend يدافع عن
difference الاختلاف – الفرق , excel يتفوق/ excellence امتياز- تفوق ,
بروز emergence / emerge يبرز , dependence التبعية
abhorrence مقت / abhorrent كاره / abhorrent يمقت abhor ,
. مُبجل reverent / reverence احترام / يُبجل- يحترم revere

- s = plural :   cars , wonders غرائب , actions أعمال ,

       trips رحلات , fly ذبابة / **flies** , city / cities ,

       country / countries , buses , losses خسائر ,

       wishes تمنيات , dishes , boxes صناديق ,

       taxes ضرائب , wife / wives زوجات ,

       leaf / leaves أوراق .

- en = plural : child / children أطفال , ox / oxen ثيران ,

    brother / brethren إخوة.

-en : *n→adj*   wooden خشبي , golden ذهبي , silken حريري ,

    woollen من الصوف

    n→v :   threat تهديد / threaten يهدد , hasten يسرّع

-ful : *n→adj* : careful , useful مفيد , harmful ضار ,

    wonderful رائع , hopeful متفائل , painful مؤلم , fruitful مثمر ,

    successful ناجح - موفق , powerful قوي - صاحب نفوذ ,

    thoughtful صاحب أفكار - متأمل , tactful محنّك - ماهر ,

    resourceful داهية - واسع الحيلة , mindful واعٍ .

    n → n : handful حفنة , mouthful ملء الفم , spoonful ملء ملعقة.

- ist : *n→n*   tour رحلة / tourist سائح , novelist كاتب قصة ,

    scientist عالم   cyclist راكب دراجة , dramatist كاتب دراما , biologist عالم أحياء

    , geologist عالم جيولوجيا , botanist عالم نبات ,

    terrorist إرهابي .

-less = opposite : *n* ⟶ *adj* harm ضرر /harmless غير ضار,
homeless مشرد , hopeless يائس , mindless مجنون ,
baseless لا أساس له, fruitless عديم الجدوى, toothless لا أسنان له,
painless خالٍ من الألم , aimless لا هدف له, needless لا حاجة له

n ⟶ *adv.* :doubtless بلا شك , regardless (of) بصرف النظر

- hood : *n*⟶*n* childhood الطفولة, boyhood الصبا ,
manhood الرجولة , neighbourhood الحي – الضاحية ,
knighthood الفروسية .

- al : *n*⟶*adj* national وطني - قومي , magical سحري,
logical منطقي , festival مهرجان, globe العالم / global عالمي ,
universe الكون / universal كوني , experimental تجريبي ,
instrumental فعّال – مؤثر -مفيد , detrimental ضار, natural طبيعي
regional إقليمي , formal شكلي - رسمي , original أصلي .

- ish : *n*⟶*adj* childish طفولي , sheepish خانع , selfish أناني ,
bluish زرقاوي , reddish حمراوي اللون ,
bookish ميال إلى الكتب أكثر من الجانب العملي .

- ic : *n* ⟶ *adj* historic تاريخي , symbol / symbolic رمزي ,
heroic بطولي , basic أساسي , philosophic فلسفي ,
horrific مرعب , energetic نشيط , pessimist مؤمن بالتشاؤم /
pessimistic متشائم , optimist مؤمن بالتفاؤل / optimistic متفائل

- ly : n→adj friend صديق / friendly ودي , weekly أسبوعي ,
    monthly شهري , yearly سنوي , daily يومي , manly رجولي ,
    cowardice الجبن - cowardly جبان /صفة (جبان / اسم) a coward

-y : n →adj   health الصحة / healthy صحي , wealthy ثري ,
    windy به رياح , cloudy مغيم , rainy ماطر , snowy مثلج ,
    sunny مشمس , stormy عاصف , handy سهل الاستعمال ,
    sandy رملي, muddy موحل , sleepy نعسان , needy محتاج,
    hunger الجوع / hungry جوعان , thirsty عطشان ,
    gloomy عابس – كئيب , wit الذكاء /witty ذكي ,
    vacancy وظيفة شاغرة / vacant شاغر , filthy قذر , dirty قذر

  n → energy طاقة, clergy رجال الدين , philosophy , democracy ,
      mercy الرحمة , agency وكالة / agent وكيل .

- ian: n→n history التاريخ / historian مؤرخ , library مكتبة /
      librarian أمين مكتبة, theology علم اللاهوت /
      theologian عالم لاهوت , music موسيقى /musician موسيقار
      Arab عربي / Arabian , India الهند / Indian هندي .

- ous : n→adj   dangerous خطير , courage / courageous شجاع ,
    poison السم / poisonous سام , ambition الطموح / ambitious طموح ,
    envy الحسد / envious حسود, piety التقى – الورع / pious تقي ,
    nerve عصب / nervous عصبي .

- phile: adj Anglophile tendency نزعة حب للإنجليز ,
      an Anglophile شخص محب لما هو إنجليزي
      n   Anglophobe شخص كاره لما هو إنجليزي .

* Suffixes Added to Adjectives لواحق مضافة إلى الصفات :

-al : *adj*—→*adj* historical تاريخي , fanatical متعصب ,
economical مقتصد .

-er : *adj*—→*adj* smaller , faster , poorer , richer , bigger , hotter ,
happy/ happier, easy/ easier , good/ better , far/ farther .

- est: *adj*—→*adj* smallest , fastest , poorest , biggest , happiest ,
good / best .

-en: *adj*—→*v* deepen يعمق , broaden يوسع , loosen يفك - يرخي ,
tighten يشدد , madden يجنن , deaden يميت , sweeten يحلي ,
lessen يقلل , fatten يسمن , soften يُلين –يَلين ,
flatten يسوي بالأرض- يبسط , deafen يصيب بالصمم ,
dampen يثبط العزيمة – يَهن عزمه , moisten يُرطب ,
harden يتصلب – يتشدد- يُقسّي ,

- ly : *adj*—→*adv* slowly , carefully , bravely بشجاعة , sharply بحدة ,
politely , kindly , nicely , true / truly بصدق , possible /
possibly , closely عن قرب , seriously بجدية .

ness : *adj*—→*n* sharpness حدة , cleverness مهارة ,
usefulness منفعة , happiness , hopelessness اليأس.

- ity : *adj*—→*n* originality الأصالة , humanity الإنسانية , vanity الغرور
duality ثنائية , individuality الشخصية = personality,
security الأمن , pure / purity النقاء , humidity الرطوبة ,
possible ممكن / possibility إمكانية ,

responsible مسئول / responsibility مسئولية ,
infidel كافر – خائن / infidelity كفر – خيانة زوجية

-ist : *adj* ⟶ *n*   idealist مؤمن بالمثالية, realist واقعي ,
fatalist مؤمن بالقدرية , feudalist إقطاعي , industrialist رجل صناعي
fundamentalist أصولي .

- y : *adj* ⟶ *n*   honest أمين / honesty , loyal موالٍ , loyalty ولاء ,
royal ملكي, royalty عائد مادي – شخصية ملكية – ملكية .

-ce : *adj* ⟶ *n*   different / difference , excellent / excellence ,
prudent حكيم -رزين / prudence سداد الرأي -حكمة
silent / silence صمت .

-cy : *adj* ⟶ *n* accurate / accuracy دقة , obstinate عنيد /
obstinacy عناد, fluent / fluency طلاقة اللسان , intimate حميم /
intimacy حميمية , sufficient / sufficiency اكتفاء , deficient /
deficiency النقص.

-ize: *adj* ⟶ *v*   realize , industrialize يصنّع, modernize يحدّث,
rationalize يرشّد , imperialize يستعمر , personalize يجعله شخصياً,
dehumanize يجرد من الإنسانية , vitalize يعطي حيوية لـ .

-ize : *n* ⟶ *v* computerize يُدخل في الحاسوب , character ميزة- شخصية /
characterize ميز , symbolize يرمز إلى , theorize ينظّر ,
maximum الحد الأعلى / maximize يزيد – يرفع ,
minimum الحد الأدنى / minimize يخفض – يقلل .

* **Underline the prefixes in these words :**

unlike , remark , embitter , disobey , degrade ,
inexpensive , review , preview , encamp , replace ,
displace , unripe, ex- pilot, antechamber , vice-consul ,
abnormality , irregular , misspell , improper .

* **Underline the suffixes in these words :**

severity , devotion , removal , eaten , enlargement ,
enlighten , comfortable , harmful , powerless , realism ,
childhood , bleeding , boxer , negotiator , ideas ,
entered , agrees , incredible , slowly , defendant ,
departure , pocketful , reasonable , windy , tenth .

* **Add a suitable prefix to the base word :**

practical : .... / cycle : ....

coloured : .... / figure : ....

work : .... / known : ....

sensitive : .... / accurate : ....

affirm : .... / pleased : ....

welcome : .... / take : ....

● **Say what part of speech the word is , add a suitable**
suffix to it and say what part of speech the derived word is :

Word	Part of Speech	New Word	Part of Speech
collect	verb	collector	noun
collect	....	....	....
collect	....	....	....
clear	....	....	....

clear	....	....	....
clear	....	....	....
clear	....	....	....
populate	....	....	....
populate	....	....	....
popular	....	....	....
fast	....	....	... .
speak	....	....	....
speak	....	....	....
comfort	....	....	....
comfort	....	....	... .
fluent	....	....	....
fluent	....	....	....
book	....	....	....
book	....	....	....
discover	....	....	....
deep	....	....	....
deep	....	....	....
heavy	....	....	....
heavy	....	....	....
child	....	....	....
child	....	....	....
king	....	....	....
king	....	....	....
invent	....	....	....
invent	....	....	....
discuss	....	....	....
promote	....	....	....
intend	....	....	....
defend	....	defendant	....
vary	verb	....	adjective
fight	....	....	noun
music	....	....	adjective

The Noun الاسم

The noun is one of the basic components of the clause .

It is necessary to recognize it so that we can use it in making

a meaningful sentence.

الاسم أحد المكونات الأساسية في الجملة , و يجب أن نتعرف على الاسم حتى يمكننا استخدامه في جملة مفيدة . و الاسم أنواع :

* **Kinds of the Noun** أنواع الاسم :

1- **Names of people** : Ali , Mona , John , Mary ,
   Elizabeth , Sara.

2- **Countries and towns** : Qatar , Lebanon , France,
   The United Kingdom, The United States of America , Cairo ,
   Tripoli , Rome , Tokyo.

3- **Concrete things** أشياء مجسدة : food , water , energy الطاقة ,
   wind الرياح , moon القمر , sun الشمس , money المال ,
   company شركة , tree شجرة , wood الخشب , initiative مبادرة
   sand الرمل , mine لغم – منجم .

4- **Abstract things** : wealth الثروة , power السلطة ,
   friendship الصداقة , honesty الشرف , generosity الكرم ,
   poverty الفقر , freedom الحرية , will الإرادة , choice الاختيار ,
   honour الشرف , weakness الضعف , treatment المعاملة ,
   harmony الانسجام , commitment الالتزام , promise الوعد ,
   ambition الطموح , evil الشر , innocence البراءة ,
   truth الصدق , welfare الرفاهية , misery البؤس ,
   optimism التفاؤل , conscience الضمير .

5- **Compound nouns** : newspaper , housewife ,

greenhouse بيت للزراعة المحمية , housemaid خادمة ,

policeman , milkman , seat belt , safety belt حزام الأمان ,

life jacket سترة النجاة , weatherman رجل الأرصاد ,

meddle man الوسيط , stepfather زوج الأم ,

stepmother زوجة الأب , stepbrother الأخ من الأم ,

stepson ابن الزوج أو الزوجة ,

father –in – law أب الزوجة أو الزوج ,

mother-in-law أم الزوج أو الزوجة ,

brother-in-law أخ الزوج أو الزوجة ,

sister-in-law أخت الزوج أو الزوجة ,

commander-in-chief القائد العام , chief of staff قائد الأركان

chief of protocol رئيس البروتوكول ,

Secretary- General الأمين العام ,

Assistant- Manager مساعد المدير

* **How to use the noun** كيفية استخدام الاسم :

A-The noun acts as a subject or an object:

يكون الاسم فاعلاً أو مفعولاً به في الجملة

1-Smoking causes disease. التدخين يسبب المرض.

2-People criticise high prices. ينتقد الناس الأسعار المرتفعة.

3- Good students get high marks.

4- We should find a solution to poverty. يجب أن نجد حلاً للفقر.

5-Millions of people suffer from famine.

يعاني ملايين الناس من المجاعة.

B- The noun acts as a subject complement or object complement.

يعمل الاسم كصفة للفاعل أي خبر للمبتدأ أو بمثابة صفة للمفعول به.

1- The **lessor** is a **person** who lets يؤجر a **house** to someone
   else.   ↓

اسم في محل خبر للمبتدأ (المؤجر) ┗

المؤجر هو شخص يؤجر منزلاً إلى شخص أخر.

2- The **lessee** المستأجر is a **person** who rents يستأجر a house .
3- Honesty is the best **policy** .   الأمانة أحسن سياسة .
4- Brevity is the soul of wit. . الإيجاز هو روح الذكاء/ الاختصار عبادة
5- Ali has become a famous critic . أصبح علي ناقداً مشهوراً.
6- We have made Nasser **a captain** → Object complement

كصفة للمفعول به (ناصر) ┗

7- I consider you **a friend** . → Object complement

*Choose the right word:

1- We spend a lot of money on (education-polite) .
2- He has just started his own (busy- business).
3- You speak badly to me. This bad (speak - language) is not accepted.
4- We need new (roads-road) here to improve traffic .
5- We should do something to put an end to this dangerous
   (feed-problem-different).
6- Doha is an Arab (food – city – villagers).
7- People do not have any food to eat. There is a real
   (success – famine).
8- We should work for the (evil – welfare) of our country.
9- Women are fighting for (freedom - freely).
10- (Poor – Poverty) is a big problem.

C- The noun acts as a modifier يعمل الاسم كصفة لاسم أخر :

1- His **peace efforts** have failed , so the warring parties might resume fighting soon.

إن جهوده السلمية قد فشلت وأن الأطراف المتحاربة قد تستأنف القتال قريبا.

2- Some **school** books contain out-of-date information.

اسم كصفة للكتب └

إن بعض الكتب المدرسية تحتوي على معلومات قديمة.We intend to
set up a new **information** centre in Doha.

إننا ننوي أن ننشئ مركزاً إعلامياً جديداً في الدوحة.

3- The **UN** resolutions aim at making peace.

إن قرارات الأمم المتحدة تهدف إلى صنع السلام.

4- They are discussing **family** problems.

إنهم يناقشون مشاكل عائلية.

How to form nouns
كيفية صياغة الأسماء

There are two main ways of recognizing a noun .

هناك طريقتان للتعرف على الاسم

A- Non – Derivative Nouns أسماء غير مشتقة :
**These are basic nouns that are not derived from other words. There are two kinds
in this category :** هناك نوعان

- **Both the noun and verb have the same form.**

الاسم والفعل لهما نفس الشكل.

face وجه- يواجه , change تبديل - يتبدل , fall هبوط - يهبط ,
cut يقطع - جرح , water يسقي- ماء , drop يهبط - هبوط ,
plant يزرع - نبات , need يحتاج- حاجة , plan يخطط - خطة ,

راتب - يدفع - pay , قول - يؤيد - تأييد - support , يقول say
= hire , زيادة - يزداد - increase , إهانة - يهين insult
يعذّب – تعذيب – torture , إيجار - تأجير - يؤجر - يستأجرrent
عقد إيجار – يؤجر – يستأجر lease , نهاية - ينتهي - end
aim بداية - يبدأ start , دمار - 'يدمر - damage , يهدف - هدف
hope يطبخ – طباخ – cook , المطر- تمطر rain , يأمل - أمل
form يفوض – مندوب – delegate , يصلح –إصلاح reform, يشگّل- شكل
graduate أول من تبنى – رائد pioneer , يتخرج – خريج

هناك كلمات مماثلة كثيرة تكون اسماً و فعلاً من حيث الشكل , و لكن يمكن التمييز بين الاسم و الفعل
من موقع الكلمة في الجملة .

1- You should wash your **face** . (noun اسم)

2- We **face** some problems . (verb فعل)

3- We should **support** Ali .   (verb فعل)

4- I want to thank you for your **support**. (noun اسم)

5-   We should have **a say** in this matter . (noun اسم)

6- I can't **say** that.   (verb فعل)

* **Pure nouns** أسماء صرفة : These nouns exist as nouns
only.

bread , money , food , tree , child , king ,
minister وزير , meat , game , victory النصر , peace ,
welfare رفاهية , strife قتال , wife , life , health , sun ,
law القانون , salary , prize , advice النصيحة , problem ,
nation أمة , butter , sheep , area المنطقة - المساحة,
volume حجم , family , country .

B- Derived nouns أسماء مشتقة :

These nouns are derived by adding suffixes to other

words.   هذه الأسماء تشتق من كلمات أخرى بإضافة لواحق إليـها .

1- We get a noun by adding the suffix " – ing "

   to a verb :

نحصل على اسم بإضافة ing - إلى الفعل الأصلي

go / going , play /playing , read / reading ,

write / writing , swim / swimming , lie / lying يكذب الكذب ,

feed / feeding التغذية

2- We get a noun by adding the suffix "– er – or – ee " to a
   verb :

نحصل على اسم بإضافة er- إلى الفعل.

help / helper معاون , defend / defender مدافع , read /

reader قارئ, play / player , fly / flyer , speak / speaker ,

kill / killer , founder المؤسس , producer المنتج ,

exporter المصدّر , dealer التاجر , composer الملحّن ,

act / actor ممثل , sail / sailor بحار , collect / collector جابي

invent يخترع / inventor مخترع , dictate / dictator ديكتاتور ,

edit) يوصل – يجمع , conduct المحرر / editor يحرر (صحافة

conductor الكمساري – موصل – قائد فرقة موسيقية

prosecute يقاضي - يدعي على / prosecutor المدعي العام

comment يعلّق / commentator المعلق

demonstrate يوضح – يقوم بـمظاهرة

demonstrator متظاهر – مساعد مدرس في جامعة

train يدرّب / trainer مدرّب / trainee متدرّب / training تدريب

detain يعتقل / detainee معتقل / detention camp معسكر اعتقال
/ رب العمل employer / موظف employee / يوظف employ
employment توظيف .

3- We get a noun by adding the suffix " – ment " to a verb.

treat يعالج – يعامل / treatment, govern يحكم / government الحكومة
agree / agreement اتفاق, replace / replacement بديل – استبدال encourage
, تشجيع encouragement /يشجع
develop يتطور – يطور – ينمي / development تنمية – تطور
improve يتحسن – يحسّن / improvement , manage يدير /
management إدارة , move يتحرك – يحرّك / movement حركة,
involve ينهمك – يورط – يُشغل / involvement الانشغال – التورط
, judge يحكم / judgement , judgment الحكم – القضاء
imprison يسجن / imprisonment السجن ,
embezzle يختلس / embezzlement اختلاس ,
punish يعاقب / punishment العقاب
banish ينفي (يطرد) / banishment النفي ,
establish يقيم – يؤسس /establishment
achieve ينجز / achievement إنجاز ,
bewilder يحيّر / bewilderment حيرة
announce يعلن عن / announcement الإعلان عن -إعلان
advertise يعلن عن / advertisement إعلان
invest يستثمر investment استثمار investor مستثمر
conceal يُخفي / concealment إخفاء

4- We get a noun by adding the suffix " – ance " to a verb :

rely يعتمد / reliance الاعتماد , defy يتحدى / defiance التحدي
avoid يتجنب / avoidance تفادي - اجتناب , comply يـمتثل /
compliance الامتثال , perform يؤدي / performance الأداء
endure يتحمل المشقة / endurance التحمل
tolerate يتسامح مع – يتساهل مع / tolerance التسامح – التساهل
attend يداوم – يحضر attendance الدوام
resist يقاوم resistance المقاومة
ignore يتجاهل ignorance الجهل
insist يصر insistence الإصرار
defend يدافع عن / defence الدفاع / self-defence الدفاع عن النفس
offend يسيء إلى offence إساءة

5- We get a noun by adding the suffixes " -ation " and " ion " to some verbs
.

inform يبلّع / information معلومات – إعلام – استعلامات
liberate يحرر liberation التحرير relate ينسب – يقص relation
علاقة – قرابة narrate يروي – يقص – يسرد
narration قصة – رواية قصة / **narrator** الراوي
consider ينظر في consideration اعتبار
dictate يملي dictation إملاء
found يؤسس foundation مؤسسة _ تأسيس – أساس
degrade يحط من قدر – يحقّر – يهين – ينحط
degradation الانحطاط- الاحتقار
realize يبلغ – يحقق realization تحقيق – بلوغ
modernize يجدد = يحدّث modernization التحديث

١٦٦

donate يتبرع بـ   donation التبرع

motivate يحرّك   motivation المدافعية- الدافعية

imitate يقلّد   imitation تقليد

educate يعلّم ـ يربي   education التعليم – التربية

violate يخرق   violation خرق – انتهاك

condemn يستنكر   condemnation استنكار – استهجان

qualify يؤهل – يتأهل   qualification مؤهل – تأهيل

justify يبرر   justification مبرر – تبرير

imagine يتخيل – يتصور   imagination خيال – تخيل

denounce يستنكر - يستهجن   denunciation استنكار – استهجان

pronounce ينطق   pronunciation النطق

renounce ينبذ – يرتد عن دين – يتخلى عن حق

renunciation نبذ- التخلي

declare يعلن   declaration إعلان

explain يفسر – يشرح   explanation تفسير

tempt يغري   temptation إغراء

adapt to يتكيف مع - يكيف   adaptation التكيف,

adapter

شيء /شخص مهمته القيام بالتكييف بين أمرين

cancel يلغي   cancellation إلغاء

produce ينتج   production إنتاج / **producer** المنتج

reduce يخفُض - يقلل من / reduction تخفيض

pollute يلوث / pollution التلوث , pollutant ملوث

prevent يمنع – يتقي – يحول دون / prevention المنع – الوقاية

suggest يقترح / suggestion اقتراح

distort يشوه (حقيقة) / distortion تشويه

intend ينوي / intention النية

satisfy يرضي / satisfaction إرضاء – إشباع

corrupt يُفسد / corruption فساد – إفساد

conceive تصور – تحمل بطفل / conception تصور

concept تصور

describe يصف / description وصف

attribute ... to يعزو إلى / attribution شيء منسوب إلى

contribute يساهم – يشارك / contribution مشاركة

adopt يتبنى / adoption التبني

inhibit يمنع – ينهى – يكبح / inhibition النهي – المنع

prohibit يحرّم – يمنع – يحظر / prohibition تحريم – الحظر

prosecute يقيم دعوة على – يقاضي / prosecution مقاضاة – الادعاء

promote يروج لـ – يرقي / promotion الترويج – ترقية

destroy يدمر / destruction الدمار

construct يعمّر / construction الأعمار

demolish يهدم / demolition الهدم

abolish يلغي / abolition إلغاء

attend to يهتم بـ / attention انتباه – عناية

6- We form a noun by adding the suffix " ion " to some verbs :

admit يعترف – يقبل / admission الاعتراف – القبول - حق الدخول

admittance , transmit يرسل – يبث /

transmission البث – الإرسال

omit يحذف omission حذف , permit يسمح لـ - يأذن

permission / permit رخصة إذن – تصريح

remit   يرسل (نقود) – يعفي من دين – يعفو عن , remit by cheque

remittance   حوالة مالية   ,   العفو – الإعفاء من دين   remission

recede   يتراجع – ينحسر   recession   ركود

accede (to)   يعتلي العرش – يضيف

accession   تولي السلطات – إضافة

televise   يبث بالتلفاز   television   بث تلفازي

revise   يراجع   revision   مراجعة

persuade   يُقنع – يُغري   persuasion   إقناع

dissuade one from   يُقنع شخصاً بالعدول عن

dissuasion   إقناع بالعدول عن

disperse   يشتت – يتشتت – يتبعثر– يتقزّح

dispersion , dispersal   التشتت – التبعثر

decide   يقرر   decision   القرار

divide   يقسّم   division   القسمة – الانقسام

invade   يغزو   invasion / invaders   الغزاة   غزو

conclude   يختتم – يبرم اتفاقاً   conclusion /   اختتام – إبرام

collude with   يتواطأ مع   collusion /   التواطؤ

exclude   يستبعد – يستثني   exclusion /   استبعاد

include   تشتمل على- يُضمّن (يُدرج)   inclusion   اشتمال – تضمين /

collide with   يصطدم بـ – يختلف مع   collision   اصطدام – خلاف /

compel   يجبر   compulsion /   إجبار

pretend   يدعي ملكية شيء لا حق له فيه – يتظاهر , **pretension**/

pretence , pretense   الادعاء

expand   يتمدد – يتوسع – يوسع   expansion /   التمدد – التوسع

5- **We get a noun by adding the suffix " – ness " to some adjectives.**

happy سعيد	happiness سعادة
lazy كسول	laziness الكسل – التكاسل
hopeless يائس	hopelessness اليأس
polite مؤدب	politeness الأدب
vague غامض	vagueness غموض
mad مجنون	madness الجنون
careless مهمل	carelessness إهمال
stubborn عنيد	stubbornness العناد
homeless مشرد	homelessness التشرد
serious جاد	seriousness جدية

* **We derive a noun by adding " –ship " to certain words.**

friendship الصداقة, kinship القرابة, hardship مشقة ,
relationship علاقة/ قرابة , scholarship منحة/ بعثة دراسية ,
fellowship الزمالة , companionship الصحبة

* **We get a plural noun by placing the article " the " before an adjective.**

the poor الفقراء , the sick المرضى, the weak الضعفاء ,
the rich الأغنياء , the helpless المستضعفون ,
the homeless المشردون , the hungry الجائعون

* **We can get a noun by using " -ce / -cy " with some adjectives.**

different مختلف   difference اختلاف / فرق

independent مستقل   independence الاستقلال

patient صبور   patience الصبر

ignorant جاهل   ignorance الجهل

lenient لين – متساهل   lenience , leniency اللين

resilient مرن – قادر على التكيف   resilience ,

resiliency مرونة – القدرة على التكيف

fluent طلق اللسان   fluency طلاقة اللسان

decent مـهذب – محتشم   decency الحشمة

efficient كفء   efficiency كفاءة

proficient ماهر – بارع   proficiency مـهارة - براعة

sufficient كافٍ   sufficiency اكتفاء - كفاية

private خاص – خصوصي   privacy خلوة – عزلة

pirate قرصان   piracy قرصنة

obstinate عنيد   obstinacy العناد

accurate دقيق   accuracy الدقة

prudent عاقل   prudence الحكمة - التعقل

indifferent غير مبالٍ   indifference عدم اكتراث – لامبالاة

urgent عاجل – ملح   urgency حاجة ملحة – أمر عاجل

** **We can derive a noun by adding " – ity " to**
    some words .

secure آمن   security الأمن

clear واضح   clarity وضوح

pure نقي   purity نقاء - صفاء

* honesty أمانة	honest أمين
popularity شعبية	popular محبوب
secularity شيء دنيوي	secular دنيوي – علماني
mentality عقلية	mental عقلي
reality حقيقة واقعة	real حقيقي
plurality التعدد	plural متعلق بالجمع
deformity تشوه – عيب خَلقي	deform يشوه
stupidity غباء – حماقة	stupid أحمق – غبي
individuality شخصية	individual شخصي- فردي
personality شخصية	personal شخصي
* loyalty ولاء	loyal موالي
* cruelty قسوة	cruel قاسٍ – ظالم
ability القدرة	able قادر
humanity الإنسانية	human إنساني
humidity الرطوبة	humid رطب
severity قسوة	severe صارم – قاسٍ
nobility النبل	noble نبيل
possibility إمكانية	possible ممكن
responsibility مسئولية	responsible مسئول
visibility الرؤية	visible مرئي
feasibility جدوى – فائدة	feasible له جدوى – مجدٍ
generosity الكرم – الجود	generous كريـم
curiosity حب الاستطلاع	curious شغوف- محب للاستطلاع
hospitality كرم الضيافة	hospitable مضياف
atrocity فظاعة- غاية في القسوة	atrocious فظيع – شنيع- مخزي

** We form a noun by adding " –th " to some adjectives .

deep عميق   depth العمق

long طويل   length الطول

wide واسع – عريض   width العرض

* Nouns derived from verbs أسماء مشتقة من أفعال

sign يوقع على / signature التوقيع / signatory أحد الموقعين

remove يزيل / removal إزالة , refuse يرفض / refusal الرفض

deny ينكر / denial إنكار , renew يجدد / renewal تجديد

dismiss يطرد / dismissal الطرد , approve يصادق على /

approval / fly يطير / flight رحلة جوية ,

discover يكتشف / discovery , recover يسترجع /

recovery استرجاع , lose يخسر / loss خسارة

die يموت / death الموت , succeed ينجح / success النجاح

fail يفشل / failure خلل – فشل , expire ينتهي / expiry انتهاء

grieve for يحزن على / grief الحزن / grievance مظلمة

believe يؤمن / belief إيمان – اعتقاد , relieve يغيث / relief إغاثة

bury يدفن / burial الدفن , detain يعتقل / detention اعتقال

abstain from يمتنع عن / abstention امتناع .

How to pluralize a singular noun
كيف يتم جمع الاسم المفرد

* **Countable Nouns** أسماء تقبل العد :

* They take the indefinite articles " a " and " an " in the singular form .
* They take the plural marker.

1- **Some countable nouns take an " s " in the plural.**

a book	books
a sea	seas بحار
an ocean أوشن / محيط /	oceans محيطات
a raid غارة	raids غارات

2- **Some countable nouns take " –es " .**

a gas	gases
a glass كوب	glasses
a bus	buses
a boss رئيس	bosses
a class صف- طبقة	classes
a mango حبة مانجه	mangoes (radio - radios / photo- photos)
a cargo حمولة – شحنة	cargoes
an echo صدى الصوت	echoes
a potato	potatoes
a watch ساعة يد	watches
a match ثقاب كبريت – مباراة – ند	matches
a beach شاطئ	beaches
a ditch حفرة	ditches
a pitch ملعب – مكان عام	pitches
a stitch غرزة	stitches
a dish صحن – طبق	dishes
a wish أمنية	wishes
a box	boxes

3- Some countable nouns end in " y " :

a facility منشأة – تسهيل	facilities
a country بلد	countries
a lady سيدة	ladies
a story قصة	stories
a salary راتب	salaries
a study دراسة	studies
a fly ذبابة	flies
a commodity سلعة	commodities

4- Some countable nouns with an " f " :

a life حياة	lives
a wife زوجة	wives
a loaf رغيف	loaves
a leaf ورقة	leaves
a sheaf حزمة	sheaves
* a half نصف halves ⟶	Three and a half hours.
	(3 hours and a half.)
a calf عجل	calves عجول
a shelf رف	shelves أرفف
a self نفس	selves
a belief اعتقاد	beliefs
a proof دليل	proofs
a hoof حافر الحصان	hoofs / hooves
a chief زعيم	chiefs

5- Some other irregular nouns بعض الأسماء الأخرى الشاذة :

man رجل / men , woman امرأة / women ,

foot / feet , goose ألوزة / geese ,

child طفل / children , ox ثور / oxen

vacuum الفراغ / vacua , vacuums ,

phenomenon ظاهرة / phenomena

memorandum مذكرة/memoranda –memorandums –memos

mouse فأر / mice , louse قملة / lice ,

apex رأس- قمة - apices ,

appendix ملحق / الزائدة الدودية – / appendixes , appendices

index الفهرس / indices , analysis تحليل - analyses ,

crisis أزمة / crises , thesis رسالة علمية – موضوع - theses

hypothesis فرضية – افتراض / hypotheses ,

basis أساس - bases , criterion معيار / criteria معايير ,

agendum / agenda جدول أعمال - agenda ,

datum معلومة / data معلومات – بيانات ,

medium وسط – وسيلة / media , mediums ,

erratum غلطة = error , errata = errors أخطاء ,

curriculum منهاج دراسي / curriculums / curricula ,

symposium ندوة / symposiums , symposia ,

fungus فطر / fungi , nucleus نواة / nuclei ,

stimulus مثير – باعث / stimuli , syllabus مقرر دراسي /

syllabi .

* halve (v.) ينصّف

* Nouns with " زوج من a pair of " :

a pair of binoculars منظار .... glasses نظارات
.... trousers بنطلون .... pants
.... shorts .... scissors المقص
.... pliers .... scales الميزان

* Nouns always in the plural form أسماء دائماً في الجمع

archives arms أسلحة proceeds
belongings ممتلكات / quarters مسكن / clothes
remains مخلفات / congratulations التهاني / resources الموارد
credentials أوراق اعتماد سفير / riches ثروات / shortcomings نقاط ضعف
manners سلوك / surroundings محيط - بيئة / odds احتمالات
particulars تفاصيل valuables أشياء ثمينة premises (عقار(مقر-مسكن
whereabouts مكان إقامة / logistics الإمداد والتموين (الجيش)
clippers القاطعة / goods بضائع

> * Our resources are plentiful.
> * The whereabouts of the thief have been spotted.
> * Our premises are not far from the city centre.
> * One's surroundings have an impact on his way of life.
> * The new ambassador has presented his credentials.
> * High-quality goods are exported to other countries.

* Nouns always in the plural form with a singular meaning:

chess الشطرنج economics علم الاقتصاد news الأخبار – الخبر
Mathematics الرياضيات means وسائل – وسيلة
measles (miziz) مرض الحصبة , metropolis العاصمة - الحاضرة
mumps التهاب الغدة النكفية physics الفيزياء
series سلسلة – مسلسل statistics إحصائية – الإحصاء ,
grass الحشيش , a species نوع - فصيلة species أنواع

* Mathematics **is** my favourite subject.

الرياضيات هي مادتي المفضلة .

* Statistics **shows** that the number of car accidents rises in summer.

الإحصائيات تُظهر بأن عدد حوادث السيارات ترتفع في الصيف.

* Measles **is** a serious disease .   الحصبة مرض خطير.

* The means you are using **are** far from being moral.

* The internet إن الوسائل التي تستخدمها بعيدة عن كونها أخلاقية.
has become a means of getting information.

أصبح الإنترنت وسيلة للحصول على المعلومات .

* Mumps **has** lately infected many children.

إن مرض الغدة النكفية قد أصاب الكثير من الأطفال مؤخراً.

● Some uncountable nouns do not take " a ", or "an '

هذه أسماء لا تقبل العد ولا تسبقها "an " أو "a" أو " s "الجمع.

hatred - الكراهية / honesty - الأمانة / information /
ink الحبر / oxygen / meat / sugar / cheese /
bread / chocolate / spinach السبانخ / butter /
copper النحاس / cotton / silk الحرير / leather الجلد /
gold الذهب / silver / الفضة steel الصلب /
darkness الظلام / laziness التكاسل / bitterness المرارة /
barley الشعير / wheat القمح / camping التخييم /
dancing الرقص / lightning البرق / thunder الرعد /
smoking / waiting الانتظار / peace السلام /
importance أهمية / equality المساواة / happiness السعادة /
advice النصيحة / baggage حقائب / education التعليم /
chaos فوضى / courage الشجاعة / dirt القاذورات /
garbage = rubbish = litter القمامة /
equipment المعدات / fun اللهو / furniture الأثاث /
hospitality كرم الضيافة / sadness الحزن / poetry الشعر /

١٧٨

safety السلامة / weather الجو / violence العنف /
materialism المادية / socialism الاشتراكية /
realism الواقعية / idealism المثالية /
nationalism النزعة القومية / racism العنصرية /
optimism التفاؤل / Biology علم الأحياء /
ham = pork لحم الخنزير / sand الرمل / mud الطين /
soil تربة / dust غبار/ mist = fog الضباب / smoke الدخان /
fame الشهرة / feminism الحركة النسوية ,
favouritism المحسوبية / logic المنطق / lumbago عرق النساء
lunacy (لوناسي) الجنون / bulk كمية كبيرة /
in bulk بكميات كبيرة / loot المسروقات /
sadism (سي دزم) السادية (تعذيب الآخرين للمتعة) /
salvation الخلاص / capitalism الرأسمالية /
terrorism الإرهاب /

* **Correct the mistakes :**
    1- There is reason for doing that . ...
    2- These are the real reason for winning the game.
    ....
    3- Some house are too old.   ....
    4- He writes good storys .   ...
    5- The building has five storey . ...
    6- Husbands should respect their wifes .
    ....
    7- We have strong proof of **his innocence.** براءته
    ....
    8- Childs love sweets too much. ....
    9- We should fight mouse ; they are dangerous.
    ....
    10- There are criterias that everybody must fit.
    ....
    11- We have collected a lot of datums .
    ....
    12- She has washed all the dishs and glass , and dried them.
    ....

Agreement of Subject and Verb
التوافق بين الفاعل والفعل

We have to use a singular verb with a singular noun or pronoun

We have to use a plural verb with a plural noun or pronoun.

علينا أن نستخدم فعلاً مفرداً مع اسمٍ مفردٍ أو ضميرٍ مفردٍ . كما يجب أن يأتي
فعل جمع مع اسم أو ضمير جمع

1- The Sun is a bright object. It is the main source of energy.

2- Food gives people energy.

3- Hamad has changed his plans.

4- Ali was the first to leave.

5- Books are available everywhere.

6- There is a problem with this man.

7- There are many problems in this village.

8- People say that they need more schools .

* Sometimes, the subject is a phrase consisting of two
related nouns .
In this case , we have to follow the real subject.

أحياناً الفاعل يكون عبارة مكونة من اسمين مرتبطين معاً. في هذه الحالة علينا أن نتبع الفاعل
الحقيقي .

مضاف	مضاف إليه	
the door	of	the room .
the doors	of	the room . أبواب الغرفة
the pillars	of	Islam . أركان الإسلام
the dangers	of	pollution . أخطار التلوث
the profits	of	the company . أرباح الشركة

1- The dangers of pollution (**are** - is) known to all .

إننا نتحدث عن " أخطار " و ليس " التلوث " .

2- The importance of trees (are - **is**) known to all .

إننا نتحدث عن " أهمية الأشجار " وليس عن " الأشجار " .

3- The profits of the company (**have**-has) increased a lot.

إن أرباح الشركة قد ازدادت كثيراً.   (إننا نتحدث عن " الأرباح ").

4- **The pictures** in this book **are** great.

5- **The main idea** in these books **is** that crimes does not pay.

6- **The boys** who come to our school **receive** good education.

● The following prepositions take a singular verb as shown in these sentences if the real subject is singular.

together with , along with , as well as , in addition to ,
but = except

   1- **Ali** along with his brothers **comes** by bus.

يأتي علي بالباص برفقة إخوته.

   Ali and his brothers come by bus.

علي وإخوته يأتون بالباص.

   2-**Noura** together with her friends **is** unhappy about the
   test.

   3-**Hamad** as well as you **likes** the idea.

   4-**All the players** except Ali **have** arrived.

   5-**The players** in addition to the coach **have arrived.**

   6-**The coach** along with the players **has appeared.**

ظهر المدرب بصحبة اللاعبين .

* Each of the above sentences starts with the real subject
  , so the verb has to agree with it.

كل من الجمل السابقة تبدأ بالفاعل الحقيقي ولهذا لا بد أن يتوافق الفعل معه.

* Predicate nouns do not affect the verb of the clause .

الأسماء التي تقوم بوظيفة الخبر لا تأثير لها على فعل الجملة .

   1- They have become **a powerful force** .

   2-   The problem is **the careless boys.**

   3-   Trees are **a source of food.**

   4-   Cars have become **a problem.**

   5-   Traffic jams are **a big problem.**

   6-   The focus is on **the books on the table.**

7- Some books are **on the table**. **On the table** are some books.
8- **In the garden** are some boys.
9- The emphasis is on **causes rather than effects**.

التأكيد على الأسباب وليس على النتائج.

* **Use singular verbs with these pronouns:**

1- I need anybody to help me .
2- Everybody is willing to take part.   الكل راغب في المشاركة.
3- Nobody has shown any sign of approval.

لا أحد أظهر أي علامة استحسان .

4- Somebody was feeding the cows when I left.
5- Does anyone like to help ?
6- Everyone accepts my design.   كل شخص يقبل تصميمي.
7- No one is rejecting the idea.   لا أحد يرفض الفكرة.
8- Someone has just called you.
9- Nothing of these things has happened since you left .
10-   One prefers to have a well- paid job.   المرء يفضل أن

يحصل على وظيفة ذات راتب   جيد .

11-Each of these cars is regularly checked.

كل واحدة من هذه السيارات يتم فحصها بانتظام .

 12- Neither of these people is suitable for the job.

لا أحد من هؤلاء الناس مناسب للوظيفة .

* **Use singular verbs with gerunds that are subjects of clauses** .

استخدم فعلاً في المفرد مع الشكل الرابع للفعل إذا كان فاعلا للجملةَ.

1- Camping **is** my favourite hobby.
2- **Reading** newspapers **is** interesting.
3- **Using** prefixes **is** useful.
4- **Travelling , sailing and skiing are** popular with many people.

* Use singular verbs with collective nouns and some
nouns ending in – s .

استخدم فعلاً مفرداً مع الاسم الجماعي ومع بعض الأسماء المنتهية بـ s

1- **Information** has become accessible.

المعلومات قد أصبحت ميسرة .

2- **Knowledge** is easy to reach today.   المعرفة

3- **This furniture** is too old.   الأثاث

4- **Money** is the root of evil.   النقود سبب كل شر .

5- **Physics** is an important subject.

6- This is great **news.**

7- **Economics** is a useful science.   الاقتصاد علم نافع .

8- **The government** are studying the idea. (

(الحكومة = أعضاء الحكومة)

The government is losing control . (مؤسسة الحكومة)

(Similar collective nouns : chorus, choir , band , team,
company , herd , group , party الحزب , club , flock ,
labour-force)

9- **The cattle** are in the pasture .   الماشية في المرعى.

** **Many people** are against the idea.

(Similar ones : clergy رجال الدين , police, poultry الدجاج ,
vermin حشرات طفيلية , youth الشباب / جمع ومفرد)

* Use singular verbs with quantities.

استخدم فعلاً مفرداً مع الكميات

1- **Fifty dollars** *is* a good sum.

2- **Two kilos of meat** *is* enough.

3- **Three hundred miles** is not easy to drive in an hour.

4- " *Modern Short Stories* " is a book I advise you to read

5- The secretary and store man is a hard-working person.

↓

السكرتير- أمين المخزن شخص مجتهد.

The same person is doing a double job.

* With words like : *some* , *all* , *none* , *more* , *most* , *a lot*
    , we can use a singular or plural verb according to the
    form of the noun that follows them .

مع هذه الكلمات بإمكاننا أن نستخدم فعلاً مفرداً أو جمعاً حسب صيغة الاسم الذي يتبعها.

1- Some of this information is correct.

Some of these students are interested in the project.

2- All of the project has been rejected.

All of your projects have been approved.

3- A lot of food has become sour.

A lot of people are trying to solve the problem.

4- None of this food is edible.

None of the students are willing to join the course.

5- Most of the project has been completed .

Most of the projects have been completed.

Subject- Verb Agreement in Dependent Clauses
توافق الفاعل مع الفعل في الجمل التابعة

1- If either of the students gets high marks , he can join this college easily.

2- The man who teaches you is my neighbour.

3- I know girls who speak good English.

4- We pray in a mosque which was built in the 17th century.

5- The mosque that you pray in dates back to the 19th century.

أسماء بديلة Appositives

1- My sister Noura has passed , but my cousin Ali has failed.

2- I talked to Mr. Masri , the project manager.

3- We know a lot about Shakespeare , the playwright . Too little is known about Shakespeare , the man.

4- You have to see Mrs. Karimi , the chief nurse.

5- Could I see Dr. Muhammad , the shift doctor ?

6- Mr. Ali Ramzi , a relative of mine , will run this company.

7- Miss Ramzi , a Palestinian from Ramallah , is coming to the seminar.

Countable and uncountable nouns

أسماء تـقبـل و لا تـقبـل الـعـد

glass   الزجاج , a glass كوب , glasses أكواب , cloth القماش ,

a cloth ممسحة , paper الورق , a paper تقرير – جريدة

papers تقارير – صحف , chicken لحم الدجاج , a chicken دجاجة ,

chickens دجاج, wood خشب , a wood غابة , woods غابات

light الضوء , a light نور - شعلة – إشارة ضوئية , lights أضواء .

* We get **light** from the Sun.

* Turn off the lights ! We do not need them.

* I need a light to make a fire.

* The traffic-lights control traffic.

liver الكبد : This liver is fresh. لحم الكبد طازج

This man's liver is not functioning well. I think he needs a new one (liver) .

* These people live in luxury .   هؤلاء الناس يعيشون في رفاهية .

Bread is a luxury for these hungry people.

matter مادة / a matter = topic مسألة – موضوع, matters مسائل

mass كتلة / a mass of concrete الخرسانة من كتلة /

the masses الجماهير , Mass media الإعلام وسائل /

mass murder القتل بالجملة / mass production . الإنتاج بالجملة

material مادة / This shirt is made of good material.

material / Oil is a raw material. النفط مادة خام.

We have all the raw materials .   لدينا جميع المواد الخام.

I hope that these ideas will materialize .

أمل بأن هذه الأفكار سوف تصبح واقعاً.

* activity النشاط - an activity أحد الأنشطة , activities الأنشطة

This drug will give a lot of activity.

إن هذا العقار سيمنحك الكثير من النشاط .

He takes part in many activities.   إنه يشارك في أنشطة كثيرة.

* agreement الاتفاق بـمعنى الاتفاقية , an agreement الاتفاق في الرأي

agreements .

We need agreement.   إننا نحتاج إلى اتفاق (تفاهم)

We have reached an agreement that will solve many

problems.

إننا توصلنا إلى اتفاق سوف يحل مشاكل كثيرة.

* business تجارة – أعمال , a business شركة - businesses شركات

He wants to study business.

I am running a business in Doha.   إني أدير شركة في الدوحة .

* trade تجارة , a trade حرفة , trades حرف

Trade is flourishing in my country.   إن التجارة مزدهرة في بلدي.You have to

choose a suitable trade. عليك أن تختار حرفة مناسبة.

Jack of all trades master of none.

إن من أن لديه كل الحرف لا يتقن أي منها .

* fruit فاكهة , a fruit ثـمرة , fruits ثمار

I like fruit a lot.   أحب الفاكهة كثيراً.

The fruits are ripe enough to pick.

إن الثمار ناضجة بدرجة تكفي لقطفها.

* famine الجوع – المجاعة , a famine مجاعة , famines مجاعات

Millions of people suffer from famine in many countries..

ملايين الناس يعانون من الجوع في بلدان كثيرة.

We have received reports of a famine in the North of the

country. لقد تلقينا تقارير عن مجاعة في شمال البلاد.

* pleasure متعة- لذة a pleasure ,السعادة – الرضا-اللذة pleasure

People seek pleasure everywhere.

الناس يبحثون عن السعادة في كل مكان.

This centre has made shopping a great pleasure.

إن هذا المركز قد جعل التسوق متعة كبيرة.

* fire النار , a fire نارُ – حريق fires نيران – حرائق

The early people feared fire so much.

كان الناس الأوائل يخشون النار كثيراً.

There is a fire in the store .   هناك حريق في المخزن .

Let's make a fire to roast this fish.

دعنا نوقد ناراً لنشوي هذه السمكة.

This is enemy's fire.   هذا إطلاق لنيران معادية.

* favour محاباة – محسوبية , a favour معروف – صنيع , favours

Favour means injustice to others.   المحاباة تعني ظلماً للآخرين.

It is not fair to favour some people .

ليس من العدل أن نحابـي بعض الناس.

Ali did me a favour.   إن علياً قدّم لي معروفاً.

* death الموت , a death حالة وفاة - deaths وفيات

Speed means death.   السرعة تعني الموت

The number of deaths is increasing.   إن عدد الوفيات في ازدياد.

* weakness عيب – نقطة ضعف , a weakness ضعف – عجز

Old people suffer from bodily weakness.

يعانـي كبار السن من عجز جسدي.

Ali is careless ; this is his weakness.   إن علياً مهمل . إن هذا عيبه.

* crime الجريمة , a crime جريمة , crimes جرائم

We should fight crime. . يجب علينا أن نحارب الجريمة

If you steal , this is a crime. . إذا سرقت فإن هذا جريمة

We do not tolerate war crimes. . إننا لا نتساهل مع جرائم الحرب

To torture prisoners of war is a war crime.

إن تعذيب أسرى الحرب جريمة حرب.

* fish الأسماك – لحم السمك , a fish سمكة ,
(الأسماك fishes أو fish)

salmon / سامن / أسماك السلمون – لحم سمك السلمون ,
a salmon سمكة سلمون

* sanction استحسان – تصريح – تفويض, a sanction عقوبة ,
sanctions عقوبات دولية

They are acting with the sanction of the boss.

إنهم يتصرفون بناءً على تفويض من الرئيس .

Some countries receive sanctions for breaking international law .

بعض البلدان تتلقى عقوبات لخرقها القانون الدولي .

* sanctuary / سانكت يواري / حماية , a sanctuary ملاذ أمن

We should provide sanctuary for armless people.

يجب أن نوفر الحماية للناس العزل .

This town is a sanctuary for criminals.

هذه المدينة ملاذ للمجرمين .

This island is a sanctuary for rare birds.

هذه الجزيرة ملاذ للطيور النادرة.

art الفن , an art فن طريقة لعمل شيء *

beauty الجمال , a beauty شخص-شيء جميل

brick قرميد , a brick قطعة قرميد

cake الكيك , a cake كيكة

chocolate الشيكولات , a chocolate حبة شيكولات

cloth القماش , a cloth قطعة من القماش - ممسحة

decision الحسم , a decision قرار

duty الواجب , a duty احد المتطلبات

History مادة التاريخ , a history تقرير - حدث

honour الشرف , an honour شرف - تكريم

* This brave man is an honour to his country.

hope الأمل , a hope أمل

iron الحديد , an iron المكواة

language (كلام) لغة , a language لغة من اللغات

*You are using impolite language. إنك تستخدم لغة غير مهذبة. * English is a
world language. الإنجليزية لغة عالمية.

pain الألم , a pain ألم

space الفضاء - حيز , a space فراغ

stone مادة الحجر , a stone حجر

success النجاح - التوفيق , a success نجاح

failure الفشل , a failure فشل - إخفاق - خلل

thought الفكر , a thought فكرة

war الحرب , a war حرب

work العمل , a work of art عمل فني ...of an author worry القلق , a
worry قلق, worries

democracy الديموقراطية , a democracy بلد ديموقراطي ,
democracies

clothing (الملابس (مفرد , clothes (ملابس (جمع
dancing الرقص , a dance رقصة , dances
furniture (مفرد) أثاث , furnishings (أثاث (جمع
laughter الضحك , a laugh ضحكة , laughs
reason منطق , a reason حجة – سبب
machinery (مفرد)آلآت , a machine آلة , machines
pay الأجر , a payment دفعة , payments
permission إذن – ترخيص , a permit رخصة – تصريح
sunlight ضوء الشمس , a sunbeam ضوء من الشمس
usefulness فائدة – منفعة , a use استخدام – فائدة

Choose the right word :

1- I like eating (a chicken-chicken) a lot.

2- They went into (wood-a wood), where they got lost.

3- The importance of modern inventions (are- is) certain(مؤكدة)

4- The mistakes made by the former manager المدير السابق (has – have) been
discussed in public. علناً

5- We need a factory to produce more (glass- glasses) because the building sector
قطاع البناء is using a lot of it.

6- She has brought me (glass-a glass) of fresh orange juice.

7- I have read some daily (paper-papers).

8- (an-some) egg sandwich will cost يكلف you five riyals.

9- The beaches of this area (is-are) wonderful, so tourists are
coming in great (number-numbers).

10-(a-an) crime is committed ترتكب every five minutes, and
that is horrible.

11- Spain is (an – a) NATO member.

12- The first letter in " money " is (a – an) "m".

13- Is Qatar (a – an) FOA member.

14- The new college is (a / ×) great success.

15- (a / ×) success depends on certain factors.

النجاح يتوقف على عوامل معينة.

16- The attempt was (a / ×) complete failure.

17- Nobody expects (a / ×) failure.

* **Tick the correct sentences :**

1- **Arms of mass destruction** is forbidden. أسلحة الدمار الشامل

   Arms of mass destruction are **forbidden**. محرمة   (√)

2- He has a shortcoming .   (   )

   He has many shortcomings.   (   )

3- Foxes are wild animals.   (   )

   Foxs are wild animals .   (   )

4 - The whereabout of the killer is unknown. (   )

   The whereabouts of the killer are unknown. (   )

5- This is good news.   (   )

   These are good news.   (   )

6- This is species.   (   )

   This is a species.   (   )

7- The seat belt is a means rather than an end. (   )

   The seat belt is means rather than end. (   )

8- This is an information about the old equipments. (   )

   This is information about the old equipment. (   )

9- I sent them some advices regarding the education (   )

   I sent them some advice regarding education. (   )

10- We need both money and honey.   (   )

   We are need both moneys and honeys . (   )

11- Ali together with his brothers are coming. (   )

   Ali together with his brothers is coming. (   )

12- All the girls except Noura have passed. (   )

   All the girls except Noura has passed. (   )

13- The problem is the old roads.   (   )

   The problem are the old roads.   (   )

14- On the floor are some plates.   (   )

   On the floor is some plates.   (   )

15- The man who teaches your children are Palestinian.(   )

The man who teaches your children is Palestinian. (   )

* **Correct the mistakes :**

1- Everybody have gone out.   ....

2- No body invited me.   ....

3- No one has confirmed that.   ....

4- No thing has happened so far . ...

5- Everyone of you have finished. .... / ....

6- Neither of your brothers are ready.   ....

7- Each of these films are shameful.   ....

8- Planting trees are a nice job .   ...

9- The reasons for change is good.   ....

10- None this food is good.   ....

11- Half of these donations has come from Qatar.......

12- The police is looking for the thief.   ....

13- Three million dollars are a big sum.   ....

14- We get a light from the sun.   ....

15- I hit traffic-light .   ...

16- I like the art.   ....

17- Painting is art liked by many people. ....

18- Everybody likes the beauty.   ....

19- This painting is beauty.   ....

20- My furnitures are broken. .... / ....

21- He eat a lot of fresh fruits. .... /..................

22- The fruits is ripe .   ...

23- The new project is great success .   ...

24- One of the success of this government is the flourishing   economy
....

25- The number of students are rising.   ....

26- There is a number of people in the office. ....

27- I have got a permission to start small business.
.... / ....

28- They need more woods to make more doors..............

29- You did me favour.   ....

30- Mathematics are important subject....... /..............

31- Neither Ali nor his friends is willing to take part........

The Adjective الصفة

* Adjectives modify all nouns . الصفات تصف جميع الأسماء.

    Examples : lazy – rich – polite – nice – busy – important

         – dangerous – delicious لذيذ , harmful ضار ,

         cheap رخيص

In English , adjectives are not generally subject to gender
and plural rules.

في الإنجليزية الصفات لا تتقيد بقواعد الجنس والجمع.

Examples:

1- Ali is nice .

2- Mona is nice, too .

3- The boys are lazy .

4- The girls are lazy , too .

5- Both Ali and Mona are busy .

* **How to use the adjective** : كيفية استخدام الصفة في الجملة

1- English is important .

2- This car is new .

3- The cars are old .

4- I need a new car. إني احتاج إلى سيارة جديدة.

5-She has got high marks. لقد حصلت على درجات عالية.

6-New cars are expensive. السيارات الجديدة غالية.

7- Fresh food will benefit you more.

نلاحظ أن الصفة تسبق الاسم الذي تصفه في هذا النوع من الجمل الذي أيضا سبق لنا أن تعرضنا له.

** **How to use more than one modifier to modify a noun.**

** كيفية استخدام أكثر من صفة واحدة لوصف اسم واحد :

1- Ali is **nice and polite**.

2- Mona is **tidy and kind and friendly.** → Mona is tidy, kind and friendly.

3- We need **ambitious , clever , helpful people.**

We need ambitious and clever and helpful people.

إننا نحتاج إلى أناس طموحين , أذكياء ,متعاونين .

4- **Lazy , careless , foolish** people are unwanted.

الناس الكسالى والمهملون والحمقى غير مطلوبين .

5- I think that this person is **careful, frank and hard-working.**

إني أعتقد بأن هذا الشخص حذر وصريح ومجدُ.

** **Adjectives coming only after the noun modified .**

** صـفات تأتـي فقط بعـد الاسم الذي تصفه.

1- The children are still awake.   لا يزال الأطفال متيقظين .

2- Don't make noise! Ali is asleep.

لا تحدث ضوضاءً . إن علياً نائم.

3- Some people are still alive .   بعض الناس لا يزالون أحياء.

4- He was alone when I saw him.   كان وحيداً عندما قابلته .

5- Both Ali and his father are alike.

إن كلاً من علي وأبيه متشابهان.

6- Ali is abroad at the moment.

7- I found Ali and his brothers apart.

وجدت علياً وإخوته متفرقين .

8- We are ahead of all the others.   كنا متقدمون عن كل الآخرين.

9- They are behind us.   إنـهم كانوا ورائنا .

10- I am **aware** of the difficulty.   إنني مدرك للصعوبات .

** **To intensify an adjective , we can use these words :**

so , too , very .   لتقوية الصفة استخدم هذه الكلمات

1- Ali is so busy. مشغول جدا .

2- Food is very important . مهم جدا .

3- English is too difficult. (للتذمر) صعبة جدا .

4- He is too busy.

5- The weather is too cold .

6- The price is extremely high.   إن السعر مرتفع للغاية.

7- This matter is highly important.   . إن هذا الأمر مهم للغاية

The match was highly enjoyable (interesting).

إن المباراة كانت ممتعة للغاية .

8- The injury was nearly fatal.   الإصابة كادت أن تكون قاتلة.

9- She is quite (completely) right.   . إنها مصيبة تماماً

* ملاحظة : هذه الكلمات تسمى "adverbs" تسبق الصفة لتقويتها.

so جداً , very , too جداً , extremely , highly , nearly ,

بالكامل – تماماً completely , quite تماماً, almost تقريباً

* ملاحظة : في الجمل التالية نجد بأن " so " تعني " ولهذا " وأن " too" بمعنى أيضاً :

Hamad studied well , so he got high marks.

درس حمد بشكل جيد ولهذا فإنه حصل على درجات عالية.

Ali is not the only person to have passed .

Hamad has passed the exam , too .

إن علياً ليس هو الشخص الوحيد الذي نجح . إن حمداً قد اجتاز الامتحان أيضاً.

** Adjectives coming with linking verbs .

هناك أفعال يأتي بعدها صفات :

1- This food tastes nice .   إن هذا الطعام له مذاق طيب.

2- This flower smells nice .   إن هذه الوردة لها رائحة طيبة

3- This music sounds nice.   إن هذه الموسيقى تبدو جميلة.

4- I feel ill .   إني اشعر بالمرض.

5- You look tired .   يبدو عليك التعب.

6- It seems nice .   أن الأمر يبدو ظريفا.

7- She got angry with me .   إنها غضبت مني.

8- He will get angry.   انه سوف يغضب.

9- He will run mad .   انه سوف يجـن.

10- He will go mad .   انه سوف يجن

11- The company will go bankrupt.   أن الشركة سوف تفلس.

12- He has become rich and famous .   لقد أصبح غنياً و مشهوراً.

* **Adjectives reinforce verbs**:هناك صفات تستخدم كمقويات للفعل *

* **It is necessary to** reduce the number of cars on roads.

من الضروري أن نقلل من عدد السيارات على الطرق.

* It is wrong to keep food uncovered.

من الخطأ أن نبقي على الطعام دون غطاء.

* It is dangerous to drive too fast.

* It is easy for me to do that.

من السهل علي أن أفعل ذلك.

* It is difficult for Ali to buy such a car.

من الصعب على علي أن يشتري مثل هذه السيارة.

It is impossible to raise prices. → Raising prices is impossible.

To raise prices is impossible.

It is wrong to smoke before children. → Smoking before children is wrong.

To smoke before children is disastrous.

أن تدخن أمام الأطفال كارثي.

* **Some adjectives become nouns if preceded by "the" :**

الصفة إذا سبقتها the يكون الناتج اسماً يعبر عن مجموعة:

the poor الفقراء / our poor فقراؤنا / the ill المرضى
the homeless المشردون / the blind العميان / the innocent الأبرياء
the guilty المذنبون / the rich الأغنياء / our rich أغنياؤنا
the hungry الجائعون / the young الشباب / the old المسنون
the oppressed المظلومون / the depressed المحبطون /
the successful الناجحون / the hopeless اليائسون /
their wise عقلاؤهم / the weak الضعفاء /
the helpless الناس الذين لا نصير لهم

* The wise solve problems caused by the foolish.

*العقلاء يحلون مشاكل يسببها الحمقى.

The innocent pay for crimes committed by the guilty.

* الأبرياء يدفعون ثمن جرائم يرتكبها المذنبون .

Our young care about our old. * شبابنا يهتمون بشيوخنا .

The oppressed will sooner or later conquer their oppressors.

* المضطهدون سوف يقهرون ظالميهم إن آجلاً أو عاجلاً.

Our rich can relieve our poor and our hungry.

إن أغنياءنا يمكنهم أن يخففوا من معاناة فقرائنا وجوعانا.

Compound Adjectives الصفات المركبة :

ملاحظة: الصفة قد تكون كلمة واحدة مثل nice ، happy، tired ، important ، lazy .

هناك صفات مركبة compound adjectives أي تتكون من كلمتين من صفة واسم يضاف إليه ed– :

long-haired	ذو شعر طويل	/ short-tailed	ذو ذيل قصير
good-hearted	طيب القلب	/ open-handed	كريم
open-minded	متفتح الذهن	/ big-headed	متكبـر
deep-rooted	ذو جذور عميقة	/ bad-mannered	ذو سلوك سيئ
a two–week holiday	إجازة مدتها أسبوعان	/ one- eyed	ذو عين واحدة
a three – year course	دورة مدتها سنتان	/ strong-willed	ذو إرادة قوية

1- Ali is a kind- hearted person.

2- Mona is open- minded , but Noura is close-minded.

3- Ali helps people a lot ; in fact he is open- handed.

4- I am having a three-week holiday.

5- You can join the two-year course.

The Adverb الظـرف

* The Adverb of Place ظرف المكان

This adverb shows the place where the action takes place.

هذا الظرف يبين مكان حدوث الفعل .

1- We always keep meat **in the fridge , opposite the kitchen door.**

2- He is playing **under the tree.**

3- I waited for you **at the corner of the street.**

4- I found the money **under a carpet , in the bedroom.**

5- You can put the cup **on the table, next to the big sofa.**

6- She was born **in Gaza , Palestine**.

7- I keep my books **in the bookcase** *in the sitting-room*.

8- They have rented a small flat **in a city** *to the south of the* capital.

9- He owns shops **throughout Qatar**.

10- She has put the old clothes **inside the cupboard near the window**.

* **The Adverb of Time** ظرف الزمان

This adverb shows the time at which the action happens.

يُظهر هذا الظرف الزمن الذي يحدث فيه الفعل.

1- Ali first got the job **at six o'clock , May 12 , 1990**.

2- We go to school **in the early morning**.

3- I sometimes play football **in the afternoon**.

4- We stop working **at sun-set**.

5- We usually start working **at sun-rise**.

6- He left Doha **on Monday**. (on April 12)

7-We finished the project **in 1995**. = In 1995 we finished the project.

8- I finished **after** you had called. = (After you had called, I finished.) ↓

     L (**Adverb clause** جملة ظرفية)

9- She was crying when I came in. = (When I came in , she was crying.) ↓

     L (**Adverb clause**)

10- I always have a cup of tea **during the break**. أثناء الاستراحة

11- They usually watch TV **before bed-time**.

12 - We go to bed **at mid-night**.

13- We **usually** have a break استراحة **at mid-day**.

14 - Many people leave the country for other countries **in summer**.

15- Nature looks beautiful **in spring**.= In spring …..

الطبيعة تبدو جميلة في الربيع.

16- She has just phoned.

17- She has not finished it **so far**.

18- I have **recently** got a reply from the university.

19- I **soon** used the new programme.

20 He will **soon** leave for Japan to join his father.

21- The oil prices rose **in the 1980s** . = In the 1980s the oil prices rose.

22- This poet lived **in the sixteenth century**. = In the 16th century ....

* **The Adverb of Manner** ظرف الحال :

We use the adverb of manner to modify the verb ... to show how the action takes place.

نستخدم ظرف الحال لإظهار كيفية وقوع الفعل .

1- Ali is **polite.** (مؤدب / صفة)

He speaks **politely** (بأدب/ ظرف حال) to all people.

The word " politely " describes how the person speaks.

كلمة politely تصف الكيفية التي يتحدث بها الشخص.

2- Mona is **kind.** (حنونة/ صفة)

She treats me **kindly**. (بحنان/ظرف حال)

How to form the adverb of manner
كيفية تكوين ظرف الحال

We often form the adverb of manner by adding - ly to the adjective.

غالباً يتم تشكيل ظرف الحال بإضافة ly - إلى الصفة.وهناك استثناءات.

Adjective صفة	**Adverb of Manner** ظرف الحال
polite مؤدب	politely بأدب
strong قوي	strongly بقوة

slow بطيء	slowly ببطيء
quick سريع	quickly بسرعة
exact دقيق	exactly بدقة
careful حذر	carefully بحذر
peaceful سلمي	peacefully سلمياً
haphazard ارتجالي	haphazardly بطريقة عشوائية
bad سيئ	badly بشكل سيئ
frank صريح	frankly بصراحة
fluent طلق	fluently بطلاقة
deep عميق	deeply بعمق
easy سهل	easily بسهولة
lucky محظوظ	luckily لحسن الحظ
true صادق	truly بصدق
gentle لطيف – رقيق	gently بلطف
simple بسيط	simply ببساطة
suitable مناسب	suitably بشكل مناسب
specific محدد	specifically بشكل محدد
historic تاريخي	historically من الناحية التاريخية
public عام – علني	publicly علناً

* Exceptions استثناءات

ملاحظة: هناك كلمات تؤدي وظيفتين... صفة و ظرف حال، كما في هذه الأمثلة:

1- I know that life is too **hard** (شاق /Adjective), so we
    have to work **hard** .   (بجد / Adverb)

2- Don't drive too **fast** (بسرعة / Adverb); **fast** (Adjective)
    driving is too risky.   إن القيادة السريعة محفوفة بالمخاطر

3- Ali is **well** .   بخير / Adjective

* Ali is good.   إن علياً طيب.

He does everything **well** .   Adverb / بشكل جيد

4- You are **early**   مبكر .   You always come **early**.

5- They are **late**.   متأخر   They always come **late**.

6- We buy a **daily** newspaper every morning(Adjective/صفة)

إننا نشتري صحيفة يومية كل صباح

7- I prefer to read **aloud**. (بصوت عالٍ = loudly) .

8- We come here **daily**. They pay us **daily** . Adverb

إننا نأتي إلى هنا بصورة يومية . إنهم يدفعون لنا بشكل يومي.

9- We hold a **weekly** meeting.   Adjective   إننا نعقد اجتماعاً أسبوعياً.

We meet **weekly** .   Adverb   ظرف حال

10- She is the **likely** winner .   Adjective   إنها الفائز المحتمل .

She will very (most)**likely** to win the race.

11- He is **alone**.   هناك احتمال كبير جداً أنها تفوز بالسباق.

Adjective / He likes to walk **alone**. Adverb

He is lonely. He is living in a lonely place.

12- Many things went **wrong** . (Adv.)

This answer is **wrong**.   (Adj.)

13-We should bury these dangerous objects **deep** in the

ground.   Adverb

This lake is **deep**.   Adjective   البحيرة عميقة.

14- The birds are flying **high** in the sky . Adverb

إن الطيور تحلق عالياً في السماء.

The price is too **high**.   Adjective   إن السعر عالٍ جداً.

15- You should get these things **right**. Adverb

You are **right** . I agree with you.   Adjective

16- The end is **near**.   Adjective صفة   النهاية قريبة.

17- They came **near** and began to shoot.   Adverb ظرف حال

اقتربوا وبدؤوا يطلقون النار.

18- Draw a **straight** line. **Adjective**   . ارسم خطاً مستقيما
   Go **straight** to the clock-tower. **Adverb**

سر مباشرة إلى برج الساعة .

19- Prices are too **low**.   **Adjective**   . الأسعار منخفضة للغاية
   The plane is flying too **low**. **Adverb**

إن الطائرة تحلّق على مستوٍ منخفض جداً.

He rejects **lowly** jobs. He just wants **high** ones.

Adjective

* These words are only adjectives الكلمات التالية تعتبر صفات فقط :

lonely   lovely جميل , lively نشيط – حيوي , deadly مميت ,
, worldly دنيوي , earthly ممكن – دنيوي , وحيد
friendly ودي – ودود , brotherly أخوي

How to use the adverb of manner
كيفية استخدام ظرف الحال

يستخدم ظرف الحال لوصف الكيفية التي يتم بها الفعل. ويجب عدم الخلط بين ظرف الحال والصفة.
1-I am proud of Ali. أنا فخور بعلي
   He is running the company **efficiently**. بجدارة/ظرف حال

إنه يدير الشركة بكفـاءة.

   He is **efficiently** running the company.
2-The public received the winners **warmly**.

استقبل الجمهور الفائزين بحرارة.

   The public **warmly** received the winners .
   The public received **warmly** the winners. (×)
3- We should drive **slowly** and **carefully** to avoid
   accidents.

يجب أن نسوق ببطيء وبحذر لنتجنب الحوادث.

4- You speak English **fluently**.   إنك تتحدث الإنجليزية بطلاقة .

5- The exam will be <u>hard</u> (صعب/صفة), so you should study
hard(بجد/ حال).

6- I do things carefully. ⟶ with care / in a careful manner   بطريقة حذرة

7-   I always act wisely. بحكمة ⟶ with wisdom / in a wise
   manner.   إني دائماً أتصرف بحكمة.

* The Order of Adverbs ترتيب الظروف :

When having to use several adverbs in one clause , we have
to follow this order .

عندما نضطر إلى استخدام ظروف عدة في جملة واحدة , علينا إتباع الترتيب التالي .

1- We **always** drive **slowly** *to the beach* *in the early morning*.

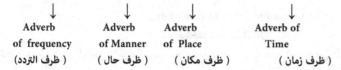

Adverb	Adverb	Adverb	Adverb of
of frequency	of Manner	of Place	Time
(ظرف التردد)	(ظرف حال)	(ظرف مكان)	(ظرف زمان)

In the early morning we always drive slowly to the beach.

2- Fatima is talking loudly *in her office* at the moment.

3- He pushed the table nervously towards the wall.

4- Ali took **carefully** all the things *outside* .

5- Suddenly I heard a noise from the floor *beneath ours*.

* **Emphasizing Adverbs** ظرف التشديد :

We use " **only** " and " **even** " for emphasis and to modify
the words that follow them.

نستخدم هاتين الكلمتين للتأكيد علي أمر ما ولوصف الكلمات التي تليها ويتغير المعنى بتغير
مكانيهما .

1- Only Ali asked for coffee.   فقط علي طلب قهوة.

2- Ali only asked for coffee.

علي فقط طلب قهوة. (أي قام بفعلٍ واحدٍ فقط.)

3- Ali asked only the maid for coffee.

طلب علي قهوة من الخادمة فقط دون سواها .

4- Ali asked the maid only for coffee.

طلب علي من الخادمة قهوة فقط.

5- I told you only to wash the car.   أخبرتك فقط أن تغسل السيارة.

6- I told you to wash only the car.

أخبرتك بأن تغسل فقط السيارة دون سواها.

7- I told you to wash the car only on Fridays.   * فقط أيام الجمع .

Adverbs that modify the whole clause ظروف تصف كامل الجملة:

We usually use these adverbs to sum up what has been
     previously mentioned.

عادة نستخدم هذا النوع من الظرف عندما نوجز ما سبق ذكره.

1- Briefly , we can say that we need more practice.

    We briefly can say that we need more practice.

2- Certainly , the radar is a trap for road hogs.

    The radar ,certainly, is a trap for road hogs.

3- Of course , we have to act quickly .

    We , of course , have to act quickly.

    We have to act quickly , of course.

4- Perhaps , the answer lies in changing our methods.

    The answer , perhaps , lies in changing our methods.

    The answer lies in changing our methods , perhaps.

5- Objectively speaking , our policy has to change.

    Our policy , objectively speaking , has to change.

    Our policy has to change , objectively speaking.

6- Therefore , we have to change our policy.

We , therefore , have to change our policy.

We have to change our policy , therefore.

We can , therefore , say that not all films are bad.

We can say , therefore , that we have to hire a new

secretary.

** Similar adverbs   ظروف مشابهة

* We have to note that these adverbs are also used to join

two related clauses.

علينا ملاحظة أن هذه الظروف تستخدم أيضاً لربط جملتين بينتهما علاقة ما.

however   , nevertheless , besides , furthermore ,
in addition , consequently , as a result .

*Choose the right word, and write what part of speech it is :

1- English is (easy-easily) to learn ………………………

2- It is (easy -easily) to do that . …………………………

3- You can do that (easy-easily) . …………………………

4- You should treat others (nice-nicely). ………………...

5- (nice-nicely) people always talk (nice-nicely) ………....

6- You drive too (fast-fastly) ; that is (dangerously-dangerous) . ..
…………………………………………

7- You breathe too (hard-hardly),………………………
and that is because you smoke (heavy-heavily).
……………

8- The rain is too (heavy-heavily) ………………………...

9- It rains (heavily-heavy) in London . ……………….......

10- He is (rough-roughly), so I always avoid him ………....

11- It is not nice to speak (rough-roughly) to others ……...

12- The knife is too (sharp-sharply) to touch……………....

13- You should drive (safe-safely) to avoid accidents.   ……………

14- (Careless-Carelessly) people never appeal to me . ...

15- He has chosen five people (haphazardly- haphazard). ....

16- The king is (frank-frankly); ....

he always speaks (frankly-frank) of our economic

problems . ...

17- You can get (high-highly) marks if you work (hard- hardly).

....

18- The rock is too (hardly-hard) to break into pieces . ...

19- The progress (التقدم) that we have so far made is   (

satisfactory- satisfactorily). ....

20- These people are (friend- friendly)........................

21- The problem was (easy-easily) to solve. ....

22- The problem was (easy-easily) solved. ....

23- The question is too (hard-hardly) to answer...............

24- A (bad-badly) done job will <u>lead to disasters</u>.

(يؤدي إلى كوارث) ....

25- You are doing a (bad-badly) job . ...

● **Correct the mistakes in these sentences:**

1- She comes always lately.

....

2- Ali always is freely.

....

3- We have freely education

....

4- They always talk free

....

5- We at school learn things useful.

....

6- Mona needs ideas new.

....

7- I found five alive people

....

8- He likes to play lonely.

....

9- He spoke friendly to me.

....

10- She does carefully things.

....

11- People young are selfishes.

....

12- Some people are carelessness.

....

13- We are in school .

....

14- He was born in March 23rd , 1996.

....

15- I go often to bed in mid-night.

....

17- They use simply language.

....

18- This is a dead disease.

....

19- We must bury the deadly man.

....

20- You work too hardly.

....

21- Sara has told I some news goods.

....

22- My parents are talking gentle .

....

23- My mother prefers to stay in home.

....

24- My camera was bad damaged.

....

25 - Don't disturb the asleep boys.

....

*   **Write what part of speech the underlined word is:**

1- The room is not <u>tidy</u> , so we should <u>tidy</u> it .

    (Adjective)   (Verb)

2- The water is <u>pure</u> ; you can <u>use</u> it for <u>drinking</u> .

    (................. , ... , ...)

3- It is <u>wrong</u> to <u>drink</u> <u>impure</u> water . In this case , you should <u>purify</u> it before <u>drinking</u> it .

    (............, ..., ... , ... , ...)

4- We have <u>discovered</u> that this <u>drink</u> tastes bad .

    (............. , ...)

5- It is mad to <u>pollute</u> water . <u>Pollution</u> is dangerous , so it is necessary to <u>reduce</u> it .

    (................. , ... , ...)

6- We welcome any <u>reduction</u> in prices . Any reduction is <u>welcome</u>.

    (.................)   (.................)

7- I <u>plan</u> to get a <u>new</u> passport . The <u>renewal</u> of the old one takes time.

    (................. , ... , ...)

8- My <u>plan</u> is useful ; I advise you to <u>accept</u> it .It can solve the problem <u>peacefully</u>.

    (................. , ... , ...)

9- The <u>agreement</u> will <u>satisfy</u> all the <u>warring</u> *parties*. (الأطراف)

    (................. , ... , ...)

10- I am <u>satisfied</u> because all the parties have <u>agreed</u> to negotiate يتفاوض على the <u>settlement</u> التسوية.

    (................. , ... , ...)

11-We must <u>settle</u> our problems <u>soon</u> .

    (............. , ...)

12- We are <u>worried</u> about the <u>settlements</u> <u>in the West Bank</u> .

(.................... , ..., ...)

13- She is <u>always</u> angry. <u>Anger</u> is something bad. It is wrong to <u>anger</u> others.

(.................. , ... , ...)

14- I don't <u>accept</u> it if you speak <u>angrily</u> to the <u>kids</u>.

(.................. , ... , ...)

15- We are <u>close</u> to <u>reaching</u> an agreement that will put an end to our <u>dispute</u>.

(.................. , ... , ...)

16-Some people <u>protest</u> against foreign <u>investments</u> , but these <u>protests</u> will fail.

(.............., ..., ...)

17-There are some <u>differences</u> , and it is our <u>duty</u> to <u>reconcile</u> the two countries.

(.............,...............,................)

* Fill in the spaces with suitable words إملأ الفراغات بكلمات مناسب

* لحل هذا السؤال ، علينا قراءة الجملة جيداً وفهم المعنى ومعرفة الكلمة المطلوبة .. إن معرفتنا بطريقة تكوين الجملة تساعدنا في معرفة الكلمة المطلوبة .. أي هل الكلمة .. اسم أو فعل .. أو صفة .. أو ظرف أو حرف جر ؟

1- Ali is ...., so we like him .

2- Ali is .... a book about the .... of oil.

3- Mona is washing her ....

4- Mona has cooked a .... meal . Everybody

.... her for it.

5- You should drive .... If you .... madly ,

you will .... your life . Don't forget that .... kills.

6- We can leave the .... any time .

7- I .... smoke because it .... wrong to smoke

8- My salary راتب is .... , and I don't .... all of it .

I .... some money because I may need it in the future .

9- Some people .... more money than they get. That is .... You

should not .... all your money . Always .... this advice.

10- Water .... important , but .... is rare . It is mad to .... it . If you

............water , you will .... many problems .

11- You .... ill , so I advise you .... see the doctor . He will .... you by

.... what is wrong with you and by .... you the right

medicine .

12- We have to .... our education system because our country cannot

.... without بدون .... education.

13- Thanks to بفضلeducation , our country will .... a lot .

14- It is necessary to .... people if they break يخرقthe law القانون . If we don't

punish them, we will have more....... We should know that ......can reduce تقلل

الجرائمcrimes من .

15- The Minister of .... has decided to increase the

.... of schools in .... areas.

16- The king is too ill to rule, so the .... have asked for

his ....

17- The Ministry of .... has asked everybody to defend the country .

18- It is wrong to .... trees. If we do that, we will cause so

much ....

19- He .... born in ..... village in the .... of Qatar.

20 - .... April 23rd 1 990 , Ali .... from his village

.... a city .... of the capital.

Degrees of comparison

درجات المقارنة

* **How to compare persons or things :**

كيف نقارن بين الأشخاص أو الأشياء :

A- The comparative degree .   درجة المقارنة بين اثنين

1- Ali is taller <u>than</u> Ahmad .   إن علياً أطول من أحمد.

    (tall + er   than)

2- My car is smaller <u>than</u> yours .

3- My house is older <u>than</u> Ali's .

إن منـزلي أقدم من منـزل علي.

4- Mona is younger <u>than</u> me .   إن منى أصغر سناً مني .

5- You drive faster <u>than</u> Ali .

6- You are bigger <u>than</u> Ali .   (big)

7- She is thinner <u>than</u> Ali .   (thin)

8- I am fatter <u>than</u> you .   (fat)

9- Doha is hotter <u>than</u> Amman .   (hot)

10- London is wetter <u>than</u> Doha .   (wet)

11- English is easier <u>than</u> Arabic .   (easy)

12- Ali is happier <u>than</u> you .   (happy)

* نلاحظ أن الصفات موضع المقارنة عبارة عن كلمات من مقطع واحد , أما إذا كانت الصفات تتكون من أكثر من مقطع ، فإننا نتبع ما يلي:

1- Health is <u>more important</u> <u>than</u> wealth .

إن الصحة مهمة أكثر من المال .

2- My house is <u>more beautiful</u> <u>than</u> yours .

إن منـزلي أكثر جمالاً من منزلك .

3- This car is <u>more comfortable</u> <u>than</u> Ali's .

هذه السيارة مريحة أكثر من سيارة علي .

4- You speak English <u>more fluently</u> <u>than</u> Ali .

إنك تتكلم الإنجليزية بطلاقة أكثر من علي .

    more +   ظرف حال(صفة الفعل) + than

B- **The superlative degree** . درجة التفضيل

ونستخدمها عندما نقارن شخص مع مجموعة من الأشخاص .

1- Ali is <u>the</u> young<u>est</u> boy in the family .

إن علياً أصغر ولد في السن في العائلة .

2- Ali is <u>the</u> young<u>est</u> of his brothers . إن علياً أصغر إخوته. 3- You are
<u>the</u> thinn<u>est</u> of all . 4-أنـت أنحـف الجميـع. Kuwait is <u>the</u> hott<u>est</u>
country in the Gulf .

5- English is <u>the</u> eas<u>iest</u> language in the world .

في حالة كون الصفة قصيرة The + صفة + est

أما إذا كانت الصفة طويلة ، فإننا نتبع ما يلي :

The + most + الصفة ⟵

1- Arabic is <u>the most beautiful language</u> in the world .

إن اللغة العربية أجمل لغة في العالم .

2- This is <u>the most difficult question</u> I have ever seen .

إن هذا أصعب سؤال رأيته في حياتي .

3- That was <u>the most dangerous adventure</u> he has ever taken .

تلك كانت أخطر مغامرة قام بها في حياته .

* **Exceptions** استثناءات :
    good-well / better than أفضل من / the best الأفضل
    bad / worse than أسوأ من / the worst الأسوأ
    far بعيد / farther than أبعد من / the farthest الأبعد
    little قليل / less than أقل من / the least الأقل
    many (much) / more than أكثر من / the most الأكثر

1- Ali is better than you . In fact , he is the best of all . He does everything better than anybody else .

2- She is worse than you . She is the worst person on earth .

3- Your house is the farthest one in the area .

4- I am **major than** Ali .

أنا أكبر مقاماً من علي . / تختلف شكلاً عما سبق ولكن نفس الوظيفة.

5-I am **senior to** Ali .   أنا أكبر من علي .

6-He is **inferior to** me.   إنه دوني منزلة.

7-He is **superior to** you.   أنه أرفع منك.

في الأمثلة السابقة وجدنا أن الصفة أو ظرف الحـال هـي موضـع المقارنة . و لا بـد مـن ملاحظـة أنـه في الأمثلة الأربعة الأخيرة نجد أن صفات المقارنة تختلف شكلاً ولكن تفيد المقارنةأما في الأمثلـة التاليـة فـإن موضع المقارنة سيكون اسم أو فعل .

1- Ali has more money than you (do) .   إن علياً يملك مالاً أكثر منك

2- I have less food than he (does) .   إني أتناول طعاماً أقل منه .

3- You preach more than you do .   إنك توعظ أكثر مما تفعل.

4- You spend less than you get .   إنك تنفـق أقـل مـما تحصـل. 5- I need more money than you do.   6-إني أحتـاج إلى مـال أكـثر مـما تحتاج أنـت. Less speed means safety. **السرعة القليلة تعني الأمان.**

7- Less energy means less pollution.   طاقة أقل تعني تلوثاً أقل.

8-You speak more than you do.   إنك تتكلم أكثر مما تعمل.

9-You eat less food than you need.   إنك تأكل طعاماً أقل مما تحتاج.

١٠- The more food you eat, the more weight you gain.

كلما أكلت طعاما أكثر كلما اكتسبت وزنا أكثر.

11-The less you speak, the better.

كلما قللت من الكلام كلما كان أفضل.

12-The more you eat , the less you think.

- **Absolute adjectives** الصفات المطلقة :

It is advisable not to compare these adjectives.

لا ننصح بإخضاع هذه الصفات للمقارنة.

dead ميت , alive حي , fatal قاتل , asleep نائم , awake يقظ ,
unique فريد , present حاضر , absent غائب , possible ممكن ,
impossible مستحيل , round مستدير , square مربع .

- **Similarity** التشابه :

Ali is as tall as his father (is).   إن علياً مثل طول أبيه.
Money is as important as management. إن المال في الأهمية مثل الإدارة.
You drive as fast as I do.   إنك تسوق بسرعة مثلي .
She speaks English as quickly as her mother does.
They left as early as I did.   غادروا مبكرين مثلي .

* Put the words in brackets in the right forms :

1- It is (easy) ....to learn Arabic than to learn English .

2- This is the (interesting) .... story I have ever seen.

3- We have (few) ....accidents than we had last year.

4-   You eat (little) .... meat than me .

5- She has (many) .... problems than you do .

6- The (important) .... point is that flies are

(dangerous) .... than cats.

7- Thanks to this road , we have the (few) .... accidents .

8- This is the (bad) ....disaster we have ever seen.

٢١٥

9- Ali runs (fast) ……….. and (well) ………….than you do .

10- We have (much) ………… pollution than we used to .

11- This is the (good) …………... story I have ever read.

12- Running is (good) …………... than walking.

13- They are getting (noisy) ………………. Than they were.

14- She has (little) …………... money than Ali does.

15- We are building (many) …………... roads than before.

16- We need (much) ………. electricity than before.

17- They speak (quickly) ………………. than others.

18- She is the (good) ………… person to do this job.

19- You ask for (little) ………… money than you need.

20 – The (much) ………… you practise , the (good)

…………………………...

21- Sweets give you (much) ……. Energy than anything else.

22- This is the (decisive) ……………… step I've ever taken.

23- The present boss is (flexible مرن) ……………… than the

former. (الرئيس الحالي / السابق)

24- My mother is the (careful) ……………………. person here.

25- Ali is the (lazy) …………… boy I have ever seen.

Determiners
أدوات التعريف (التحديد)
* The Articles : the - a – an *

* The Demonstratives أسماء الإشارة *

this   - that - these – those

The possessives صفات الملكية
my- his –her – your – our – their –its

أدوات التعريـــــف : The articles / determiners

" the , a , an "

The articles are a kind of adjective .

أدوات التعريف هي نوع من الصفات

1- We use the definite article before a noun that is
   already known to us. (The book on the table. / The
   man sitting under the tree.)

أداة التعريف أو التخصيص " the " تستخدم قبل الاسم عندما يكون هذا الاسم ذاته معروفاً لدينا
مثال : the book الكتاب أي المقصود الكتاب المعروف لدى الأشخاص الذين يتحدثون عنه .

Names of people are not preceded by any of the above articles.

* أسماء الأشخاص لا تُعرّف بأي أداة من الأدوات السابقة .

Ali , Huda , James , Henry , Mary .

Names of one-word countries and cities are not generally
 preceded by an article .

* أسماء البلدان والمدن لا تُعرّف .

Qatar , Doha , Kuwait , Jordan , Damascus , Palestine ,
Hebron الخليل , Lebanon, London, Mecca , Saudi Arabia , India, Beirut , Cairo, Tunis.

* Determiners are not used with common nouns unless they are
  related to other nouns.

* الأسماء الشائعة لا تعرّف إلا إذا تم ربط الاسم بشيء آخر .

wool الصوف, wood الخشب , iron الحديد , copper النحاس
cheese الجبن , hunger الجوع ,oxygen , air , food , water , milk ,
sugar , salt , information معلومات , knowledge المعرفة ,
Arabic اللغة العربية, English اللغة الإنجليزية , oil , power ,

health الصحة , nature الطبيعة , science العلم education التعليم ,
success النجاح , disease المرض , prevention الوقاية ,
speed السرعة , smoking , reading القراءة , ink الحبر , sand الرمل
blood الدم , ice الثلج , life الحياة , death الموت , Math الرياضيات ,
physics فيزياء , music الموسيقى .

* **Examples** أمثلة :

* I like **milk** and **tea** .
* **Water** is necessary to **people** .
* **The water in this country** is polluted . الماء في هذا البلد ملوث
* We should protect **nature** .
* I can describe **the nature of this element** .

أستطيع أن أصف طبيعة هذا العنصر .

* We don't use " the " if we talk about " water" in general.

ملاحظة : من الأمثلة السابقة ، نرى أنه لا داعي لاستخدام أداة التعريف " the " إذا تحدثنا عن "
الحليب والشاي " عموماً .
أما إذا حدث تخصيص .. الماء في هذا البلد .. فلا بد من " the " .

ملاحظة: يجوز تعريف knowledge بـ a إذا جاء بعدها of :

* Knowledge is important , so we should have easy access to it.
* A knowledge of English is necessary.
* Many people live in the North of the globe. (region)
   Oil is found in the South of the country.
   Most people prefer to live in the West .
* Doha is west of Qatar. (position)
   Aqaba is south of Jordan.
   Haifa is north of Palestine.
* Go westwards . On seeing a mosque , walk south for two
   miles.(direction)

* We have to use " the" with these nouns:

بعض الأسماء الشائعة تُعرَّف بـ the :

the sun , the moon , the earth , the environment , the weather ,

the climate المناخ

* The Smiths are coming to visit us tonight. عائلة سميث قادمون لزيارتنا.

* The Ali Nasser who works for your company is different from the Ali Nasser who teaches French.

● 	The Netherlands هولندا , the Philippines, the United States ,

● 	the Black Sea , the Dead Sea , the Indian Ocean , the Suez Canal ,

	the River Nile , the Alps جبال الألب ,

	the Queen Elizabeth II , the Gulf Times , The Hague لاهاي .

The following nouns usually come without " the":

الأماكن التالية عادة تأتي بدون أداة التعريف.

1- 	We go **home** after we finish **work.**

2- 	We are at **home** in the evening.

3- 	They are at **work** now.

4- 	I want to go to **university** after I finish **school.**

5- 	You must take him to **hospital.**

6- 	The thief must go to **prison.** اللص يجب أن يذهب إلى السجن.

7- 	Do you go to **church** ? هل تذهب إلى الكنيسة؟

8- 	Trees make oxygen.

9- 	Dogs are animals.

10- 	Japanese cars are popular.

11- 	We need electricity a lot.

12- 	Man likes peace and hates war.

13- 	God forgives sinful people if they repent.

	Man proposes ; God disposes. الإنسان في التفكير و الـلـه في التدبير .

14- 	All my friends are doctors.

15 – 	We have breakfast , lunch and dinner at home.

16- 	*Man and wife* consult one another.

17- 	*Father and son* work together.

18- 	These two children are *brother and sister*.

19- 	You can buy *lock and key.*

20- I like to get information about *sun , moon and stars*.

21- He talks a lot about *heaven and hell*.

22- We are at war. (at peace , at ease , at rest , at sea , at lunch

in danger , in need , in reply , in love ,

in difficulty , in trouble , on purpose , on fire,

on sale , on duty , on land , by accident ,

by heart , by mistake ,by chance ,

out of control , out of date , out of print ,

اصطلح على استخدامها بهذا الشكل.

23 – Thank you , Father. Thank you , Teacher.

Another / other

● We usually use " another " as a determiner before a singular
noun or pronoun .

1- I have sent Ali **a book** , but he is asking for <u>**another one.**</u> كتاب أخر

2- She has written **an article** مقالة and the teacher wants **another one**.

3- **A student** left at five o'clock. **Another student** left an hour later.

* We can use " **another**" as a pronoun.

1- I gave Ali **an apple** , but he asked for **another.** ⟶

(replacing the " apple")

2- Ali has got **an increase in his salary** زيادة في راتبه, but he is asking for
another. زيادة أخرى

٢٢٠

* We usually use " other" with a plural noun or pronoun.

* نستخدم "other" مع اسم أو ضمير جمع.

1- I have read some **articles** , and I will read **the other ones** soon.

2- Some **people** don't agree with me. **Other ones** do.

3- **These cars** are cheap. **The other ones** are not.

هذه السيارات رخيصة. والسيارات الأخرى ليست كذلك.

* We use " **other**" as a pronoun.

1- **Some of your friends** are willing to come. **The others** are not.

2- Three of these **apples** are soft لينة . **The others** are too hard.

3- Some **people** care about **others**.

4- It is not nice to offend **others**. ⟶ people

5- I have seen two people. The first one knows a lot about computing. The **other** one does not. (singular / المفرد أحياناً مع)

6- The **other** day I was talking to my friends when Ali rushed in

* Put " the " if necessary عند الضرورة " the " ضع :

1- ...... pollution التلوثis a big problem . ... pollution of our beaches will destroy ....sea birds and animals .

2- .... hard work العمل الجاد leads to يقود إلى .... success .
I can say that ....success of .... company is **due to** راجع إلى ....co-operation of .... staff with .... management .

3- .... speed can kill . ... speed of a car can cause يسبب an accident .

٢٢١

4- I need .... information about .... English and Arabic . ...
information Ali has given me is not *enough* . كافية

5- We need .... blood and .... medicine . ... blood in this bottle is not
good , and .... medicine we have got from abroad is too old .

6- We need ...... fresh air and ...... clean water.

7- .... water in this glass is not fresh.

8- .... prices of petrol are expected to rise which means that .... rate of
.... inflation التضخم will rise too.

9- .... food gives people .... energy . All .... energy that we need is easy
to get.

10- .... price of this bread is high. We should complain to .... owner of
.... bakery.

11- .... freedom is dear , we should fight for it .

12 - .... *constitution* الدستور ensures .... freedom of .... opinion.

13- .... women call for .... equality and .... right to vote.

14- .... crime happens because .... young cannot find .... jobs.

15- In .... early morning all of .... family members have .... breakfast
in .... back garden .

16- .... accidents occur because .... police do not punish .... mad
drivers.

17- .... money makes .... money.

18- .... people of my country do not drink .... wine .

19- We have .... milk , ... tea and .... coffee.

20- .... economy of .... country is sound.

The indefinite articles " a " and "an" modify countable nouns.
أدوات التعريف تسبقان الأسماء القابلة للعد. " an " / " a "

Singular مفرد	Plural جمع
a book	books
a tree	trees
a room	rooms
a car	cars
a door	doors
a man	men
a child	children
a tooth ضرس	teeth
a foot	feet
an ox ثور	oxen ثيران
a life روح إنسان	lives
a knife سكين	knives
a thief لص	thieves
a loaf رغيف	loaves
a leaf ورقة	leaves

هناك أسماء شائعة قلنا أنها لا تعرّف بـ " the " وكذلك لا تقبل " a " أو " an " قبلها حتى ولو كانت مفردة .

food (✔)   , a food (×)

information (✔) , an information (×)

oil (✔)   , an oil (×)

= I need <u>food</u> and <u>water</u> .   إني أحتاج طعاماً وماءً.

= We need <u>a food centre</u> and <u>a water filter</u> .

إننا نحتاج إلى مركز للغذاء ومصفاة للمياه . إن وجود " a " ليس من أجل " food " و " water " بل مـن أجل " centre " و " filter " .

* Put " a " or " an " when necessary :

1- .... oil is the main source of .... income in .... oil-producing country .

2- They have recently started ..... new oil refinery in .... area in the North .

3- You can write .... letter to .... information centre if you want to know more about .... country .

4- .... apple .... day keeps the doctor away .

5- .... intelligence الذكاء is innate. فطري

6- .... student must take .... intelligence test before we

accept him .

7- Coal الفحم is .... energy source , but we also get ...... energy from .... gas.

8- Ali is showing ..... interest in building ..... new power station

in ..... area close to .... factory in the south of Jordan.

9- ..... dogs bark at ..... strange people.

10- ...... alphabet can have more than one sound.

الأداة " an " تسبق اسم مفرد يقبل أن يُجمع ، بشرط أن يكون الحرف الأول في هذا الاسم , a , e , i

o , u

* يجب مراعاة النطق.

an apple تفاحة , an area منطقة , an amateur هاوي , an egg بيضة ,

an effort جهد , an elephant فيل , an interest اهتمام-مصلحة ,

an ink-pot محبرة , an infant رضيع , an orange ,

an *hour* (تنطق : أوا), an oasis واحة ,

an offer عرض , an uncle عم-خال , an umbrella مظلة .

إذا " u " نطقت " يو " , فلا ينطبق على الكلمة الكلام السابق . خذ مثالاً :

1- I need a *used* car , not a new one. (مستعمل / يوزد)

2- We are fighting for a *united* country. (متحد / يونايتد)

3- A *uniform* can solve the problem. زي موحد / يوني فورم

4- Many workers have joined a *union*. إتحاد / يونيان

5- The park is a **utility** where people can relax. (مرفق - منشأة / يوتالاتي)

6- * I asked an **upholster** to repair the seats of my car. منجّد

7- * An **uprising** broke out in Gaza three years ago. انتفاضة / أبرايزنق)

)

8- * He has an **urge** to succeed. رغبة قوية / أيرج

When a singular noun is preceded by an adjective , the indefinite articles " a " and "
an " agree with the adjective.

في حالة وجود صفة قبل الاسم المفرد , فإن أدوات التعريف النكرة تنسجم مع الصفة

* I have got **a new car** , but Ali has got **an old one**.

* Qatar is **a Gulf country**.

* Ali is **an excellent student** at **an English school**.

* He is an *honest* person. (تنطق : أُنست).

In case of abbreviations and acronyms , we have to use the " a " and " an " carefully.

في حالة الاختصارات والأسماء المشتقة من الحروف الأولى المكونة لاسم مكون من أكثر من كلمة،علينا أن نستخدم أدوات التعريف النكرة بحذر. إن الأمر يتوقف على نطق الحرف الأول.

OPEC is an acronym for the Organization of Petroleum- Exporting Countries .

(an يأخذ حرف علة ← a vowel يعتبر " o " حرف)

* Iraq is an OPEC member.

* This man is an FBI agent. (إف " يتم نطقه "f"حرف (ef

FBI = The Federal Bureau of Investigations

مكتب التحقيقات الفيدرالي.

NATO = The North Atlantic Treaty Organization .

(تنطق n نَ)

* France is a NATO member.

* Qatar is a GCC member.   قطر عضو في مجلس التعاون الخليجي .

GCC = Gulf Co-operation Council.

* This man was a CIA agent .

هذا الرجل كان عميلاً لوكالة الاستخبارات المركزية.

* He is a BBC editor.

* He is a one-time hero. (النطق : وَن)

* I attended a one- hour meeting.

حضرت اجتماعاً دام ساعة واحدة.

* Correct the mistakes :

1- We need a sugar a lot. ....

2- She has a old car. ....

3- Ali is an QBC broadcaster. ....

4- This is a R.A.F officer. ....

5- They took him to an hospital in the Doha.

....

6- We have reached a agreement. ....

7- He has a hour's duty. ....

8- He has a excellent plan.   ....

9- She is a honest person. She wants history book.

....

10- They have an excellent ideas .   ...

11- Qatar is a Arab League member.   ....

12- Egypt is a African country.   ....

13- Britain is an European country .   ...

14- An Asian countries seek to set up a alliance.

....

15- What a ugly idea ?   ....

● **Put the right articles when necessary**

ضع أدوات التعريف عند الضرورة :

1- We have chosen ..... applicant , and ...... manager will meet him .... next day .

2- I talked to ... advocate of ...... project . He showed me ...... advantages we would

get .

3- .... opponents معارضوا of .... project talked about .... problems we would

face if .... project was started .... opponent said he would burn himself to

.... death if they went ahead قدماً مضوا with ....project .

4- We are for ...... peace السلام because .... war الحرب benefits nobody.....peace-

keeping force will start arriving tomorrow

5- .... infant died of cholera ...... last night . ... infant's mother had died five

days ago .

6- .... number of .... accidents is rising آخذ في الارتفاع ,which means that ......

people do not follow .... safety rules.

7- It is possible to put .... end to our traffic problems.

8- ...... young man helped ...... old man cross .... road.

9- ..... books provide ...... people with ...... useful things.

10- ....accidents could drop if ...... drivers reduced...... speed

ا لضما ئـر Pronouns

Pronouns stand for nouns .

الضمائر تحل محل الأسماء وتؤدي نفس الوظيفة .

الفاعل Subject		المفعول به Object
I أنا	$\rightarrow$	me
he هو	$\rightarrow$	him
she هي	$\rightarrow$	her
it إنها – إنه	$\rightarrow$	it
you أنت – أنتم – أنتن	$\rightarrow$	you
we نحن	$\rightarrow$	us
they هم – هن	$\rightarrow$	them

Examples :

1- **I** visit **you** , and **you** visit **me** .

الفاعل قبل الفعل ، والمفعول به بعد الفعل .

2- Ali helps **me** , and **I** help **him** .

He always offers to help **me** .   (he = Ali)

3- Mona helps **me** , and **I** help **her** .

She is always to help **me** .   (she = Mona)

4-Ali and Nasser have asked **us** for help.

إن علياً وناصراً طلبا منا المساعدة.

5- **We** should help **them** if **they** help **us** . (them = Ali and Nasser)

6- I like this road because **it** is wide . واسع   (it = road)

7- The teacher punished the students because **they** didn't

   follow **him** . (they = students الطلاب / him = teacher)

8- We should stop these films because **they** spoil young

   people.   (they = films)

   * **Choose the right pronouns** :

1- The coach told the players that (he – him) would show

         (they – them)   his new tactics.

2- Mona said that (he - her – she) had won a race.

3- Hamad is a friend of (my – me – mine) ;

   (him – he – his) always gives (I – me – my) useful advice

4- Ali and (he – his- her) sister , Noura think that

   (he – them – they) will get high marks.

5- Ali says that (his – him – he) cannot buy the car because

   (she – he – it)   is too expensive.

The possessives

تستخدم ضمائر الملكية " صفات الملكية " لتدل على أن شيئاً مملوكاً لشخص ما .

   Examples :

1- I want **my book** . أريد كتابي

2- **Your car** is black , but **mine** (my car) is white .

سيارتك سوداء ولكن سيارتي بيضاء .

3- **My** car is white , but **yours** (your car) is black .

4- Ali is **my friend** . **His house** is not too far from **mine**.

5- Ali is **my friend** . **My car** is the same colour as **his** .

إن علياً صديقي . إن سيارتي نفس لون سيارته .

6- Mona is <u>Ali's sister</u> . <u>Her hair</u> is as fair as <u>his</u> , but mine is

   different from hers .

إن منى أخت علي . إن شعرها أشقر مثل شعره ، ولكن شعري مختلف عن شعرها .

7- The boy's hair is fair. إن شعر الولد أشقر.

8- The boys' hair is black . إن شعر الأولاد أسود.

9- They are on a three months' holiday.

إنهم في إجازة مدتها ثلاثة أشهر.

10- The teachers' salaries are paid on time.

إن رواتب المدرسين تدفع في حينه.

11- A teacher's salary is too low to mention.

إن راتب المدرس منخفض جداً بحيث لا يمكن ذكره.

* Pronouns and Possessives الضمائر وصفات الملكية

Pronouns	**Relevant Possessives**
I / me	my car = mine .
You	your car = yours.
he / him	his car = his .
she / her	her car = hers.
it	its colour = its.
we / us	our house = ours.
they / them	their house = theirs.

ملاحظة :

١- بعد صفات الملكية my , your , his , her , its , our , their لا بد مـن وضع الشيء الـذي يخص المالك .

٢- بعد ضمائر الملكية ours , theirs , mine , yours , his , hers , its لا نضع الشيء الـذي يخص المالك لأنه يفهم ضمناً من السياق ولأننا استبدلناه بـ " s " الملكية .

٣- إذا أردنا أن نذكر المالك شخصياً والشيء الذي يخصه فلا بد من إتباع ما يلي :

1- I took Ali's book . أخذت كتاب علي.

2- Mona's teacher is ill today .

3- The teacher's room is closed . غرفة المدرس مغلقة.

4- The teachers' room is tidy . غرفة المدرسين مرتبة.

5- The children's room is untidy . غرفة الأطفال غير مرتبة.

6-This is Ali's father's car . هذه سيارة والد علي.

* Avoid confusion. ٤- لا بد من تفادي الخلط في هذه الحالات

1- Ali's car is new . سيارة علي جديدة.

    Ali's busy . ⟶ Ali is busy .

    Ali's got one . ⟶Ali has got one .

2- **Its** advantages are beyond doubt . مزاياها لا شك فيها.

It's nice to mention its importance. من الجميل أن نذكر أهميتها.

 It is nice to mention its importance .

3- I walk to **their** house . Mine isn't far from **theirs** .

إني أسير مشياً إلى منـزلهم . إن منـزلي ليس بعيداً عن منـزلهم .

4- **There's** something wrong . ⟶There is something wrong

5- There's been something wrong . ⟶ There has been

    something wrong .

6- I took **your** book . أخذت كتابك.

7- **You're** a friend of mine . You are a friend of mine.

إنك صديق لي .

٥- يجب عدم الخلط بين (هناك) there) و (صفة ملكية) their .

8- I like my school a lot . I go **there** every day .

9- There is a book on the table . هناك كتاب على الطاولة

10- Ali and Nasser have got new bags, but **mine** is unlike **theirs**.

11- Ali and Huda are my friends . I know **their** father well .

إن علياً وهدى أصدقائي . إني أعرف والديهما جيداً .

12- I sympathize with the Palestinians ; their country is usurped.

إني أتعاطف مع الفلسطينيين . إن وطنهم مغتصب .

** **The possessives**   صيغ الملكية :

There are two possessive forms .   هناك صيغتان للملكية

1- Sunday is the first day **of** the week .

2- Sunday is the **week's** first day.

3- My study is next to my **parents** ' bedroom.

Possessive adjectives صفات الملكية (**Possessive Pronouns**) :

my لي / his له / her لها / its (لغير العاقل) له / your لك /
our لنا / their لهم /

هذه الكلمات تدل على الملكية ويأتي بعدها الشيء المملوك كما سبق ذكره .

mine = my car / his = his car / hers / its / yours / ours /   theirs /

هذه أيضاً تدل على الملكية ولكن لا يجب وضع الشيء المملوك بعدها .

*من أجل التأكيد على ملكية الشخص لشيء ما , فإننا نستخدم own قبل صفة الملكية

* This is **my own.**   هذه سيارتي

It is different from **yours** . (yours = your car) سيارتك الخاصة بي .

Mine is white , but yours is red.   (mine = my car   )

* I saw **Ali's own** father last night .

My father (mine) is taller than his. (his = his father)

* Mona gave **her** brother a watch. أخيها

Your brother is taller than **hers.**   (hers = her brother)

* You can change **your own** house. بيتك ـ بيتكم

Yours is too old.   (yours = your house)

* We have sold our own old car . سيارتنا القديمة

   Ours is 20 years old.   (our = our car)

* I know Ali and Nasser's house.

   Theirs is close to Hamad's.   (theirs = their house)

* When to use the apostrophe 's or only the apostrophe :

We usually use the apostrophe " 's" with possessive nouns like :

   Ali's father , the manager's office ,

   the ministry's lawyer محامي الوزارة ,

   the coach's plan خطة المدرّب , the parents' council مجلس الآباء .

1- This is **Ali's car**.

   The man's idea is easy.

   We will pay you for **a day's work**.

   The team's coach is firm .   مدرب الفريق حازم .

   We have to study **Qatar's history**.

   The university's policy is to accept excellent students.

      سياسة الجامعة هي أن تقبل الطلاب الممتازين .

   The children's car needs repairing.

      سيارة الأطفال تحتاج إلى تصليح.

   Ali's English is better than Mona's.

2- The Johns' house is far from here. . منـزل عائلة جون بعيد من هنا

   The girls' room is big.   غرفة البنات كبيرة .

   The girl's room is small.   غرفة البنت صغيرة .

   We follow the coach's plan.   إننا نتبع خطة المدرّب.

   Everybody must attend the coaches' meeting.

      كل شخص يجب أن يحضر اجتماع المدربين.

* We notice that nouns related to people accept the 's form.

علينا أن نراعي بأن الأسماء التي لها صلة بالناس هي التي تقبل صيغة الملكية السابقة.

*Generally , nouns not related to people accept the *of* form.

the number of cars , the advantages of tourism   مزايا السياحة ,
the effect of inflation on low- income people

تأثير التضخم على أصحاب الدخل المنخفض.

The costs of the project   تكاليف المشروع ,
the freedom of opinion   حرية الرأي

* **Double possessives** الملكية المزدوجة :
1- This is **a book of Ali's.**
2- I liked **a painting of Picasso's** . لوحة لبيكاسو
3- Nasser is **a friend of mine.**
4- Nasser is not **a friend of yours.**
5- These are **friends of ours** .

* **Use the right possessive form :**

1- I have two friends , Ali and Nasser . They are true friends of ....
.

2- This is not .... book . I think that it is ....

3- You should wash .... own hands .

4- Noura cleans .... own teeth daily.

5- Ali is a friend ...... yours. You know .... house .

6- Mona is a sister .... Hamad ..... .

7- The teacher ..... house is next to ....

8- Ali and Nasser are brothers . I like .... way ...... doing things.

9- The price ...... the car is too high.

10- The smell .... this flower is fantastic.

* Correct the mistakes :

1- The people needs must be considered. ....

2- The students's choices are considered. ....

3- I have seen the childs father. ....

4- I have talked to all of the children parents. ....

5- We need to wash the floor room. ....

6- Nasser is a true friend of me . ...

7- Is Ali a brother of you ? ....

8- She isn't a sister of Ali. ....

9- There school is not far from hers. ....

10- Here mother is coming. ....

11- My school is next to there's. ....

12- He's English is perfect . ...

13- My English is better than her. ....

14- Our farm is in the North the country. ....

15- The horse' mane is terrific. ....

* Write what the underlined words mean :

1- My picture appeals to everybody , but <u>Huda's</u> doesn't . ...

2- Have you seen my mother's picture ?

   <u>Mine</u> is completely different from <u>hers</u> . ... /

   ....

3- Your house is not as large as <u>ours</u> . ...

4- We have decided to renew our house , not <u>theirs</u> . ...

5- Ali's sons , as well as <u>mine</u> , want to join this university . ...

* **Choose the right word** : اختر الكلمة المناسبة

1- Nasser is a member (at – for – of) this club.

2- Your car is similar to (my – mine – me).

3- Nasser has sold (he – him – his) camera.

4- Noura has found (her – she – hers) money.

5- I am sorry for (me - my – mine) mistakes.

6- You do not care for (you – yours – your) children.

7- We help friends of (us – ours – our).

8- They intend to redecorate (there –their – theirs) house.

9- The cat has eaten (it's – its – it) food.

10- The people (of – on – about) the area need real change.

Reflexive Pronouns & Verbs
الأفعال والضمائر المنعكسة

* **We use reflexive pronouns when both the subject and object are the same.**

نستخدم الضمائر المنعكسة عندما يكون الفاعل والمفعول متشابهين
أي لا بد من انسجام بين الفاعل والمفعول. وهي تأتي مع أفعال منعكسة .

Examples :

1- I *enjoy* myself at the sea-side. أمتع نفسي على شاطئ البحر.

2- Ali *regards* himself the best boy.

إن علياً يعتبر نفسه أحسن ولد.

3- Mona will *cut* herself.   إن منى سوف تجرح نفسها.

4- The cat has hurt itself.   القطة قد آذت نفسها.

5- Don't *deceive* yourselves.   لا تخدعوا أنفسكم .

6- We *respect* ourselves .   إننا نحترم أنفسنا .

7- They *help* themselves.   إنهم يساعدون أنفسهم .

8- Don't *endanger* yourself .   لا تعرّض نفسك للخطر.

* **We use reflexive pronouns only with reflexive verbs like :**

1- I always *control* myself when I have problems.

أنا دائماً أتحكم في نفسي عندما أواجه مشاكل.

2-She *keeps* herself familiar with new things.

إنها تجعل نفسها على دراية بأشياء جديدة.

3-You have to *adapt* yourself to the new situation.

عليك أن تكيف نفسك مع الوضع الجديد.

4-We should *change* ourselves.

يجب أن نغير أنفسنا .

5-They *prepare* themselves for the final exams.

إنهم يعدون أنفسهم للامتحانات النهائية.

* **We use a reflexive pronoun to emphasize the subject .**

نستخدم الضمير المنعكس للتأكيد على الفاعل .

1- I saw it myself.   2- Ali himself called the police.

3- Mona did it herself.   4- You yourself agreed to come.

* **by myself = on my own = alone** بمفردي :

1- I can study and revise on my own.

إنني أستطيع أن أدرس وأراجع بمفردي.

2- You have to come by yourself.   عليك أن تأتي بنفسك.

3- I advise her to do things by herself.

4- Everybody has to come on their own.

5- We need to plant the trees by ourselves.

علينا أن نزرع الأشجار بأنفسنا.

* **Correct the mistakes :**

1- She wants to do things by himself.   ....

2- I looked at himself in the mirror.   ....

3- I like to do my homework in my own.   ....

4- We would rather enjoy ourself on the beach. ....

5- Mona himself showed me the way.   ....

6- Ali has washed the car by hiself.   ....

7- I wrote the letter meself.   ....

* **Choose the right possessives :**

1- I talked to Ali a lot . He asked me to study (her - him - his) plan .

2- Ali damaged (mine - my - me) book because I damaged (him - his - he) .

3- I phoned (my - me - mine) friends to make sure if
    (them - there - their) father had arrived .

4- We asked the headmaster المدير to replace (his - our - mine) English teacher with (
    your - you - yours).

5- (hers - my - mine) father promised to lend me (he - him - his) car .

* **Write what the underlined word means :**

1- My car is not like Ali's . ...

2- My idea is better than yours . ...…..............

3- Her house is far from mine ....

4- We like our teachers , but my brothers don't like theirs ....

5- My plan is different from Mona's ....

3- She has allowed her sons to go out with your ....

4- Ali agreed to employ me son . ……...........................

5- The manager has decided to increase us salaries ....

6- The manager promised the employees to improve there working conditions .

....

7- Your salary is higher than Ali is....................................

8- My salary is not as high as you .   ...

9- This house is as big as their .   ...

10- Ali's car is not as small as my .   ...

11- Mine camera is less expensive than yours.   ....

12- My teachers room is next to your classroom.   ....

13- Mona picture is wonderful.   ....

14- This car is Ali is.   ....

15- These books are my , not yours.   ....

16- We house is not far from her .   ...

17- My room is next to parents.   ....

18- A bee makes honey for we , but it's sting is bad.

....

19- Yousif visits I , and I visit he. ....

20- Book ' s are useful , so I read a lot of it .

....

21- Him likes to visit she family.   ....

22- He's house is near my.   ....

23- Alis house is big than yours.   ....

24- English is easier than Arabic. ....

25- Ali's marks are high than Mona. ....

26- Mona's car is expensive than Ali. ....

27- This is the good cat in the world. ....

28- You can run more fast than Ali does. ....

29- She is singing gooder than you do. ....

30- She has got better marks than me do. ....

٢٣٩

** " *every* كل and " *each* كل " are determiners functioning as
   adjectives صفات :

1- Every student has got a book.
     No student has got a book.

2- Each student is free to join the team.
     No student (no one) is …..

3- <u>Every one of</u> you can say what **they** like.
     <u>Everyone</u> **has** done **their** homework .
     Everybody *is* washing **their** dishes.
     Nobody (no one) **has** shown **their** approval.

     * everybody يأتي معها ضمير يدل على الجمع وفعل يدل على المفرد.

4- Everyone wants to buy it.
     Every one **of** you wants to pass.
     Each one **of** the boys has got a ticket.

5- I understood every **single** word. (single = intensifier / every   للتضخيم)
)

6- Ali and Nasser always help **each other** .
     Ali and Nasser always visit one another.
     The students always greet **one another**.

7- You can come every other day. (**Monday ,Wednesday**)

8- We usually meet **every day**. (كل يوم / adverb ظرف)

9- We meet to discuss our **everyday problems.** (adj.صفة)
                  مشاكل يومية L

Conclusion :
every car , everyone , every one of you ⟶ (√)
everyone of you (×) .
each person (√) , each one (√) / eachone (×)

Quantifiers محددات الكم

* some – any   / * many – much – most
* a few - a little / * a lot of – lots of
* numbers   / * all   / * several - both

Some بعض / any

* I have talked to some people at the party.
* I have some food in the morning.
* I don't have any food in the morning.

(المقصود : لا أتناول أي طعام)

* I don't have some kinds of food .   (إني لا أتناول بعض أنواع الطعام.)
* She has not done anything.
* Have you got anything?
* Does your father need any money?
* Any person can do this job.
* I want **some** money   (some تسبق اسم لتحديد الكم determiner)
* She wants some books.
* I don't eat **any** butter.
* She doesn't buy any books .   إنها لا تشتري أي كتب.
* I didn't find anything .   إني لم أجد أي شيء.
* He found something .   إنه وجد شيئاً ما.
* They went somewhere .   إنهم ذهبوا إلى مكان ما.
* We went nowhere .   إننا لم نذهب إلى أي مكان.
* We didn't go anywhere .

غالبا نستخدم some (بمعنى بعض) في حالة الإثبات ،
ونستخدم any بمعنى (أي – أية) في حالة النفي .

٢٤١

* I don't like **some** people .   إنني لا أحب بعض الناس.

* I don't like **any** people.

إني لا أحب أياً من الناس .   (أي أنني لا أحب أحداً من الناس)

* He can't remember **some** words.

إنه لا يستطيع أن يتذكر بعض الكلمات.

* He can't remember any words.

إنه لا يستطيع أن يتذكر أي كلمة(ولا كلمة).

* <u>Put " some " or " any " in the right place</u> :

1- We need ……….. information about ………. countries in
   the Middle East .

2- ……………….. students have passed with high marks.

3- I didn't get ………… money .

4- She has bought …………. vegetables .

5- They cannot help …………… people .

6- ……….. applicants have a perfect knowledge of English,
   others know ………… of it.

7- He hasn't got ………. idea of what we intend to do.

● في بعض الأحيان ، يجوز استخدام " any " في حالة الإثبات .

* Anybody can solve this problem .

أي شخص يستطيع أن يحل هذه المشكلة .

* You can do anything to relieve them .

بإمكانك أن تقوم بأي شيء للتخفيف من معاناتهم

* He is too hungry ; he is ready to eat any food.

1-   I learn <u>some words</u> every day.

   (...some of the words / some of these words)

2-   <u>Some students</u> come late. (...some of the students)

3-   She drinks <u>some milk</u> in the morning.

                     (some of this milk)

4-   You can add <u>some sugar</u>.

إذا جاء بعد some اسم يجوز وضع of بعدها بشرط أن تسبق الاسم الذي يليها أحد أدوات التعريف مثل the / this / these / my كما هو واضح من الأمثلة السابقة والتالية . أما إذا جاء بعدها ضمير فلا بد من استخدام of .

*   I want to read some of these books. (√)

*   I have eaten some of it. (√)

*   I want to take some of you. (√)

*   We will take some food.   (√)

*   She has taken **some of the food.** (√)

*   She will take some it .   (X)

*   She will take **some of it.** (√) (it ضمير)

*   I watch films. **Some of them** are useful. (them ضمير)

●   ملاحظة : any تسبق اسماً في حالتي المفرد والجمع .

●   She has not found <u>any</u> food.

●   I did not see <u>any</u> student.

●   Ali has not got <u>any</u> books yet.

*   I haven't eaten any food for days.

إنني لم أتناول أية طعام منذ أيام .

●   I haven't eaten some food for days.

إنني لم أكل بعض الأطعمة منذ أيام.

*   I haven't seen any of your friends yet.

*   You can take any of these books.

معظم most   /   كثير much   /   كثير many

1- Many people have left the village for the town.
2- She is facing many problems.
3- I helped many of you.
4- He has helped many of those people.

تأتي **many** مع اسم يقبل العد أو ضمير مثل السيارة / الكتاب / المشكلة .

many cars / many books / many problems/ many of you / many of these

    1-   You drink too much coffee. That is bad.
    2-   Don't eat too much meat.
    3-   Too much sugar is bad for health.
    4-   We need as much water as possible.
    5-   You can take much of it.

نستخدم **much** مع اسم لا يقبل العد مثل القهوة / الماء/ المال / اللحم / أو مع ضمير فنقول :
much money / much food / much meat / much heat
much of that / much of it / much of this food.

1- She has taken most (of the) books.
2- Most people prefer to stay at home.

معظم الناس يفضلون أن يبقوا في البيت.
3- Most of these cars are old.   معظم هذه السيارات قديمة.
4- Most of this food comes from outside the country.
5- Most food is good for people.
6- Most of you are good at English.   معظمكم جيد في الإنجليزية.
7- We have plenty of oil. Most of it has come from the Middle East.

نستخدم most وتعني / معظم / مع اسم يقبل العد أو اسم لا يقبل العد أو مع ضمـير
فنقول :

most cars / most of the cars / most money / most of it

الكثير من plenty of / lots of / a lot of

1- A lot of people came to the concert.

الكثير من الناس جاءوا إلى الحفلة الغنائية.

2- Lots of people come to see the play.

3- You eat a lot of food.

4- They have lots of food.

5- We need a lot of that (it – these).

نستخدم / lots of - a lot of بمعنى / الكثير / مع اسم يقبل أو لا يقبل العد أو مع ضمير فنقول :
a lot of cars / a lot of food / a lot of it / lots of cars / lots of that /

1- I have plenty of money .   عندي الكثير من المال.

2- Plenty of people have voted for the new project.

الكثير من الناس قد صوتوا لصالح المشروع الجديد.

3- Plenty of water is urgently needed.

4- We have water in plenty.   لدينا مياه بكثرة.

5- People do not have problems in years of plenty.

لا يواجه الناس مشاكل في سنوات الوفرة.

a few / a little قليل

1- I meet a few people.

2- Very few boys came to the concert.

3- Too few people want to learn from mistakes.

4- He has invited a few friends. That is not bad.

5- He has invited too few people. Nobody will enjoy the party.

6- I drink a little milk.

7- You eat too little meat.

8- A few of the students agree with you.

9- The few agree with you. الأقلية تتفق معك.

10- You can eat a little of this honey.

11- A little of this material can suffice .

إن القليل من هذه المادة قد يكفي.

نستخدم a few مع اسم أو ضمير يقبل العد فنقول:
a few cars / (a) few people / a few of you قلة منكم / a few of them.

* نستخدم few للدلالة على قلة قليلة يستهان بها . أما a few لقلة لا يستهان بها
* نستخدم a little مع اسم أو ضمير لا يقبل العد فنقول a little milk / a little of it /
a few people (قلة مقبولة) قليل من الناس
few people , not enough people . (قلة غير مقبولة) قلة من الناس

٢٤٦

الخلاصة   Summary *

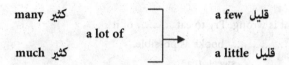

a few قليل   many كثير
a lot of
a little قليل   much كثير

1- I have got **many letters** .

2- She drinks too **much tea** .

3- **A few people** came to the party .

4- We have got **a few problems** .

5- Ali can speak **a little English** .

6- We just need **a little sugar.**   إننا فقط نحتاج إلى قليل من السكر.

* many / a few يأتي مع كل منها اسم جمع مفرده يقبل العدد مثل car- cars /

* much /a little يأتي معهما اسم مفرد لا يقبل العدد مثل/tea- information /

* لاحظ وجود of / بعد أي من محددات الكم determiners. في هذه الحالة فإن الاسم الذي يأتي بعدها يمكن أن نضع قبله أداة تعريف أو اسم إشارة كما هو موضح أدناه . أما إذا جاء بعدها ضمير فلا داعي لوضع أي من أدوات التعريف أو أسماء الإشارة :

** Many of students (✕) , many of **the students** (√) , many of you (√) , many of those people (√) , many them (✕) , much of the food (√) , a little of the food (√) , a little of it (√) , much of it (√) , a few of my friends (√) , a few of those trees (√) .

1-   **Many of the students** have passed with high marks.

2-   I need **a little of this cheese**.

3-   **Much of this honey** will be kept in a cool place.

4-   **Many of you** know this fact.

5-   **A few of my students** have got bad marks.

6-   We consume too much gum. **A lot of it** comes from Africa.

إننا نستهلك الكثير جداً من الصمغ . إن معظمه يأتي من أفريقيا.

*** Put " many, much, a few, a little, a lot of " or any
suitable quantifiers:**

1-You eat too ...... food. That is wrong. Try to eat .... of it .

2- I advise you to read as .... books as possible.

3- You shouldn't drink too .... sweet tea.

4- We don't need .... car-parks. We only need ...... of them.

5- I drink .... milk every day. I like it so ....

6- She knows ...... English words , so she can speak English .

7- They know too .... languages, so they can't mix with

.... people from other countries.   8- Too

...... people support your idea, so I advise you to give it

up.

9- Too .... students are against my plan , so the minister will drop it.

10- We need ....sugar . We don't have any of it.

11- You have to do ...... things if you want to get better results.

12- I have read ....of the books you sent me last month.

13- She has made .... of these cakes.

14- She needs .... of this food.

15- We will allow .... of you to go out at the weekend.

16 .... of these people are ready to help me.

17- I don't need .... of this information.

18- ....of your friends are unhappy about it.

19- .... problems still exist.

20- We have solved .... of our problems. We will

solve the remaining ones soon. سوف نحل المشاكل المتبقية قريباً.

* He has (much /a great deal of) experience.

يفضل استخدام العبارة الثانية بدلا من much في حالة الإثبات.

* Many visit this area. (اسم / الكثيرون / ويقصد بها الناس أوالسائحين)

* You eat much. (اسم الكثير / ويقصد بها الطعام وهي اسم مفرد)

كلا both / عدة several / كل (جميع) all

1- All (of these) apples are ripe.

جميع / (هذه) التفاحات ناضجة .

2- **All people** are equal .   كل الناس متساوون . (بشكل عام) All

3-   **the boys** in this class have passed .   (للتحديد)

All of you can come .

4- Not all food is good for us.

5- Several people were killed in the blast.

قتل العديد من الناس في الانفجار .

Several of these apples are too soft.

6- Both Ali and Nasser are coming.

7- I would like to see both (of) Ali and Nasser.

8- I would like to see both.

9- I would like to buy both (of)these cars.

10- Both of you are suitable .   كلاكما مناسب .

11- Both of them are willing to join you.

كلاهما راغب في اللحاق بك.

11- Mona has got two brothers and a sister.

Both of her brothers are university students.

Both (of) Mona's brothers are university students.

Ali and Hamad are Mona's brothers. Both of them
go to university.

Both of you. (√) كلاكما / Both you. (X)

Both boys (√)   / Both of the boys. (√)

All the apple . (X) / All (of / the) apples. (√)

a number of عدد من = some / **the number of cars**

1- The number of books is not enough.

2- The number of accidents is rising .   إن عدد الحوادث يتزايد .

3- There is a big number of mistakes.

4- There are a number of mistakes in your letter.

هناك بعض الأخطاء في رسالتك.

5- A number of people have accepted the idea.

إن بعض الناس قد قبلوا الفكرة .

6- The number of births has risen over the last 20 years إن عدد المواليد قد ارتفع خلال السنوات العشرين الأخيرة .

7- Tourists are coming to this area in great numbers.

السائحون يفدون إلى هذه المنطقة بأعداد كبيرة.

*إذا كانت / a number of / بمعنى : بعض / فإنها تكون في حالة الجمع و بناءً على ذلك يجب أن نراعي مطابقة الفعل للجمع .

* أما إذا كانت / the number of / بمعنى / عدد / فإنها تكون في حالة المفرد وبناءً عليه يجب أن يكون الفعل مطابقاً للمفرد .

tens / hundred / thousand / million

ten out of one hundred /

1- <u>Tens</u> of people have become homeless.

عشرات من الناس أصبحوا مشردين.

2- <u>Hundreds</u> of people are coming to the city.

مئات من الناس يأتون إلى المدينة.

A (one) hundred of people have already arrived.

Three hundred of them are expected to arrive on Monday.

I have done that hundreds of times.

3- <u>Thousands</u> of homes were destroyed .

آلاف ا لبيوت دمرت.

4- <u>Millions</u> of people are leaving the rural areas.

ملايين الناس يغادرون المناطق الريفية .

Three million of them are farmers.

There are a million of people living in this city.

* الكلمات التي تحتها خط عبارة عن أسماء ولهذا فإنها تقبل / s / الجمع .

1- Five <u>hundred</u> people live in this area.

2- Twenty <u>million</u> people live in this country.

3- I need three <u>thousand</u> Riyals.

* أما إذا تم استخدامها كصفة كما في الأمثلة الثلاثة الأخيرة فإنها لا تجمع .

1- Three millions of people. (X)

2- Three million people . (√)

3- Hundreds of cars. (√)

4- Hundreds cars . (X)

5- One hundred car. (X)

6- One hundred cars. (√)

7- Ten out of every hundred people. (√)

8- Five out of every million people is illiterate. (X)

9- Five out of every million people are illiterate. (√)

إن خمسة من كل مليون شخص أميون .

● I have received **a tenth** of the amount. (عشر / .n)

* This is the **tenth** attempt. (العاشر / .adj)

*هذه هي المحاولة العاشرة. This is the

fourth largest city in the world.

*هذه رابع أكبر مدينة في العالم. He came

fifth in the race. جاء في المركز الخامس في السباق.

* He can pay you **a hundredth** of the money.

*إنه يستطيع أن يدفع جزءاً واحداً من المئة من النقود. Only a

millionth of the people rejected the plan.

* Three **thousandths** (3/1000) of people are poor.

* **Scores** of people are coming here. (اسم .n)

There are (is) **a score** of people . (20 people)

This event happens every three **score** years. (60 years)

* There is a **dozen** eggs. (adj.)

There are a **dozen** eggs. هناك در زن من البيض.

* There are three **dozen** eggs.

* How many **dozen** do you want ?

* * I have seen the play **dozens** of times. (اسم .n)

Dozens come here to enjoy the beauty of nature.

How many **dozens** of eggs do you want ?

We sell eggs in **dozens**.

ملاحظة :   dozen / score   تجمع إذا كانت ضميراً (اسماً) .أما إذا كانت في محل صفة فلا تجمع كباقي الصفات.

too أيضاً / either

1- Ali likes music , and I (like it) **too** .

2- They came on time , and you (did) **too** .

3- She can sing. Ali can (sing) **too** .

إنها تستطيع أن تغني وعلي يستطيع أن يغني أيضاً .

4- I can read and write too.

5- Mona has retired . Ali has retired too.

6- I have got a visa. Have you got one too ?

7- Mona doesn't like American films , and I don't like them

either .   8-إن منى لا تحب الأفلام الأمريكية وأنا لا أحبها أيضاً.   Ali didn't get

anything , and I didn't get anything either .

9- I can't jump . I can't dive either.

نستخدم too بمعنى (أيضاً) في حالة الإثبات . ونستخدم either بمعنى (أيضاً) في حالة النفي.

Demonstrative Pronouns   ضمائر الإشارة

* this -هذا /   this man / this car/ this idea: اسم إشارة يسبق اسم مفرد/ *

   this food / this information / this cheese / this coffee .

this → يشير إلى اسم قريب وقد يقوم مقام الاسم

* This is my house.

*   This will help you a lot.

* You can benefit from this.   يـمكنك أن تستفيد من هذا .

* that ذاك - ذلك / اسم إشارة يشير إلى اسم بعيد ويجب أن يكون الاسم مفرداً
  that man – that house – that road – that book – that building .
* You can find it next to that building.
* Doha is the main town in Qatar. Everybody knows *that*. →

أخذت مكان اسم.

* these (منا قريب جمع اسم تسبق)هؤلاء / these boys / these cars
  these men / these people / these children /
  these ideas الأفكار هذه / these books الكتب هذه .
* We need to help these homeless people.
* These children have damaged the flowers.
* I help *those* who help themselves. (اسم)
* those (عنا بعيد جمع اسم يسبق) أولئك / those boys / those girls/
  those books.

  Those trees protect my farm.

  We have to solve these problems.

جميع أسماء الإشارة تقوم مقام الاسم .

That is boring. ممل شئ ذلك / I don't accept that.   إني لا أقبل ذلك.
These are interesting stories.   هذه قصص مشوقه.
Those will cause a lot of trouble.

تلك الأشياء (أولئك الناس) سوف تسبب كثيراً من المتاعب.
You can use these and those.   يمكنك أن تستخدم هؤلاء وتلك .

How to make a question

كيف تصنع سؤالاً ؟

It is important to know question words like :

لا بد من معرفة أدوات الاستفهام (السؤال) وهي :

١- what ماذا - ما ،ونستخدمها للسؤال عن شيء .

٢- when متى ، ونستخدمها للسؤال عن الزمن الذي حدث فيه الفعل.

٣- where أين ، ونستخدمها للسؤال عن المكان الذي حدث فيه الفعل .

٤- why لماذا ، ونستخدمها للسؤال عن سبب قيامنا بالفعل أو الهدف من وراء قيامنا بالفعل .

٥- who من ، ونستخدمها للسؤال عن شخص أو أشخاص .

٧- how كيف ، ونستخدمها للسؤال عن الطريقة التي تم بها الفعل.

٨- how old كم عمر ، للسؤال عن العمر .

٩- how often كم مرة ، للسؤال عن عدد مرات وقوع الفعل .

١٠- how long كم طول المدة ، للسؤال عن طول المدة التي استرقها حدوث الفعل .

١١- how many كم عدد ، للسؤال عن العدد .

١٢- how much كم كمية ، ما مقدار ، للسؤال عن الكمية أو المقدار .

١٣- how far كم المسافة ، للسؤال عن المسافة والبعد .

١٤- which [بـمعنى – أي _ للاختيار بين أمرين] –

Which book do you need ?

١٥- whose [بـمعنى _ لمن _ للسؤال عن صاحب الشيء] –

Whose book is this ?

هناك نوعان من الأسئلة .. نوع الإجابة عليه بـ " Yes " أو " No " .. ونوع تتطلب الإجابة معلومات عن الزمن أو المكان أو الهدف .. وكلاهما يخضع إلى نفس طريقة التكوين .

(دعنا نطلق عليها مقويات مقيمة) نضع المقوي قبل الاسم أو الضمير فنحصل على سؤال الإجابة عليه
بـ Yes أو No . وإذا أردنا أن نصنع المزيد من الأسئلة فإننا نضع أدوات سؤال مثل what , where ,
when , who.

1- Ali **can** go to the party .

    Can Ali go to the party ?   Yes , he can .

    Where can Ali go ?   → He can go to the party .

    What can Ali do ?   → He can go to the party .

2- Mona **will** phone tomorrow .

    Will Mona phone tomorrow ?   Yes , she will .

    When will Mona phone?   → She will phone tomorrow.

    What will Mona do   ?   → She will phone tomorrow.

3-   Ali **is** going home .

    Is Ali going home ?   Yes , he is . (No , he isn't) .

    Where is Ali going ?   →   He is going home .

4- They **were** going with Ali .

    Were they going with Ali ?   Yes , they were .

    Who were they going with? →   They were going with Ali.

 5- I <u>was</u> driving slowly .

    Were you driving slowly ?   Yes , I was .

    How were you driving ?   →   I was driving slowly

6- I <u>am</u> going on my own . بمفردي

    Are you going on your own ?   Yes , I am .

    How are you going ?   →   I am going on my own .

7- I <u>have</u> seen Ali at the park .

    Have you seen Ali at the park ?   Yes , I have .

    Who have you seen at the park ?   من رأيت في المنتزه؟

    Where have you seen Ali ? → I have seen him at the park.

    What have you done ?   ماذا فعلت ؟ → I have seen Ali .

    You are ←→   I am   ملاحظة :

    You were ←→   I was

** لكي نكون سؤالاً نضع المقوي مثل can/ will / is / are was/ were / have /
قبل الاسم فنحصل على سؤال الإجابة عليه بـ Yes أو No وإذا أردنا أن
نتوسع في طرح أسئلة أخرى , فإننا نضع أدوات سؤال قبل المقوي.

٢ - In the absence of auxiliaries في حالة عدم وجود المقويات السابقة:

أ - إذا كان الفعل شكل أول بدون " s " الغائب نستعين بـ do قبل الاسم .

¹

1-   I   **come** by car .

↓

Do you come by car ?   ؟   هل تأتي بواسطة السيارة

Yes , I do .   (No , I don't .)

How do you come ?   ⟶   I come by car .

¹

2-   They **arrive** at six .

Do they arrive at six ?   Yes , they do .

When do they arrive ?   متى يصلون ؟

What time do they arrive ?   ⟶   They arrive at six .

* عند طرح السؤال .. علينا أن نأخذ الإجابة بعين الاعتبار لأن ذلك يسهّل علينا عملية تكوين السؤال كما
هو واضح من الأمثلة السابقة .

ب- إذا كان الفعل شكل أول فيه " s " الغائب فإننا نستعين بـ does قبل الاسم بشرط حـذف " s "
الغائب .

¹

1-   Mona **speaks** five languages .

Does Mona **speak** five languages ?   ؟   هل منى تتحدث خمس لغات

Yes , she does . (No , she doesn't .)

How many languages does Mona speak?   ؟   كم لغة تتحدث منى

She speaks five languages .

لاحظ أنه عند الإجابة نحذف does ونعيد " s " الغائب .

2- He **goes** to the club <u>twice a week</u> . مرتين في الأسبوع

$$\downarrow$$

Does Ali **go** to the club .... ? ⟶ Yes , he does.

How often does Ali go <u>to the club</u> ?

He goes there هناك إلى|twice a week .

₁

3- I **have** a small car.

Do you have a small car ? ⟶ Yes , I do .

What **do** you have ? ⟶ I have a small car.

What kind of car do you have ? ما نوع السيارة التي تـمتلكها ؟

Have ⟶ اسم معها لأن السابقة المقويات من تعـتبر لا وهنا " يـملك " بـمعنى

4- She **has** a big car. تـمتلك

$$\downarrow \qquad \downarrow$$

Does Mona have a big car ? ⟶

Yes , she does. (No, she doesn't.)

What kind of car does Mona have ? She has a small car.

جـ- إذا كان الفعل شكل ثانٍ ، فإننا نستعين بـ did مع تبديل الفعل من شكل ثانٍ إلى شكل أول .

₂

1- I **walked** three kilometres .

$$\downarrow$$

Did you **walk** .... ? ⟶ Yes , I did . (No, I didn't)

₁

How far did you walk ? ⟶ I walked three kilometres .

2- She **paid** 20 Dinars for the book .

$$\downarrow$$

₁

Did she pay .... ? Yes , she did . (No , she didn't .)

How much did she pay for the book ? كم دفعت ثمناً للكتاب؟

She paid 20 riyals .

2

3-   They left at noon.

Did they leave at noon ?

When did they leave?

* In the above questions we expect the answers to focus on the object :

في الأسئلة السابقة نتوقع أن تتركّز الإجابات على اسم يكون مفعولاً به . أما إذا كنا نرغب في طرح سؤال الهدف منه معرفة الفاعل فتكون أسئلتنا على النحو التالي :

* In case we ask about the doer of an action , our questions are
similar to these :

1-   Who is coming ?   coming   / هنا نستفسر عن فاعل الفعل

2-   What is happening ?   ما الذي يحدث ؟

What are happening ? (×)

يجب التعامل على أساس توافق الفعل مع المفرد .

3-   Who comes on time ?

Ali does.

Ali and Mona do.

4-   Who has got the best marks ?

من الذي (الذين) حصل على أحسن الدرجات؟

Ali has.

Ali and Mona have .

5-   What has happened ?

Ali has damaged Mona's toy.   إن علياً أتلف لعبة منى ؟

Ali and Mona have passed the English test.

إن علياً
ومنى قد نجحا في اختبار الإنجليزية.

** الخلاصة : السؤال يكون صحيحاً إذا بدأ بمقوٍ مقيم مثل /have / was / is / can / will / أو مقوٍ مستورد مثل /do, does , did / أو نضع أداة سؤال قبل المقوي.

* Is Mona coming ?   / * Where is Mona going ?
* What has she got ?
* Does Mona help you ?   / * Who does Mona help ?
* What did she get?   / * How far did you run ?

The above are direct questions الأسئلة المباشرة هو شكل هذا .
But in case of indirect questions that are planted in other sentences ,
we need not follow the normal way of forming the direct questions.

ولكن في حالة الأسئلة غير المباشرة التي تزرع داخل جملٍ أخرى , فإننا لا نتبع الطريقة المعتادة في تكوين الأسئلة المباشرة.

Examples :

1- Is *Ali* coming ? (Direct question سؤال مباشر)
    I want to know if *Ali* **is** coming . (Indirect question)

2- Where **was** *Ali* at five o'clock ?
                                    I need to know where *Ali* **was** at five o'clock .

* was / is مقويات موجودة وكنا نعتمد عليها في تكوين السؤال بوضعها قبل الاسم .
أما في حالة الأسئلة غير المباشرة نقوم بوضعها بعد الاسم فتكون النتيجة جملة خبرية وليس سؤالاً.

3- What **does** Ali like to do ?
    I would like to know what Ali likes to do .

4- Where **do** you prefer to go ?
    We want to know where you prefer to go.

5-   How **did** Mona get her copy ?
    I want to know how Mona got her copy.

٢٥٩

من أجل تكوين do / does / did مقويات مستوردة لم تكن أصلاً موجودة في الجملة الخبرية ونستعين بها أسئلة مباشرة في حالة غياب المقويات الأصيلة . ونقوم بحذفها في حالة الأسئلة غير المباشرة .

6- Who finished ? (هنا سؤال عن فاعل الفعل وهذا النوع من الأسئلة يكون هكذا)

    I want to know who finished.

7- What was happening ?

    You can tell us what was happening .

8- What should be done ?

    We need to know what should be done.

* **Write questions based on these answers :**

1- I am ten years old .

    ....

2- I am checking my car .

    ....

3- I was waiting for Mona .

    ....

4- He is angry because I always annoy him .

    ....

5- They were walking to the beach .

    ....

6 - I meet him at school .

    ....

7 - She leaves at six .

    ....

8- Ali is.

    ....

9- I have found it in the box .

    ....

10- We should drive carefully .

    ....

11- I am studying hard to succeed .

....

12- She won twice .

....

13- He wants a small car.

What kind of car ....?

14- Yes , I am .

....

15-   No , he hasn't.

....

16 - Ali has .

....

17- Mona did .

....

18- Ali and Nasser are .

....

19- It is Mona's.

....

20- It takes three hours.

....

21- I think it will take four years.

....

22- No , they aren't.

....

23- She always comes by come.

....

24- No , she didn't.

....

25- You could go on the Underground

....

* Supply the missing verb ضع الفعل المفقود :

1- Do you ………….. Hani ?

2- Does Ali ………… English ?

3- ……… Ali phone last night ?

4- ………… you visit Ali ?

5- …………… Ali visit you ?

6- Where ………you go in the afternoon ?

7- When …………… Mona come ?

8- How did you ………….. here yesterday ?

9- What ………. Ali ……………yesterday

10- Why …………… Ali leave tomorrow ?

11- How …………… they do it ?

12- Where was Ali ……………….. ?

13- Why …………. you running ?

14- How long …………… you been studying ?

15- Can you …………. me where Ali lives ?

16- How often ……….. Hamad phone you ?

17- Where did you …………….. Ali?

18- …………….. you coming to Ali's party?

19- …………….. Ali free now?

20- …………… Mona at home when you phoned?

21- What kind of music …………… Ali like ?

22- What ………. the weather like today ?

23- What ……….. the weather like yesterday ?

24- Who ……… shouting ?

25- Who has ………….. this door ?

* __Answer these questions :__

1- How long did you take to do it ?

....

2- How long has Ali been waiting ?

....

3- Who did you tell ?

....

4- Who phoned you last night ?

....

5- Are you free ?

....

6- Have you watched the match ?

....

7- Why are you running ?

....

8- Why did Ali go to the bank ?

....

9- Why does Mona drink a lot of milk ?

....

10- Does Ali drink wine ? why ?

....

11-What do you think of Ali ?   ما رأيك في علي ؟

....

12- What is happening ?   ما الذي يجري ؟

....

13- What happened ? ماذا جرى ؟

....

14- What are you doing ?

....

15- What sort of job do you do ?   ما نوع العمل الذي تقوم به؟

....

16- What has Ali done ?

....

17- What did Mona do ?

....

18- What are they doing ?

....

19- What were you doing ?

....

20- How did Hamad improve the standard of his English?

....

* **Correct the mistakes :**

   1- What Ali is doing ? ....
   2- How you came last night ? ....
   3- Why you are angry ? ....
   4- Where did Ali went ?   ....
   5- When do Ali usually arrive ?..........................
   6- Who are crying ?   ....
   7- What have happened ? ....
   8- What happening ?   ....
   9- I know what is Ali doing. ....
   10- I do not know why are you late . ...

The question – tags الأسئلة البُعْدية

* Tag-questions follow statements for emphasis .

هذا النوع من الأسئلة يأتي بعد جملة خبرية تأكيداً لمحتواهـا ، وتشبه إلى حـد كبير الأسـئلة العاديـة في تكوينها .

* There are two ways of forming tag- questions.

هناك طريقتان لتكوينها.

A- In the presence of auxiliaries (الأفعال المساعدة) **في وجود المقويات**

1- Ali **is** talking to your father , **isn't he** ?

إن علياً يتحدث إلى والدك ، أليس كذلك ؟

قمنا بوضع المقوي في حالة النفي ثم الضمير "he " بدلاً من " Ali ".

2- Mona **isn't** free at the moment , **is she** ?

أما إذا كان المقوي في حالة نفي ، فإننا نحذف علامة النفي فقط ثم نستخدم الضمير المناسب بـدلاً مـن الاسم " Mona " .

3- You **are** a student , **aren't you** ?

أنت طالب (طالبة) ، أليس كذلك ؟

4- I **am** right , **aren't I** ?   أنا محق ، أليس كذلك ؟

5-Ali and Mona **will** do it for you , **won't they** ?

(will not = won't)

6- I **will** explain the matter to Hamad, **shall I** ?

7- Ali **has** passed , **hasn't he** ?

8- Your parents **have** left for London , **haven't they** ?

9- Your mother **had** got one , **hadn't she** ?

10- Ali **had better** study abroad , **hadn't he** ?

(had better من المقويات التي تأتي مع شكل أول)

* have / has / had تعتبر من المقويات لأن بعدها جاءت أفعال في الشكل الثالث

B- In the absence of auxiliaries في غياب المقويات :

      1

1- You **accept** my idea , **don't you** ? ‏إنك تقبل بفكرتي ، أليس كذلك ؟‏

2- Ali and Mona **don't agree** with you , **do they** ?

‏إن علياً ومنى لا يتفقان معك ، أليس كذلك ؟‏

3- Ali **appeals** to you for help , **doesn't he** ?

‏إن علياً يناشدك طالباً المساعدة ، أليس كذلك ؟ Hani and -4‏

Huda saw it **, didn't they** ?

5- You **didn't get** one , **did you** ?

* **Have** ⟶ 1- **an auxiliary** (مقوٍ لفعلٍ أخر) فعل مساعد /
                               2- **lexical verb** فعل له معنى

  1-You **have got** a car , **haven't you**?

‏have (هنا مُقوٌّ لفعل شكل ثالث.)‏

2- You **have** a problem with your boss **, don't you** ?

‏(هنا ليست مقوٍ) have (3- Ali **has** a‏

problem , **doesn't he** ?

4- Mona **had** a phone call last night , **didn't she** ?

5- You **have to tell** your father, **don't you**?

(haven't you?) (هنا مقوٍ لفعلٍ شكل أول.)

6-Ali **has to do** that, **doesn't he**?   (hasn't he?)

7-Mona **had to** sell her car, **didn't she**?   (hadn't she?)

* **Supply the missing question - tags :**

1- I have sent you a copy , ...?

2- You have a cup of coffee every day , ... ?

3- Huda has got her book back , ... ?

4- Ali has a nice car , ... ?

5- You have had your lunch , ... ?

6- Mona likes music , ... ?

7- You haven't taken it , ... ?

8- You are against ضد smoking , ... ?

9- I am your neighbour , ... ?

10- You can settle the matter , ... ?

11- Ali had his lunch an hour ago , ... ?

12- Mona is at home , ... ?

13- Ali reads this newspaper every day , ... ?

14- He read the article المقال yesterday, ... ?

15- She hardly got it , ... ?

* **hardly** أداة نفي وتعني " لم " .

16- You have got no money , ... ? (لاحظ وجود النفي)

17- You saw nobody , ... ?

18- You have to write this sentence, ... ?

19- Ali has to buy a new car, ... ?

20- Mona doesn't write stories , ... ?

21- I will show you how to do it , ... ?

22- Ali had a cold last night , ... ?

23- You had better leave it ,................... ?

24- Mona will come with you , ... ?

25- Ali enjoys skating , ... ?

26- You had to cancel the trip, ... ?

27- You don't have to do that, ... ?

28- He has no idea, ... ?

29- They are having a good time, ... ?

30- Ali and Mona won't come to the meeting, ... ?

31- Mona forgot her book, ... ?

32- I am with you , ... ?

33- The weather is clear , ... ?

34- Our newspapers are free , ... ?

35- Our newspapers call for freedom of speech , ... ?

* Put these words into the correct order :

1- are / going / Where / you /

.... ?

2- does / father / out / your / go / When /

.... ?

3- has / Ali / What / you / told /

.... ?

4- was / Why / late / brother / your /

.... ?

5- is / with / wrong / you / What /

.... ?

6- have / working / How / here / been / long / you /

.... ?

7- can / change / How / it / he ?

.... ?

8- money / this / is / Whose ?

.... ?

الكلام غير المباشر Indirect speech

نلاحظ المراسلين ينقلون لنا كلاماً صادراً عن أشخاص آخرين ، ونحن غالباً مـا نقـوم بـنفس الـدور .. دور الوسيط بين طرفين ، وهذا الوسيط يبدّل في الكلام المنقول .

أمثلة Examples

1- " I will leave Doha tomorrow ." (كلام مباشر Direct speech

     ↓ ↓   ↓

Ali said that he would leave Doha the next day .

(Indirect speech كلام غير مباشر)

في الجملة الأولى نشاهد كلام علي كما هو دون تبديل فيه .

وفي الجملة الثانية قمنا بنقل كلام علي ، ومن طبيعة ناقل الكـلام أن يبـدّل في الكـلام ، ومعظـم التبـديل ينصب على الكلمات التي تحتها خط .

Huda said that she would leave Doha the next day.

* في الحالة الأولى نُسب الكلام إلى علي , وأنا نقلت كلام علي .

* في الحالة الثانية نُسب الكلام إلى منى , وأنا نقلت كلامها .

2- " I can meet you at school tomorrow ."

     ↓   ↓   ↓   ↓

Mona said that **she could** meet **me** at school **the next day** .

Mona told Ali that she could meet him at school the next day .

Ali told Huda that he could meet her at school the next day .

* في الحل الأول الكلام منسوب إلى منى , وأنا قمت بنقل كلامها حيث أنها توجه الكلام لي .

* في الحل الثاني الكلام منسوب إلى منى موجهة كلامها إلى علي , وأناقمت بنقل الكلام .

* في الحل الثالث الكلام منسوب إلى علي موجهاً كلامه إلى هدى , وأنا قمت بنقل كلامه لها.

3-   " You have helped me a lot ."

                     ↓   ↓   ↓

Ali told me that I had helped him a lot .

Mona told Hani that he had helped her a lot .

Ali told Mona that she had helped him a lot .

I told Ali that ………………………………… . (complete.)

I told Mona that ……………………………… .

4- " I have convinced my father of my idea".

Mona told me that **she had** convinced **her** father of **her** idea

Ali informed me that **he had** convinced **his** father of **his** idea .

Mona assured Huda that **she had** convinced **her** father of **her** idea . منـى أكّـدت لـ هـدى

بأنها قد أقنعت والدها (والد منى) بفكرتها (فكرة منى).

5- "I am busy today" .

Ali confirmed أكّدthat he was busy **that day** .

Ali assured me that **he was** busy **that day** .

Mona said that **she was** busy **that day** .

I assured my father that I was busy that day.

6- Mona said, "I am discussing my plan with my father" .

Mona said **she was** discussing **her** plan with **her** father .

Mona **says** (شكل أول / الفعل مضارع) that she is discussing her plan with her father.

إذا كان الفعل الرئيسي في الماضي (شكل ثان) , فإنه يتم تغيير الفعل التالي إلى الماضي.أما إذا كان

في حالة المضارع , فلا داعي لتغيير الفعل الآخر.

7- "You <u>broke</u> <u>my</u> window <u>yesterday</u> " , Ali said .

Ali said that **I broke** (**had broken**) **his** window **the day before** . Ali told Mona that **she broke** (**had broken**) **his** window the day before .

8- Ali : "<u>I</u> <u>am</u> studying <u>here</u> <u>now</u>" .
Ali says that he is studying here now.

Ali said (that) he was studying **there** <u>**then**</u> . ⟶ . في ذلك الوقت

9- Ali asked ," Have you seen your brother ? "
Ali asked me if I had seen my brother.
Ali asked Hamad if he had seen his brother.
Ali asked Mona if she had seen her brother.

10- Mona asked , " Do you see my brother at school ?"
Mona asked me if I see (saw) her brother at school.
Mona asked Ali if he sees (saw) her brother at school.
Mona asked Huda if she sees (saw) her brother at school.

11- Mona : " Can I get one more ? "
Mona asked if she could get one more.
Mona asked to get one more.
Mona asked for permission to get one more.

طلبت مني إذناً بأن تأخذ ......

12-Ali asked , " Where can I meet you tomorrow ? "
Ali asked me where he could meet me the next day.
Ali asked Mona where he could meet her the next day.

1- Ali asked , " When did my father call you ? "
Ali asked me when his father (had) called me.
Ali asked Mona when his father (had) called her.
Ali asked Hamad when his father (had) called him.

* عندما ننقل سؤال شخص , فإننا نتبع ما يلي :

١- إذا كان السؤال لا يبدأ بأداة سؤال مثل why , where , what , فإننا نضع if
بعد فعل النقل .

٢- نبطل السؤال بوضع المقوي المقيم قبل الاسم أو نحذف المقوي المستورد ثم نطبق نفس
خطوات النقل المتبعة في حالة الجمل الخبرية العادية.

٣- إذا كان الكلام المراد نقلة يعبر عن حقيقة فلا داعي لتغيير الفعل إلى شكل ثانٍ.

2- Ali asked , " Is Qatar a GCC country ? "

    Ali asked if Qatar is (و ليس was) a GCC country.

3- Ali said , " Mix with my people as much as you can ."

    لاحظ أن فعل الجملة المراد نقلها هو في صيغة أمر إثبات (شكل أول).

    Ali advised me to mix with his people as much as I could.

    Ali told Mona to mix with his people as much as she could.

    Ali asked Mona and Rashid to mix with his people as much
       as they could.

    Ali ordered his children to mix with his people as much as
       they could.

    Ali suggested that we should mix with his people as much as
       we could.

    Ali suggested that we mix with his people as much as we
       could .

    الشك في إمكانية العمل بالاقتراح على حاله في الشكل الأول تعبيراً عن (المثال الأخير).

    نلاحظ أننا أبقينا على mix

16- Ali : " Don't smoke ! "

    نلاحظ أن الفعل في صيغة أمر منفي . لاحظ كيف يتم التعامل مع هذه الحالة.

    Ali told me not to smoke.

    Ali advised me not to smoke.

    Ali asked me not to smoke.

* When reporting what others say , we have to make certain
   changes :

عند نقل ما يقوله الآخرون, تتم بعض التغيرات .

1- We use a speech verb like : said , told , stated ,
   pointed out أوضح , added أضاف, stressed شدد,
   emphasized أكد, assured , explained .

2- We change the pronouns according to the people whose words we are
   reporting. يتم تغيير الضمائر حسب الشخص الذي ننقل كلامه

I ⟶ he , she / me ⟶ him , her / my ⟶ his , her /

You (في بداية كلام الشخص)⟶ I , he , she /

You (مفعول به) ⟶ me , him , her /

Your ⟶ my , his , her / We ⟶ they / us ⟶ them /

our ⟶ their /

3- We change the verb tense . . نقوم بتغيير زمن الفعل

   1 ⟶ 2   1 ⟶ 2

   will ⟶ would / can ⟶ could

   may ⟶ might / must ⟶ had to

   have ⟶ had / am , is ⟶ was

   are ⟶ were / go ⟶ went

   visit ⟶ visited / 2   3

           visited ⟶ visited , had visited

4- We change some time indicators. نقوم بتغيير بعض مؤشرات الزمن

   tomorrow ⟶ the next day

   yesterday ⟶ the day before

   last week ⟶ a week earlier

   now ⟶ then في ذلك الوقت

   (place : here ⟶ there هناك)

* Report the following :

1- Ali said , "I took my son to London last year".

   Ali told me that ………………………………………….

2- Mona promised , "I will inform you of my father's reply رد tomorrow".Mona

   promised وعدت me that …………………...

3- "I have seen your book here".

   Hani assured me أكد لي that ……………………………… .

4- "I am teaching my children now".

   Huda said (that) ……………………………………… .

5- "When do you see your boss ?".

   Ali asked me when ………………………………… .

   Mona asked Hamad ……………………………………

6- Mona : "Where did you go with my son ?".

2   3

   Mona asked me where I went (had gone) with her son .

في حالة السؤال ، فإننا نتعامل معه وكأنه ليس سؤالاً .. أي نعيد الكلام إلى ما كان عليه قبل السؤال .. أي نتخلص من صيغة السؤال .. ثم نجري التغييرات المعتادة في حالة نقل الكلام .

7- Ali asked, "Why is Mona shouting now ?"

   Ali asked ……………………………………….…… .

8- Mona asked , "Is Ali coming to my party tomorrow ?"

   Mona asked …………………………………………

9- Hani asked , "Can you see my father tomorrow ?"

   Hani asked me ……………………………………….

   Hani asked Mona ……………………………………….

   Hani asked Ali ……………………………………….

10- Hani asked , "Did your brother win the race last year ?"

Hani wanted me to tell him ....

Hani asked Mona ....

11- Hani asked , "How did you get one yesterday ?"

Hani asked me ....

Hani asked Mona ....

12 Ali said , "Study well before the exam ."

Ali advised me ....

Ali told me ....

Ali suggested that ....

13- Mona said , "Wash your hands before you eat".

Mona ....

14- Mona : "Don't eat too much".

Mona ....

15- Teacher : "Don't write while listening to me !".

The teacher ordered us أمرنا ....

16- Hamad said, "I will sack you if you don't do your job well ."

Hamad warned حذّر Hani that ....

Hamad warned the pilots that ....

Hamad warned Mona that ....

Hamad warned me that ....

17- Ali said , " Don't read aloud ."

Ali advised me not to read aloud.

* **Complete these sentences :**

1- My father said that ....

2- The police confirmed that ....

3- Ali denied أنكر ....

4- Hani admitted اعترف بـ his ....

5- Hani admitted the ....

6- Hani admitted to ....

7- Hani admitted that ....

8- I told my friends ....

9- The teacher asked ....

10- The police say ....

* **Which is correct ?**

1- Ali says that he is the last to come. (   )

   Ali says that he was the last come. (   )

2- Mona said that her father has left for London. (   )

   Mona said that her father had left for London. (   )

3- Ali asked where can he get more information. (   )

   Ali asked where he could get more information. (   )

4- Hamad asked me I got the money

   Hamad asked me if I got the money

5- Mona advised Ali not drive too fast .

   Mona advised ali not to drive too fast .

Ways of Joining Sentences (Clauses)

طـرق ربـط الجـمـل

عندما تكون هناك علاقة ما بين جملتين ، فإننا نقوم بربط تلك الجملتين مستخدمين أدوات ربط مناسبة
connectives.

A- **Addition** الجمع والإضافة : The aim is to combine two
   independent clauses. الهـدف هو ربط جملتين كل واحدة منهما مستقلة

1- I bought apples . I bought <u>grapes</u> . عنب

   I bought apples **and** grapes .

2- I watched TV . I read a story .

   I watched TV **and** read a story, <u>**as well**</u>. ⟶ أيضاً

   I watched TV , and I   read a story.

   I watched TV . I **also** read a story . أيضاً

   I watched TV . I read a story , <u>**too**</u> . ⟶ أيضاً

   I watched TV . **In addition** , I read a story .

   I watched TV . **Furthermore** , I read a story . . وعلاوة على ذلك

   I watched TV . **Besides** , I read a story . . وعلاوة على ذلك

   (**beside = next to**)

3- I saw a man . I saw a woman . I saw a policeman .

   I saw a man and a woman , as well as , a policeman.

   I saw a man and a woman , together with a policeman.

   I saw a man and a woman , along with a policeman.

   I saw a man , a woman , and a policeman.

4- Noura is friendly . Noura is helpful.

   Noura is friendly and helpful.

   Noura is friendly in addition to (her) being helpful.

5- I want to join the sports club. I want to go camping .

   I want **to join the sports** club and **to go camping**.

أنا أريد القيام بعملين ..وكل عمل مكون من أكثر من كلمة , ولـهذا فإننا نستخدم ... to go . أما إذا كان كل عمل مكون من فعل واحد فقط فلا داعي استخدام to write كما في(٦)

6- I want to read and write.

7- I want to read , and Ali wants to play music.

B- - either .... or أو .. أن إما / neither .. nor ولا ..... لا /

1- You play football . You watch TV .

   You either play football or watch TV .

2- You play football . You play basketball .

   You play either football or basketball .

3- The parents like the idea. Ali likes the idea.

   Either the parents or Ali likes the idea.

4- The teachers are right . I am right.

   Either the teachers or I am right.

5- I don't eat rice . I don't eat meat .

   I eat neither rice nor meat .   إني لا أكل رزاً ولا لحماً.

   I don't eat rice , **nor do I eat meat.** →   يجب أن تكون في

   هذا التراكيب على هيئة سؤال.

6- I don't eat pork . I don't drink wine .

   I neither eat pork nor drink wine .

   I don't eat pork , **nor do I drink wine.**

7- The girls are not coming. Ali is not coming **either** أيضاً.

   Neither the girls nor Ali is coming.

7- My sisters have not seen the film. Nasser has not seen the film either.

   Neither my sisters not Nasser has seen the film.

   Note : after " **or** " and " **nor** " the verb has to agree with the noun closest to it.

   بعد " or " أو " nor " يجب أن يتوافق الفعل مع الاسم الأقرب له.

* Join these sentences :

1- He didn't see Ali . He didn't see Mona .

....

2- She doesn't dance . She doesn't sing .

....

لاحظ أنه لا بد من إدخال تعديل مناسب على الفعل بعد التخلص من النفي .

3- You sing . You dance .

....

4- He got a book . He got a pen . He got a rubber .

....

5- She cooked the lunch . She tidied the rooms .

....

Adverbial clauses of time :

** as soon as (بـمجرد) , **no sooner ... than** (ما أن ... حتى)

*   I saw a lion . I screamed and fainted . (**Two main clauses**)

<u>As soon as</u> I   رأيت أسداً . صرخت وأغمي عـليّ.
<u>saw a lion</u> ,   <u>I screamed and fainted</u> .

         ↓   ↓
Subordinate clause جملة تابعة   Main clause جملة رئيسية

الجملة التابعة تتبع أداة الربط و لا تؤدي معنى إلا بوجود الجملة الرئيسية .
(توضع as soon as قبل الحدث الأول)

I **no sooner** saw a lion **than** I screamed and fainted .

* Join each pair of sentences using (as soon as) or (no sooner...than) :

1- I finish. I go out.   ....
2- I arrive. I will ring you.   ....
3- He arrived. He phoned me. ....
4- She received the new car. She paid the price..............
5- We left the stadium. The match was over...............

٢٧٩

عندما When

1- I feel ill . I see my doctor .

             1   1

    When I **feel ill** , I **see my** doctor .

         ↓   ↓

    Subordinate   Main

2- When I saw Ali , I told him everything .

3- When I arrived , he finished .

4- When I arrived , he had finished .

5- When I arrived , he was finishing .

تعليق: عند استخدام فعلين في الشكل الثاني (كما في المثال ٣) نجد بأن الفعلين حدثا في الماضي وفي نفس الوقت تـقريباً.

وفي حالة استخدام فعل شكل ثان وأخر شكل ثالث (كما في المثال ٤) فإن الفعل في الشكل الثالـث يكون قد حدث واكتمل حدوثه قبل وقوع الفعل في الشكل الثاني.

وفي حالة استخدام فعل شكل ثان وأخر شكل رابع كما في المثال ٥ فإن الفعـل في الشـكل الرابع كان لا يزال مستمراً لحظة وقوع الفعل في الشكل الثاني.

بينما While = as

     2   4

1- Ali **came in** while I **was watching** TV .

2- While I **was watching** the match , he **left** .

3- While we **were walking** , we **met** Ali .

    While walking , we met Ali .

    هذه عبارة وليست جملة : Phrase ↓

* يمـكن تحويل clause إلى phrase إذا كان نفس الفاعل في الجملتين ويتم ذلك بحذف فاعل الجملة الثانية والفعل المساعد .

\# ملاحظة: يجب وضع while قبل الجملة التي يكون فعلها شكل رابع.

before قبل / بعد after

1- I **wash** <u>before</u> I **go out** . (main clause / subordinate clause)

   I **wash** <u>**before going out**</u> . → Phrase

   يجوز التحويل إلى phrase   إذا كان الفاعل نفسه في الجملتين.

2- I **phone** my friends <u>after</u> I **finish** .

3- I **will tell** you <u>before</u> I **leave** .

4- She **met** Ali <u>before</u> she **left** .

   She **met** Ali <u>before</u> leaving .

5- I **had phoned** Ali <u>before</u> I **went out** .

6- Ali **left** <u>after</u> he **had got** his salary .

   Having got his salary , Ali left.

since مـنـذ

1- I **have been studying** the case <u>since</u> you **left** .

2- He **has been** ill <u>since</u> he **arrived** .

3- They **have not phoned** <u>since</u> they **left** .

* Join these sentences :

1- It has been raining . We arrived .

   ....

2- She has been busy . You phoned .

   ....

3- You phoned . I was writing .

   ....

4- I will hit Ali . I see him .

   ....

5- You should wash your hands . You start eating .

   ....

6- I shouted . They escaped . هربوا

....

7- It rained . We went home .

....

8- She had tidied the room . She went out .

....

9- I was reading . I heard a man shouting .

....

10- Ali phoned . We were doing the homework .

....

* **Correct the mistakes :**

1- I wrote a letter before left . ...

2- As soon as I finished , I call Ali. ....

3- He washed after repaired the car. ....

4- She met Ali while he is going home. ....

5- While paint a picture , Ali sneezed. ....

6- When I saw Mona , she cry. ....

7- She has been painted this picture since last April. ....

8- While it stopped raining , we left. ....

9- I have been studying since you arrive. ....

10- Mona has been writing since my arrive . ...

٢٨٢

Connectives showing cause and result .

أدوات ربط توضح السبب والنتيجة

The main clause contains a very important idea .

The subordinate (dependent) clause contains a less important

idea , so we can change it into a phrase.

الجملة الرئيسية تحتوي على فكرة هامة جداً التي يريد الشخص أن يشدد عليها.

الجملة التابعة تحتوي على فكرة أقل أهمية , ولـهذا مِكننا أن نحولـها إلى عبارة

1- I didn't buy the car *because it was too old* .

    └ main clause   └ subordinate clause

إني لم أشتري السيارة لأنها قديـمة جداً.

I didn't buy the car *because of* (*due to*) *its being too old.*

    └ main clause   └ phrase

إني لم أشتري السيارة بسبب قدمـها (بسبب كونـها قدمِة).

I didn't buy the car , for it was too old. (هنا التشديد على الفكرتين)

    └ main clause   └ main clause

2- The car was too old , so I didn't buy it .

إن السيارة كانت قديماً جداً ولـهذا فإنني لم أشتِرها.

3- The car was too old ; therefore , I didn't buy it .

4- The car was too old ; I , therefore , didn't buy it .

   The car was too old ; I didn't buy it , therefore.

إن السيارة كانت قديـمة جداً ولـهذا السبب فإنني لم أشتِرها.

5- He didn't study well ; as a result , he failed .

إنه لم يدرس بشكل جيد ، ونتيجة لذلك فإنه رسب .

  He didn't study well ; consequently , he failed.

6- He didn't go to school *because he was ill* .

    └ main clause   └ subordinate clause

He didn't go to school *because of his illness* .

           (بسبب مرضه) └ phrase

He didn't go to school *due to his illness.*إنه لم يذهب إلى المدرسة بسبب مرضه

           └ phrase

He didn't go to school *owing to his illness* .

           └ phrase

He didn't go to school *on account of his illness* .

           └ phrase

* نلاحظ أنه بعد because of ، due to ، owing to ، on account of لا بد من وضع اسم يشـتق مـن الصفة أو من الفعل لأن الكلام الذي يليها لم يعد جملة بل أصبح شبه جملة .

7- We are sad **because** Ali has failed .

We are sad **because of** Ali's failure. إننا حزينون بسبب رسوب علي.

8-They cancelled the trip **because of** the bad weather conditions

هم ألغوا الرحلة بسبب الأحوال الجوية السيئة .

9- He resigned his job **due to** bad management .

إنه استقال من عمله بسبب الإدارة السيئة .

10- Some people are driving too fast , **thus** endangering others .

إن بعض الناس يسوقون بسرعة كبيرة جداً وهم بذلك يعرضون الآخرين للخطر .

11- People are cutting trees , **thus** increasing CO_2 in the air.

إن الناس يقطعون الأشجار وهم بهـذا يزيدون من ثاني أكسيد الكربون في الهواء .

12- The earthquake destroyed many houses , **thus** making thousands of people homeless .

إن الزلزال دمر الكثير من البيوت وهو بذلك جعل آلافاً من الناس مشردين .

* بعد thus تأتي نتيجـة العمـل الأول ، ويكـون الفعـل شـكل رابـع شريطـة أن يكـون نفـس الفاعـل في الجملتين الأصليتين .

* The earthquake الزلزالdestroyed houses . (main clause)

* The earthquake made thousands of people homeless.

(main clause)

الفاعل مشترك في الجملتين ، ولأن الجملـة الثانيـة ناتجـة عـن الجملـة الأولى فيمكننـا أن نسـتخدم thus بشرط حذف الفاعل في الجملة الثانية وتحويل الفعل فيها إلى شكل رابع .. كما هو واضح فيما يلي :

The earthquake destroyed houses , *thus making thousands of people homeless* .
L phrase

The earthquake destroyed houses , making thousands of people homeless.

* Ali made too much noise , so I had to move to another place.
  Ali made too much noise , **thus** I had to move to another place.
    └ main clause   └ main clause

    * Join the sentences using different connectors :

* We sell oil to many countries . We get a lot of hard currency.
  We sell oil to many countries , so (thus) we get a lot of hard
  currency.
  We sell oil .... , thus getting a lot of hard currency.
  We sell oil ...... ; therefore , we get ....
  We get a lot of hard currency because we sell oil to many
  countries.
  We get .... because of our selling oil to ....
  We get .... because of our oil sales to ....
  We get .... by selling oil to ....

1- Ali gets up late every day . He makes me angry .
    * ....
    * ....

2- Mona explains everything . She encourages تشجع us to attend يحضر her lecture.
    * ....
    * ....

3- People drive slowly . They have fewer accidents .
    * ....
    * ....

4- We save نقتصد energy . We have less pollution التلوث .

   * ....

   * ....

5- We are causing too much pollution. We are using too much energy.

   * ....

   * ....

6- We see wars everywhere these days. People are selfish.

   * ....

   * ....

7- You eat too many sweets . You are getting fatter.

   * ....

   * ....

8- Ali took many pictures of the view. The view appealed to him .

   * ....

   * ....

9- You mix with native speakers. Your English is improving
    remarkably.

   * ....

   * ....

10- Ali is angry. You mistreat him.

   * ....

   * ....

٢٨٦

أدوات ربط توضح النتيجة * Connectives showing result

The tea is very hot . I cannot drink it .

The tea is **so hot that** I cannot drink it .

إن الشاي حار جداً لدرجة أنني لا أستطيع أن أشربه.

It rained so heavily that many houses collapsed.

أمطرت بغزارة شديدة لدرجة أن الكثير من البيوت انهارت.

صفة adj./ adv ظرف ◄━━ that ◄━━

وهناك طريقة أخرى لربط الجملتين :

The tea is **too hot to** drink .

too ━━► صفة adj. ━━► to

إن الشاي حار جداً لدرجة أنه لا يمكن شربه .

■ (that ◄━ صفة ◄━ to) / (so ◄━ صفة ◄━ too) يقومان بنفس الوظيفة وهو ربط جملتين تكون الجملة الثا

ناتجة عن الأولى، ولكن يجب أن نلاحظ بأن to ◄━ صفة ◄━ too تستخدم فقط إذا كانت الجملة الثانية تفيد النفي .

English is **so difficult that** only few people can learn it .

English is **too difficult to** learn .

إن الإنجليزية صعبة للغاية بحيث لا يمكن تعلمها .

The question is **too difficult to** answer .

The road is **so busy that** we cannot cross it .

The road is too busy to cross .

The road is too busy to cross it . (X)   (it لا داعي لاستخدام)

It is too difficult a question for me to answer.

He had **such an accident that** ten people were killed.

She painted **such a lovely picture that** she won the best prize

She has **such good ideas that** we- إنـها رسمت صورة جميلة جـداً لدرجـة أنـها فـازت بأحسـن جـائزة.

always consult her.

such ━━► اسم ━━► that

كافٍ enough

1- Ali has enough experience.   إن علياً لديه خبرة كافية .

Ali is experienced enough to do this job .

إن علياً ذو خبرة تكفي للقيام بهذه الوظيفة.

Ali is experienced enough for the job.

2- You are not fit enough for this sport.

You are not fit enough to play this sport.

إنك لست لائقاً لياقة تكفي لأن تلعب هذه الرياضة.

3- We do not have enough money for the picnic.

4- He is old enough to get married.   إنه في سن يكفي لأن يتـزوج.

نضع enough قبل الاسم ولكن بعد الصفة .

* Join these sentences using suitable connectors :

1- Mona worked hard . She passed with high marks .

....

2- The exam was very difficult . Most of the students failed.

....

3- The workers are angry . The manager has refused to increase their salaries

....

4-Inflation التضخمis going up. We spend ننفق too much .

....

5- We can't go sailing . The weather is too bad .

....

6- The sea is very rough . It is mad to go fishing .

....

7- They won the match . They played well .

....

8-The king ousted عزلthe Education Minister وزير التعليم . His

policy proved faulty ثبت فشل سياسته .

....

9-She asked a silly question . She angered all the students .

* ....

* ....

10- Ali wrote a wonderful composition . Everybody admired it .

* ....

* ....

11- The suitcase الحقيبةwas very heavy. She could not carry it.

* ....

* ....

12- He is extremely للغاية obstinate عنيد . It is useless to argue with him.

* ....

* ....

13- The problem is very hard. We can't solve it.

* ....

* ....

14- The food was very hot. I could not eat it.

* ....

* ....

15- He spoke very quietly. We got everything he said.

* ....

* ....

16- He doesn't smoke at all. He doesn't have any health
problem.

* ....

* ....

17- She listens to the BBC programmes regularly . Her English is improving.

* ....

* ....

18- He is very fat . He can't move easily.

....

Connectives showing purpose
أدوات ربــط توضح الـهـدف

1- I am studying hard . I want to pass .

إنني أدرس بجد . لماذا ؟ ما هو الهدف ؟

I am studying hard **so that** I can succeed .

I am studying hard **so that** I will succeed .

I am studying hard *so that* I may succeed .   إني أدرس بجد حتى أنجح   └ main
clause   └ subordinate clause

2- She worked hard **in order that** she could succeed .

She worked hard **in order that** she might succeed .

3- She went to the bookshop **in order to** buy a book .

She went to the bookshop **to buy** a book .

إنـها ذهبت إلى المكتبة لكي تشتري كتاباً .

4- I came to the library **to borrow** a book .

جئت إلى المكتبة لكي أستعير كتاباً .

5- I came to the library *with a view to borrowing a book* .

└ main clause   └ phrase

٢٩٠

6- I came here *with the aim of borrowing a book* .

        L phrase

- ملاحظات : في (١،٢) استخدمنا (so that ، in order that) لربط الجملتين في (٣) استخدمنا to بمعنى لكي لربط الجملتين وتم استخدام الفعل في الشكل الأول.

- في (٥،٦) استخدمنا with a view to ، with the aim of بمعنى "بهدف" واضعين بعدها اسماً مشتقاً من فعل لأنه تم تحويل الجملة التابعة لأداة الربط إلى عبارة.

* Join these sentences :

1- I always get up early . I want to get to school on time.

....

2- She read the article thoroughlyبدقة. She wanted to grasp يستوعب the writer's view رأي .

....

3- They got ready well . They wanted to win the race .

....

4- He is working hard . He wants to make a fortune .ثروة

....

5- We are building wide roads . We want to overcome يتغلب علىour traffic problems

....

6- We have to boil the drinking water. We want to kill germs.

....

7- The government refuses to increase salaries. They want to control inflation التضخم.

....

8- He runs 10 km every day. He wants to lose weight.

....

9- She is learning a lot of words. She wants to improve her

English..

10- She was driving slowly on the icy road. She wanted to avoid

accidents..

* **Complete these sentences :**

1- We provide نوفر green area مناطق خضراء so that.................

2- We provide schools so that ....

3- We provide schools with a view to ....   4- We are

using the radar in order to ....

5- They are fighting with the aim of ....

6- Ali is doing a lot of exercise in order that ....

7- We have to impose more taxes in order to ....

نحن مضطرون لأن نفرض مزيداً من الضرائب لكي.......

8- I have joined this university with a view ....

9- She ran fast so that ....

10- The doctor examined the patient well so that ....

....

أحياناً يقوم الإنسان بعمل ما خوفاً من شيء ما . وفي هذه الحالة نستخدم lest بمعنى " خشية أن " أو for fear of بمعنى "خوفاً من ".

1- **Mona eats a little food** *lest she should get fat* .
   L main clause   L subordinate clause

إن منى تأكل قليلاً من الطعام خشية أن تسمن .
لاحظ أننا استخدمنا should قبل الفعل في الجملة الثانية (الجملة التابعة) .

2- Mona eats a little food *for fear of gaining extra weight* .
    L main clause   L phrase

إن منى تأكل قليلاً من الطعام خوفاً من (تحسباً من) اكتساب وزن زائد .

* تذكّر أننا دائماً نستخدم بعد حرف الجر اسماً قد يكون على شكل فعل شكل رابع.

Complete these sentences :

1- He is studying hard lest ....

2- She eats a little food lest ....

3- You have to get a visa in advance مسبقاً for fear of ....
....

4- We should get our children vaccinated for fear of ....
....

5- I advise you to wear warmer clothes lest you ....

* Join these sentences :

1- Mona washes daily . She fears تخشى that she might get
    sick. ....

2- Nasser is studying well. He fears that he may fail.
....

3- You should read the question carefully . I fear that you
    may give the wrong answer .
....

4- We should solve the poverty problem. يجب أن نحل مشكلة الفقر
We fear that it might threaten تهدد our country's stability استقرار
....

5- I always drive carefully. I don't want to have an accident.
....

6- I study hard . I don't want to fail.
....

٢٩٣

7- We pray . We do not want to displease Allah.

    ....

8- I do not mix with bad people. They might spoil me.

    ....

9- Noura practised a lot. She did not want to lose the race.

    ....

10- He avoids يتجنب fatty food . He does not want to gain

    weight. ....

Connectives showing contrast
أدوات ربـط تفيـد التناقـض

1- The car was too expensive . Ali bought it .

نلاحظ وجود تناقض بين الجملتين.. إذ أن السيارة غالية جداً. ولا نتوقع أن يبادر علي بشرائها .

Although the car was too expensive , **Ali bought it** .

     L subordinate clause   L main clause

Ali bought the car **although** it was too expensive .

Ali bought the car **even though** it was too expensive.

إن علياً اشترى السيارة على الرغم أنها كانت غالية جداً .

2- The weather was too bad . They went sailing .

The weather was too bad , but they went sailing .

الطقس كان سيئاً للغاية ولكنهم أبحروا .

3- He had bad marks . The university admitted him .

He had bad marks , yet the university admitted him.

     L main clause   L main clause

كان لديه درجات سيئة ومع ذلك فإن الجامعة قبلته .

He had bad marks ; **even so** , the university accepted him.

4- She had high marks . She was not admitted to the university .

• **She had high marks . Nevertheless ومع ذلك , she was not admitted to the university .**

* She had high marks ; **nevertheless** , she was not admitted to the university .

5- He is too fat . He can run faster than you .

●   He is too fat . **However** ومع ذلك , he can run faster than you.

    He is too fat ; however , he can run faster than you.

    L_{main clause}   L_{main clause}

6- He was ill . He came to the party .

    He came to the party *in spite of his illness* .

    L_{main clause}   L_{phrase}

جاء إلى الحفلة على الرغم من مرضه .

    He came to the party despite his being ill .

جاء إلى الحفلة على الرغم من كونه مريضاً .

Complete these sentences:

1- Although they are getting bad salaries, ...

2- The manager refuses to increase our salaries although

....

3- The sea was so rough هائج ;however, ...

4- She was dismissed طردت despite ....

5- They went on driving in spite of ....

* Join these sentences :

1- Ali didn't prepare well for the exam . He passed .

....

2- The sun was too bright . She went out for a walk.

....

3- It was raining heavily . They went on playing .

....

4 -She was so ugly قبيحة. Ali agreed to marry her .

....

5- Prices are too high . Nobody has complained . اشتكى

....

7-Ali is wealthy ثري. He isn't generousكريم .

....

8 - You eat too much.. You never gain extra weight. وزن زائد

....

9- She gets up early. She comes late for school.

....

10- He died a poor man. He worked hard all through his life.

....

11-His articles are full of good ideas. Too few people read them.

....

* Complete these sentences :

1- Although they work hard , ...

2- Mona is polite , but ....

3- I respect you even though ....

4- You offend me تسيء لي ; nevertheless , ...

5- I bought a new car in spite of the fact that ....

6- We will send them food and money despite ....

7- They went swimming although ....

8- You treat me badly even though ....

9- People hate Ali in spite of ....

10- People love Hani despite ....

11-She runs and jumps although ....

12-He eats too much food; however, ...

13-The sea was rough; nevertheless, ...

14-Although the exam was too difficult, ...

15-The weather was too hot; nevertheless, they ....

16-Although he uses simple language, ...

17-The road was covered with ice, but ....

الجمل الشرطية Conditional Clauses

● نستخدم " if " بمعنى " إذا " أو " إنْ " أو " لو " لربط جملتين ... الجملة التابعة لـ " if " تحتوي
على الشرط والثانية تحتوي على ما يترتب على تحقيق الشرط .

Examples :
1- If you help me , I will help you . . إن ساعدتني فإنني سوف أساعدك .
2- They will succeed if they study well .

إنهم سوف ينجحون إنْ هم درسوا بشكل جيد .

** **There are three types of " if " clauses :**

هناك ثلاث حالات للجمل الشرطية:

* **First type** الحالة الأولى :

           1   1

*   If you **play** well , you **will win** إذا لعبتم جيداً فإنكم سوف تفوزون
      ∟ subordinate clause   ∟ main clause

* You **will suffer** a lot if you **smoke** .   *إنك سوف تعاني كثيراً إذا دخّنت .   If you
smoke , you will **suffer** a lot .

* If he **smokes** , he **will destroy** his life . إذا دخن فإنه سوف يدمر حياته

* **Unless** you <u>stop</u> smoking , you <u>will suffer</u> a lot .

ما لم تتوقف عن التدخين فإنك سوف تعاني كثيراً .

* **Unless** you <u>study</u> hard , you will not <u>(won't) pass</u> .

ما لم تدرس بجد ، فسوف لن تنجح .

* If you **don't** study , you won't pass.

If he **doesn't** study , he will fail.   (unless = if not)

* * If we **heat** water , it **boils** . (Fact **حقيقة**)

  If we **mix** oxygen with hydrogen , we **get** water .

  If you have a problem , tell me . (Instruction إرشادات)

  If there is a fire , call the fire brigade.

إذا كان هناك حريقاً اتصل بالإطفائية.

  If there is a fire , don't use the lift .

In case the house burns down , switch off electricity.

في حالة أن يحترق المنزل , اقفل الكهرباء.

  In case you find a difficulty , you can contact me.

في حالة أن تجد صعوبة , يمكنك أن تتصل بي.

إذا وجدت صعوبة , يمكنك الاتصال بي.

* Complete these sentences :

1- If you succeed , I will buy you a car .

  If you succeed , you can join the university .

2- If you fail , ...

3- He will come to the party if ....

4- I will hit Ali if ....

5- Unless we improve the roads , ...

6-As long as طالما you are careless , ...

7- You must study hard , or (otherwise و إلا) ....

8- Unless you come , ...

* Replace " unless " with " if " :

1- Unless we act quickly , a disaster will take place.

....

2- Unless she gets high marks , we won't accept her.

....

* Second type : النوع الثاني *

           2   1

*   If it **rained**   ,   I **would stay** at home .

      L subordinate clause   L main clause

* If you helped me , I would help you.. إن ساعدتني , فإنني سوف أساعدك
هنا أفترض أمراً أشك في حدوثه.

* He **would buy** it if he **had** money. إنه سوف يشتريها إن كان يملك مالاً.

     2

* If I were you , I **would do** it .

لو كنت مكانك فإنني سوف أفعل ذلك .(أننا نعبر عن حالة عدم يقين)

● هذه حالة شاذة .. إذ أننا استخدمنا were بدلاً من was لأن هناك استحالة في أن أكون مكانك .

* If I were the king , I would not sign the decree .

لو كنت الملك ، فإنني سوف لن أوقع على المرسوم .

ملاحظة : إذا جاء بعد have أو has اسم , فإننا نتعامل معهما على أنـهما فعل شكل
أول . وكذلك had إذا جاء بعدها اسم فإننا نتعامل معها على أنـها فعل شكل ثانٍ.
أما إذا جاء بعد had فعل شكل ثالث , فإنـها تكون مقوياً لفعل شكل ثالث.

* Complete the sentences :

1- If Ali plays , ...

2- If Hani played , ...

3- We would not come if ....

4- She would change her mind if ....

5- If I were Ali , ...

6- If he had a problem , he ....

7- If I have a problem , I ....

8- If she has a car , ...

9- Unless we do something , ...

10- If she didn't succeed ....

* Correct the verbs in brackets :

1- If I (have) .... extra money , I will lend you .

2- She will come if she (have) .... time .

3- If I had time , I (come) ....

4- I would forgive him if he (stop) ....attacking me.

5- If you forget , I (remind) .... you .

6- If you forgot the appointment , I (remind) ....you .

7- If I (be) .... Mona , I (not buy) .... that ring.

8- Should you study hard, you (succeed) ....

   (Should = if)

9- Unless we do something , we (see) .... more accidents.

10- Unless she (run) .... , she (miss)..............the bus.

11- If she (have) .... money , she will buy one.

12- If she (have) ....money , she might buy one.

13- We would do something if we (have) ....directions.

14- If you (have) .... an electricity problem , don't

repair it yourself. If you (do) .... it yourself, you may

endanger your life.

16- In case you (see) ....the red traffic-light, stop.

17- In case you see the green traffic-light , (cross) ....

18- Unless she (take) ....exercise regularly , she
won't get fit.

19-   She wouldn't lose weight unless she (take) ....
a lot of exercise.

20- He won't be able to be fluent at the language unless he (mix)...................
with native speakers.

*   **Third type**   النوع الثالث

3   3
* If it **had rained** , I **would have cancelled** the trip .

(had ـب مسبوقاً ثالث شكل فعل) / (ـب مسبوقاً ثالث شكل فعل   would have)

* If Ali **had played** , we **would have won** the match .

لو أن علياً لعب ، لفزنا بالمباراة .

لاحظ أن علياً لم يلعب ، وأننا لم نفز .

* If she **had studied** well , she **would have passed** .

لو أنها درست بشكل جيد ، لنجحت .

نفهم من هذه الجملة : إنها لم تدرس ولهذا فإنها لم تنجح.

She didn't study well , so she didn't pass .

●   ولكن عند استخدام if يجب أن يكون شكل الجملة كما هو موضح في المثال السابق .

●   If the price had been too high, I would not have bought the car .

لو كان السعر مرتفعاً جداً ، لما اشتريت السيارة.

في الأصل السعر لم يكن مرتفعاً ، وبناءً على ذلك فإنني اشتريت السيارة .

- We **would have accepted** you if you **had had** high marks .

لو كان لديك درجات عالية لقبلناك.

- If you **had come**, I **would have told** you. =

  Had you come, I would have told you. (had = if)

* Had you invited me , I would have come. **لو دعوتني لجئت.**

  If you **had invited** me, I (**would** وأ**could** أو **might**) have
  come.

* **Complete these sentences :**

1- If he smokes , he ………………………………….

2- If he smoked , he …………………………………...

3- If he had smoked , he …………………………….

4- Had she been busy , ……………………………… .

5- I would not have gone there if ………………………..….

6- He would come if he ………………………………. .

7- If he had a good time , ……………………………… .

8- If I had had a problem , ……………………………… .

9- She wouldn't have come if ……………………………. .

10- If the terms were unfair, ……………………………. .

لو كانت الشروط غير عادلة.

* **Correct the verbs inside the brackets :**

1- Unless you have high marks , we (not accept) …………you .

2- If she (have) ……… bad marks , she cannot join this college.

3- If she (have) …………… high marks , we would accept her .

4- We would have employed him if he (have) ....
experience خبرة .

5- If he has experience , he (get) .... the job .

6- If she had been ill , she (not leave) .... the company .

7- But for our money problems لولا, the business (not fail)
....

8- But for education لولا التعليم, we (not develop) ....

9- You (improve) ....your language provided that بشرطyou
make more effort. أن تبذل مزيداً من الجهد.

10- As long as you (run) .... the company well , your
profits أرباحك will increase. سوف تزداد

11- If I (be) .... free, I would have joined you.

12- They (resign) .... their jobs had the
management objected to the new system.

13- If there (be) .... good roads , we won't have too many accidents.

14- If there were a problem, they (let)............. you know.

15- If there (be) .... any trouble , they might
have stopped the job.

16- If we don't improve the system , there (be) ....
serious problems arising from that.

17- There might have been better results if we (plan) ....
the project well.

18- If she (not break) .... the window , I
wouldn't have hit her.

19- She (not get)............. bad marks if she had studied well.

20- I would cancel the trip if the weather (change)............

Adjectival (Relative) clauses الجمل الوصفية

* We use relative pronouns ضمائر موصولة like : " who , whom , which , that , where, whose " to join two clauses . The clause following the relative pronoun is called dependent clause.

الجملة التي تأتي بعد الاسم الموصول تسمى جملة تابعة.

● We usually use a comma before the relative pronoun if the dependent clause contains non-essential information . " that " marks a clause containing essential information.

عادة نضع فاصلة قبل الضمير الموصول إذا كانت الجملة التابعة تحوي معلومة غير أساسية. أما في حالة that فلا داعي لاستخدام الفاصلة.

Relative clauses contain extra information هذه جمل تتضمن معلومات إضافية

A- who / whom الذي – التي – الذين – اللاتي: **They replace people.**

1- I respect <u>people</u> . <u>They</u> treat me politely .

     I respect people **who treat me politely .** → Relative clause

      └ main clause   إني أحترم الناس الذين يعاملونني بأدب.

2- I insult <u>people</u> . <u>They</u> insult me .

   I insult people **who insult me .**   إني أهين الناس الذين يهينونني.

        └ Relative clause (و تحتوي على معلومة أساسية)

3- I know <u>the man</u> . <u>He</u> teaches you .

   I know the man , **who teaches you .** إني أعرف الرجل الذي يدرّسك

                     ↓

هنا لا تحتوي على معلومة أساسية لأن التركيز على معرفة الرجل ولهذا وضعنا فاصلة قبلها.

4- I met <u>the woman</u> . <u>She</u> had phoned last night .

I met the woman , who had phoned last night .

5- <u>The man</u> is my neighbour . <u>He</u> teaches Ali .

The man ,who teaches Ali , is my neigbour .

إن الرجل الذي يدرّس علياً هو جار لي .

6- <u>The boy</u> is my neighbour. You teach <u>him</u>. (مفعول به)

The boy , (whom) you teach , is my neighbour .

The boy you teach is my neighbour .

ملاحظة : نستخدم whom إذا كان الضمير في موقع المفعـول بـه ويجـوز في هـذه الحالـة الاسـتغناء عـن whom .

* نستخدم who و whom بعد الاسم العاقل .

* Complete these sentences :

1- I hate the people who ………………………………………………...

2- I admire the students who ……………………………………………...

3- The policeman who saw the accident ……………………………...

4- The girl (whom) Ali loves ……………………………………………...

5- I talked to a man who ……………………………………………...

* Join the sentences using " who " or " whom "

1- I will fire all the workers . They are careless .

……………………………………………………………...

2- The manager wants to promote يرقّي the employees الموظفين They work hard .

……………………………………………………………...

3- The employees will get promoted . They have long experience .

……………………………………………………………...

4- They want to thank the doctor . He saved their son's life .

……………………………………………………………...

5- The police should punish the drivers . They break the traffic rules . قوانين المرور

....

6-The man is a university graduate. I have employed him to run my company.

....

B- which / that الذي – الذين – التي : They replace things.

1- I read the book . You had sent it last week .

    I read the book , (which) you had sent last week.

          * قرأت الكتاب الذي كنت قد أرسلته في الأسبوع الماضي .

          * نستخدم which بعد اسم غير عاقل .

          * هنا يجوز الاستغناء عن " which " لأنها حلّت محل ضمير في موقع مفعول به .

2- This is the road . It leads to Ali's house .

    This is the road which leads to Ali's house .

3- I like films . They teach us good things .

    I like the films (that) which teach us good things .

4- The car is too expensive . Ali has bought it .

    The car , (which) Ali has bought , is too expensive .

5- Ali sent me a copy of the book . He had written it .

    Ali sent me a copy of the book ,(which) he had written.

    Ali sent me a copy of the book that he had written .

6-You want to buy the car. Ali is talking about it.

    You want to buy the car , which Ali is talking about.

    You want to buy the car about which Ali is talking.

    You want to buy the car that Ali is talking about.

في حالة استخدام that لا يجوز تقديم حرف الجر about .

* Join these sentences :

1- The water is polluted . We drink it .

....

2- We should drink water . It contains minerals .

....

3- You should give me questions . I can answer them easily .

....

4- The policy is disastrous مدمرة . You follow it .

....

5-The earthquake destroyed thousands of houses . It hit the

North of the country .

....

** Study these sentences to see how the relative pronoun
" which " is used.

* You talk too much , <u>which</u> makes me angry .

* هنا which تعود إلى الجملة السابقة لها (You talk too much) . هناك بعض الكتاب يعترضون على
هذا الاستخدام , وهناك آخرون يـميلون إلى هذا الاستخدام .
* إنك تتكلم كثيراً جداً الأمر الذي يجعلني أغضب .
* هنا which تقوم مقام فاعل للفعل " make " .

* They study well , which means that they
will certainly succeed.

إنـهم يدرسون بشكل جيد الأمر الذي يعني بأنـهم سوف ينجحون بالتأكيد .

* **Complete these sentences in the same way :**

1- They are taking the matter seriously بجدية, which means that
....

2- She speaks politely to everybody , which
....

3- He speaks English fluently بطلاقة , which
....

4- It is raining heavily , which ....
....

5- Ali refused to lend me his car , which ....

C - **where** حيث : It replaces a place.

We went to <u>a park</u>. We had a good time <u>there</u>.

لربط الجملتين.. نلاحظ وجود there (معنى هناك) في الجملة الثانية.. وهي تشـير إلى a park في الجملة الأولى. نقوم بشطب there ونستبدلها بـ where التي يجب أن نضعها بعد park .

We went to a park, where we had a good time.

ذهبنا إلى متنـزه حيث قضينا وقتا ممتعاً.

Join each pair of sentences using " where ":

1- Ali joined a London university. He studied chemistry there.

....

2-We soon came to a lake. We saw hundreds of ducks there.

....

3- We have schools. Young people can study foreign languages there.

....

4-The government has provided first-class hospitals. Sick people get free treatment there.

....

5-The police sealed off the area. A crime was committed there last week. طوقت الشرطة المنطقة .

....

6- The teachers took the pupils to the school garden. They planted trees there.

....

7 Ali took us to a modern shopping centre. We found everything there.

....

D- **whose** صاحب الشيء : It replaces the owner of a thing.

I know **the man**. You have borrowed **his car** .
I know the man **whose car** you have borrowed.

1- I mix with **young people** . **Their parents** speak good English.

....

2- We respect women . Their children are polite.

....

3- People like a wife . Her house is always tidy.

....

4- This is the man . His son was killed in last night's accident.

....

5- We reward students . Their performance is excellent.

....

* Find the error and correct it أوجد الخطأ وصححه :
1- We like people which work hard. ....
2- The hotel which we will stay is not too far . ...
3- The hotel where was built last year collapsed . ...
4- The cat who killed the mouse is black. ....
5- I like people who English is perfect. ....
6- The book , that you are looking for , is on my table.

....

7- The man, whom teaches you , is a friend of mine.

....

8- He comes first will receive a gift. ....
9- Cars are made in Japan are strong. ....
10- People salaries are too low are angry. ....
11- People high salaries are comfortable. ....
12- People live in glass houses should take care. ....
13- People who living in glass houses have to take care. ....
14- The money is on the table is Ali's. ....
15- The girl , lives in the opposite flat, speaks good English.

....

Noun clauses الجمل الاسمية

* A noun can function a subject or object .

* قلنا إن الاسم في الجملة إما أن يكون فاعلاً أو مفعولاً .

1- Ali likes Mona .

2- They are coming to the concert .

3- The students have got their books .

* يمكن استبدال الاسم بجملة ا سمية كما في هذه الأمثلة :

1- I know Ali .

I know that Ali is a student . إني أعرف بأن علياً طالب.

↓

هذه جملة اسمية

2- I don't know where they live .

I like to go wherever you take me .

3- Mona knows what I want . إن منى تعرف ما أريد.

I accept whatever you say. إني أقبل مهما تقول.

4- He knows if I am busy . إنه يعرف عما إذا كنت مشغولاً.

5- I think that you are wrong .

6- They say that Mona has decided to resign .

إنهم يقولون بأن منى قد قررت أن تستقيل .

7- I know who can repair the car .

إني أعرف الشخص الذي يستطيع أن يصلح السيارة.

I need whoever can do it for me.

إني أحتاج إلى من يستطيع أن يقوم بذلك لي.

8- I don't know how Ali came to school .

إني لا أدري كيف جاء علي إلى المدرسة .

9- I can tell you when I will finish it .

10- Can you tell me why Mona is angry ?

ملاحظات :

* الجملة الاسمية تحل محل الاسم في الجملة .

* الجملة الاسمية يمكن أن تبدأ بكلمات السؤال مثل :

what , where , when , who , how , why

* الجملة الاسمية يمكن أن تبدأ بـ " if " بمعنى " عما إذا " .

* You know where Mona lives .

* I don't know if Mona can do that .

* الجملة الاسمية لا تكون على هيئة سؤال :

* I know where does Ali want to go . (✗)

* I know where Ali wants to go . (✔)

* Change these questions into noun clauses :

1- How long will Ali stay there ?

<u>I don't know</u> how long Ali will stay there .

ملاحظة: نضع الجزء الأول الذي تحته خط ثم نتخلص من السؤال بإعادة الجملة إلى ما كانت عليـه قبـل السؤال.

2- How old is Mona ?

<u>Tell me</u> how old Mona is .

3- How far is Doha from here ?

I don't know how far ………………………………………..

4- When will Mona arrive in London ?

Can you tell me ………………………………………?

Please let me know ……………………………………

5- What have you done ?

I want to know what ………………………………………

6- Why do you walk to school ?

I want to know ……………………………………………

7- Who does Ali visit ?

I know who(m) <u>*Ali visits.*</u>

8- When does Mona go out ?

I want to know …………………………………………..

9- What did Mona say to her mother ?

I don't know <u>*what Mona said to her mother.*</u>

10- When did they begin to play ?

Tell me ....

11- Can you do that for me ?

Tell me <u>if</u> you ....

12- Did you find your book ?   (لا بد من وضع if في الجواب)

I want to know ....

13- Has Ali sold his car ?

I don't know ....

14- Does Mona agree with you ?

I want to know ....

15- Do you intend to join the university ?

I want to know ....

16- Where did Ali find his watch?

I want to know ....

17- How does Mona come to school?

Can you tell me how .... ?

18- Has Mona phoned you?

I want to know if ....

19- Are you busy?

Ali wants to know ....

20- Were you at home last night?

Ali asked me ....

أتمنى / يا ليتني   I wish ...

١- عندما نتمنى شيئاً في زمن الحاضر ونعرف أنه من الصعب تحقيق هذه الأمنية فإننا نقول :

1- I wish I <u>had</u> a car .

* بعد wish تأتي جملة اسمية فعْلُها شكل ثانٍ .
* تفيد هذه الجملة أنني لا أملك سيارة في زمَن الحاضر ، وأتمنى أن أمتلك واحدة .

2- I wish I <u>could</u> do that .   3- He wishes he had more money
يا ليتني أستطيع أن أفعل ذلك.
إنه يتمنى أن يمتلك مزيداً من النقود

4- I wish I <u>were</u> free .

5- She wishes she <u>were</u> able to speak English .

٢- أما في حالة الماضي ... فإننا نتحدث عـن شيء لم نفعلـه ونتمنى الآن أننا قمنا بـه ، أو شيء فعلنـاه
ونتمنى أننا لم نفعله . فماذا سيكون شكل الجملة ؟

1- I didn't go to the concert .   لم أذهب إلى الحفل الغنائي.

    I wish I <u>had gone</u> to the concert .   يا ليتني ذهبت إلى الحفل الغنائي

* بعد wish تأتي جملة فعْلُها شكل ثالث مع had .

2- She <u>went</u> to the zoo .

    She wishes she <u>hadn't gone</u> to the zoo .

إنها تتمنى لو أنها لم تذهب إلى حديثة الحيوان .

3- I told Ali about the accident .

    I wish I hadn't told Ali about the accident .

* <u>Conclusion</u>   الخلاصة

١- في حالة الزمن الحاضر بعد wish يكون الفعل شكل ثان .

I wish I had time .   يا ليت أن يكون عندي وقت
أتمنى أن يكون عندي وقت.

٢- في حالة زمن الماضي بعد wish يكون الفعل شكل ثالث مدعوماً بـ had

I wish I had phoned Ali .   يا ليتني اتصلت بـ علي.

I wish I hadn't gone there .   يا ليتني لم أذهب إلى هناك.

*Change each sentence expressing a wish :

1-   I don't have a ticket .

    ....

2-   I have a problem with my boss .

    ....

3- Ali doesn't know how to dive .

....

4- Huda doesn't have a good salary .

....

5- Ali can't speak English .

....

6- Mona isn't at the party .

....

7- Ali didn't attend the debate المناظرة.

....

8- I spent all my money .

....

9- Mona didn't finish high school .

....

10- Nasser wasn't free yesterday .

....

11- Hamad didn't buy a small car.

....

12- Sami didn't accept the job offer.

....

13- Ali doesn't know the answer to this question.

....

14- I can't do anything for you.

....

15- I failed to inform my father of the changes made to the party's schedule.

....

* Correct the verbs in brackets :

1- I travelled by car to Dubai . I wish I (travel) .... by air .

2- I miss my family . I wish they (be) ....here now .

3- The kitchen is awful . I wish that I (wash) .... the dishes last night .

4- I wish that I (know) .... more English .

5- I'm tired today . I wish that I (not stay up) .... late last night .

6- The car I bought last week was too bad . I wish I (not buy) .... it .

7- The exam was too difficult . The students wish they (have) .... an easier

   one .

8- Ali isn't well . I wish he (be) ...... all right. I need him now

9- Mona is sad. She wishes she (buy) .... the ring.

10- Ali was angry. He wishes he (watch) .... the match.

* The infinitives   الأفعال في حالة المصدر

* infinitive هو الفعل الأصلي مسبوقاً بـ to مثل :

to play , to fly , to accept , to change .

* الفعل في حالة المصدر يمكن أن يأخذ مكان الاسم في الجملة .

أمثلة :

1- I want a car .

     I want to buy a bike to buy هو المصدر و أخذ مكان الاسم: أي مكان المفعول به

2- I intend to apply for this job.   أنا أنوي أن أتقدم لهذه الوظيفة.

3- They decided to move to London.   هم قرروا أن يرحلوا إلى لندن

4- She agreed to attend the conference .   وافقت على أن تحضر المؤتمر

5- He refused to sell me his car .   رفض أن يبيعني سيارته

* وهناك أفعال أخرى تقبل أن يأتي بعدها فعل مصدر ... نذكر بعضاً منها .

1- I asked Mona to help me .   طلبت من منى أن تساعدني.

2- She promised to help me .   إنها وعدت بأن تساعدني.

3- He **promised** me *to come* . إنه وعدني بأن يأتـي.

4- I **persuaded** Ali *to travel* by air. أنا أقنعت علياً بأن يسافر بالجو.

5- He **forced** me *to sell* everything . He **compelled** me *to sell*

everything . ٦ إنه أجبرني على أن أبيع كل شيء . He **caused** me

to cancel the trip . إنه جعلني ألغي الرحلة.

7- You **encourage** us *to learn* English . إنك تشجعنا على أن نتعلم الإنجليزية

8- He **offered** *to help* me . عرض بأن يساعدنـي.

9- She **declined** *to give* more details.

امتنعت عن إعطاء مزيد من التفاصيل.

10- I **would like** *to do* something else .

11- I **prefer** *to stay* . إنـي أفضّل أن أبقى.

12- I **would prefer** *to stay.*

* هناك صفات تقبل أن يأتي بعدها فعل في المصدر .. نذكر منها :

1- I am **happy** to tell you .

2- He is **sorry** to say that . إنه آسف لأن يقول ذلك.

3- He is **glad** to come . إنه مسرور لأن يأتـي.

4- I am **willing** to do that . إني راغب في أن أفعل ذلك.

5- She is **unwilling** to buy this car إنـها غير راغبة في شراء هذه السيارة

6- It is **important** to fight smoking . من المهم أن نـحارب التدخين.

7- It is **necessary** to fight crime. من الضروري أن نـحارب الجريـمة.

8- It is **right** to do that . من الصواب أن نفعل ذلك.

9- It is **wrong** to say that . من الخطأ أن نقول ذلك.

10- It is **mad** to smoke . من الجنون أن ندخـن.

11- It is **easy** to smoke , but it is **difficult** to give it up .

من السهل أن ندخن ولكن من الصعب أن نتركه.

* ذكرنا أن infinitive الفعل في حالة المصدر يمكن أن يحل محل المفعول به .

* الفعل في حالة المصدر يمكن أن يحل محل الفاعل أيضاً .

1- **To smoke** is mad .   . أنْ تدخـن جنـون

2- **To steal** is wrong .   **.أنْ تسرق خطأ**

3- **To destroy** nature means **to destroy** life

أن تدمر الطبيعة يعني تدمير الحياة.

4- **To love** means a lot .   . **أنْ تـحب يعني كثيراً**

5- **To forgive** is great .   .أن تصفح شيء رائع

6- **To save** a life is a noble goal.   .أن تنقذ حياةً هدف نبيل

7- My ambition is **to become** a doctor.

إن طموحي هو أن أصبح طبيباً.

8- **To love** is something , but **to love** and **to be loved** is

everything.   أن تحب شيء ولكن أن تحب وأنْ تُحب لهـو كـل شيء

* **Fill in each space with a suitable infinitive:**

1- They plan .... a modern town in the North of the

country. They believe that .... the housing problem,

they need .... something

2- .... good food is the best way ....healthy.

3- .... less food can lead to a loss of weight.

4-........ too many cigarettes a day is.........your health.

5- We want .... a solution حل to this problem.

* **Find what is wrong and correct it :**

1- It is nice help the poor .

....

2- It is stupid eat more than you need .

....

3- She has decided taking the driving test .

....

4- I advise you thinking before you write .

....

5- She promised me **take part in** تشارك في the race .

....

6- It is your duty tell the truth.

....

7- He has just started do his homework.

....

8- Cross this busy road is too dangerous.

....

9- She offered take me to the party, but I refused go with her.

....

10-   Eat good food means a lot.

....

*Arrange the words in such a way that you produce good sentences :

1- dangerous / is / to / too / drive / **It** / fast .

....

2- means / **To** / too / drive / death / fast .

....

3- fair / is / to / **It** / energy / save .

....

4- waste / is / mad / **It** / energy / to .

....

5- you / wants / to / **Ali** / somewhere / play / else .

....

6- you / advise / to / English / **I** / learn .

....

7- will / me / **He** / to / cause / everything / lose .

....

8- agreed / **She** / come / to /to/party/ my .

....

9- are / willing / **We** / watch / match / to / the .

....

10- don't / you / **I** / to / smoke / here / allow .

....

11- to/ promised/ **He**/ smoking/ give up/

....

12- unacceptable/ **To** / is/ others/ lie/ to

....

13- compel/ can't/ to/ **You**/ me/ do/ hate/ I / things/

....

14- impossible/ me/ is/ to/ these/ **It**/ for/ terms/ accept/

....

15- / failed/ **They**/ to/ problem/ a solution/ find/ have/ this/ to

....

16- trees / cut / **To** / to/ life / is / destroy /

....

17- unfair / **It** / to / nature / destroy / is /

....

18- are not / leave / allowed مسموح / **They** / before / noon/ to /

....

الشكل الرابع للفعلThe gerund

هو عبارة عن الفعل الأصلي مضافاً إليه " ing - " .

أمثلة : going , playing , swimming , driving

* gerund يقوم بدور الاسم سواء كان فاعلاً أو مفعولاً به .

Examples   أمثلة

1- I like to read . (✔)

  I like reading . (✔)   إنـي أحب القراءة.

2- I prefer swimming .

3- **Smoking** is dangerous .   التدخين خطير .

4- **Reading** books can benefit you a lot .

إن قراءة الكتب يـمكن أن تفيدك كثيراً

5- **Destroying** the environment is wrong.   إن تدمير البيئة خطأ .

فيما يلي أفعال تقبل أن يأتي بعدها gerund بوظيفة اسم .

1- I **don't mind coming** with you .   إني لا أمانع في المجيء معك.

2- He **missed talking** to you .   إنه اشتاق إلى الحديث إليك.

3- We can **go fishing** .

4- They **went swimming** yesterday .

5- I can't **stand smoking** .   إنـي لا أستطيع أن أتحمل التدخين.

6- We **have a problem** teaching these children .

لدينا مشكلة في تعليم هؤلاء الأطفال.

7- I **spent** too much time **trying** to repair the fault .

أمضيت كثيراً من الوقت في محاولة إصلاح العطل .

8- I can't **help doing** that.   لا يمكنني أن أتـجنب فعل ذلك .

9- I always **avoid coming** late .   إنـي دائـماً أتـجنب المجيء متأخراً.

* هناك أفعال يأتـي بعدها مصدر infinitive وفعل شكل رابـع gerund وتوصـل لنـا نفـس المعنى .

أمثلة :

1- He **started to write** .

   He **started writing** .   بدأ بالكتابة.

2- We **began to build** it in 1990 .

   We **began building** it in 1990 .   بدأنا في بناءه في عام ١٩٩٠.

3- I **like to play** football .

   I **like playing** football .

4- I **prefer to drive** than <u>to fly</u> .

   I **prefer driving** to flying .   إني أفضل ركوب السيارة على السفر جواً.

<u>ملاحظة</u> : في الحالات التالية لا يجوز إلا الشكل الأول أي المصدر infinitive :

* I **would like to go** fishing .
* I **would prefer to watch** the match .
* I **would love to** come.

* أفعال يأتي بعدها فعل المصدر infinitive وفعل في الشكل الرابع gerund ولكن المعنى مختلف في الحالتين .

1- When I saw my father , I **stopped smoking** .

عندما رأيت والدي ، توقفت عن التدخين .

التعليق : كنت أدخن وعندما رأيت والدي توقفت عنه . *هنا الإنسان يترك عملاً كان يعمله

2- I was painting my room .When I got tired , I **stopped to smoke**.

كنت أدهن غرفتي . وعندما تعبت ، توقفت لكي أدخن .

<u>التعليق</u> : كنت أقوم بدهان الغرفة ، وعند التعب ، توقفت عن الدهان لكي أقوم بالتدخين . هنا الإنسان يترك عملاً لكي يقوم بعملٍ غيره .

3- I was fishing when I saw Mona. I **stopped to ask** her how she was .   كنت أقوم

بالصيد عندما قابلت منى. وتوقفت لكي أسألها عن حالها.

4- He **tried to kill** Ali .   **إنه حاول أن يقتل علياً.**

التعليق : إنه قام بالترتيب لعملية القتل ، ولكنه لم يباشر بالتنفيذ .

5- He **tried killing** Ali .   **حاول قتل علي.**

التعليق : بعد أن رتب لعملية القتل ، قام بالتنفيذ ولكن عملية تنفيذ القتل لم تنجح

6- I **remembered to visit** Ali .   **تذكرت أن أزور علياً.**

التعليق : كان عندي نية لزيارة علي ونسيت أن أقوم بالزيارة ، ولكنني في لحظة ما تـذكرت أن
أقوم بالزيارة. " الزيارة لم تتم " .

7- I **remembered visiting** Huda .   **تذكرت زيارتي لهدى.**

التعليق : الزيارة تمت ونسيتها ثم تذكرتها .

8- He has **stopped me leaving** the office before noon.

لقد منعني من مغادرة المكتب قبل الظهر.

* أفعال يأتي بعدها infinitive فعل في المصدر ولكن بدون to .

1- He **made me write** the sentence twice .   إنه جعلني أكتب الجملة مرتين

2- They will **make** you **cancel** the booking .

إنهم سوف يجعلونك تلغي الحجز .

3- I can't **let** you **go out** alone.   لا أستطيع أن أدعك تخرج وحيداً.

4- She **let me come in** .   **دعتني أدخل.**

5- She **helps** me **do** my homework .   * (✔)

   She **helps** me **to do** my homework . * (✔)

6-We **were made to cancel** the trip .   **أجبرنا على إلغاء الرحلة**

7- The grass **was let to grow.**   ترك العشب لكي ينمو

* **Use the right verb - forms :**

1- He agreed (come) .... although he (be) ....busy.

2- You can (tell) .... me what (do) ...., but   you can't

  compel me (do) .... things I don't like (do) ....

3- I'd like (say) ...... that Ali (be) ......better than the others .

4- You can't make people (accept) ....your ideas .

5- This policy will cause many students (drop out) .... of school .

6- When it started (rain) ...... , we had to (go) .... home .

7-When I saw my father , I stopped (write) .... to

(greet يحيي) ....him .

8- He tried (steal) .... the money; he just planned to do that.

9- I can't stand (live) .... in the city centre.

10- While I was (go) .... home , I (see) ....some beautiful flowers . I

  stopped (look at) .... them . But my brother didn't let me (look)

  ....n , and that made me (get angry) .... Things like that

  always (happen) .... to me .

11- I stopped (wash) .... my car when I heard the telephone ring.

12- As soon as the building collapsed انهار , we started (look for) .... any

  survivalsناجين .

13- I was (drive) .... home when I (see) .... the accident.

I had to stop (drive) ....to see what (happen) ....

14- We should stop (talk) ....to follow what Ali is (say)......

15- We still have problems (find) .... the real cause of

the fire .

16- They have no difficulty (restore) ....order and

peace to the area.

إنهم لا يجدون صعوبة في استعادة النظام والسلام إلى المنطقة.

The prepositions   حروف الجر

يشكو الكثيرون من العرب الذين يتعلمون الإنجليزية من حروف الجر لأن حروف الجـر في اللغة العربية
تختلف تماماً عن مثيلاتـها في اللغة الإنجليزية .
مثلاً حرف الجر " من " قد يعني " from " أو " with " أو " of " .
وبناء على ذلك .. فإننا ننصح بحفظ حروف الجر عن طريق الممارسة .

1- Adjectives with prepositions   صفات مع حروف جــر :

angry (with people / angry about (at) something) غاضب من
happy with my wife = pleased with .... من مبسوط
displeased مستاء / delighted with مبتهج من - مسرور
satisfied with راضٍ عن / disappointed with يائس من
ashamed of خجل من / jealous of غيور من =
envious of (envy يحسد - الحسد) / jealous for غيور على
full of = filled with مملوء بـ / devoid of خالٍ من
good at جيد في ✕ bad at   / good for صالح لـ ✕ bad for
excellent at بارع في   / absent from متغيب عن
next to بجوار   / close to قريب من ✕ far from بعيد عن
tired of متمل من متعب من , متمل من = bored with = fed up with . من متملل

٣٢٤

sorry for (person) حـزين على / sorry about (something) أسف لـ

responsible for مسئول عن = in charge of

responsible to مسئول أمام / guilty of مذنب بـ

afraid of = scared of = terrified of خائف من / proud of فخور بـ

free from = safe from - في مأمن من / free of duty معاف من الرسوم independent of

تابع لـ subordinate to / مستقل عن

suspicious of = doubtful of = sceptical of متشكك من

واعٍ بـ - على دراية بـ aware of = conscious of / موالٍ لـ loyal to

منـزعج من / upset about قلق حيال worried about

مساوٍ لـ equal to / قوي -ضعيف فـ strong , weak in

على دراية بـ - على إطلاع على / familiar with = acquainted with

كـريم تجاه / polite to / generous to / good to / kind to / nice to

قليل الأدب مع / rude to / impolite to / unfriendly to / friendly to

مـماثل لـ similar to / مخصص لـ _ مخلص لـ devoted to

مختلف عن / opposed to معارض لـ / different from

متورط في - ضالع في involved in / مـهتم بـ interested in

ميال نحو inclined to / مستعد لـ ready for

مخطوبة لـ engaged to / مـتزوج من married to

متعطش لـ thirsty for راغب في willing to X unwilling to /

جاد بخصوص serious about متأكد من sure of /

معادٍ لـ hostile to حريص على keen on / مدين لـ indebted to

غيـر مبالٍ بـ indifferent to

مولع بـ fond of قادر على - قابل لـ capable of /

مذكّر بـ reminiscent of / معبّر عن expressive of

مشهور بـ famous for / impressed (by – with) مفتون بـ

separate from منعزل عن / related to =

٣٢٥

connected to (with) / على صلة بـ / adequate to مناسب لـ

relevant to لـ صلة بـ / مناسب- مطابق لـ- له صلة بـ / suitable for مناسب لـ

independent of مستقل عن / subject to معرّض لـ خاضع لـ-

superior to أعلى من / أسمى من – inferior to أدنى من

according to حسب / طبقاً لـ- distant from بعيد عن

far from بعيد عن / responsive to مستجيب لـ

sensitive to حساس لـ

susceptible to معرّض لـ / حساس – سريع التأثر -

prone to ميال / معرّض لـ - عرضة لـ-

in short = in brief وباختصار / in particular وبشكل خاص

in general وبشكل عام

هذه صفات ولقد سبق أن ذكرنا كيف يتم استخدام الصفة في جملة .إليكم هذه الجمل:

1-I am **familiar with** your problems.

إني على علم بمشكلاتك.

2- He is **proud of** his country . إنه فخور بوطنه.

3- She is **married to** a rich man . إنها متزوجة من رجل ثري.

4- I am **sorry for** Huda ; She has failed twice .

إني آسف لأجل هدى . إنها رسبت مرتين .

5- I am **sorry about** the harm I have done you .

إني آسف للضرر الذي صنعته لك .

6- He is **sorry for** coming late.

7- You are **different from** Ali , but Ali is **similar to** his father.

إنك مختلف عن علي ولكن علياً مشابه لأبيه.

8- This object is **identical to** this one.

إن هذا الجسم مشابه لهذا الجسم.

9- She is **weak in** Maths , but **strong in** English.

إنها ضعيفة في الرياضيات ولكنها قوية في الإنجليزية .

10- We are **committed to** the project.

نحـن ملتزمون بالمشروع .

* Put the right prepositions in the spaces :

1- She is ashamed .... what she has done .

2- It is good to be jealous .... your wife , but it is bad to be jealous .... others .

3-The Minister is responsible ...... the king .... his ministry .

الوزير مسئول أمام الملك عن وزارته

4- The road is full .... cars .We are aware ....this traffic problem

5- I hope that they are serious .... solving this problem .

6- Both Ali and Nasser are different .... you .

7- Your car is similar .... mine .

8- We are satisfied ....the progress التقدمyou have made .

9- I am not interested ....this subject .

10- We are opposed .... what you are saying.

11- I am afraid .... this wild animal.

12- We are worried ...... Ali; he has not returned home so far.

13- The road is devoid .... any cars.

14- We are unaware .... the wealth of our country.

15- They are blind ....our complaints شكاوى.

16- He is indifferent .... my warnings .

17- Ali is rude .... me , and I don't like that.

18- She is envious .... her friend's beauty .

19- We are loyal .... our beliefs.

20- We are committed ..... making peace. نحن ملتزمون بصنع السلام.21- I will take part in the race and I am sure ...... winning.

22- You are always late .... school.

23- I am pleased .... you ; you are working hard.

24- He is getting tired .... doing this job.

25- She has been absent ...... the school meetings for days.

26- He is unwilling .... leave his old father alone.

27- This man is married .... an Englishwoman.

28- She has been involved.....these investigations for months

29- They are free .... any guilt.

30- We are not inclined .... this idea.

2- Nouns with prepositions : أسماء مع حروف جـر

1- I go to school by bus . I stay at school till لغاية one o'clock .

2- I always get up at six o'clock in the morning .

3- In the afternoon , I do my homework . If I have a problem with it , I always ask
    my father for help .

4- In the evening , I usually watch TV with my family.

5- On Friday , I often go out with friends .

6- Jassim is on holiday .   إن جاسماً في عطلة .

7- Ali is on leave , too .   إن علياً في إجازة أيضاً.

8- We go swimming at (on) week-ends .

        إننا نذهب للسباحة في عطلة نهاية الأسبوع.

9- They started to feel at home.

10- We are at ease.   إننا مرتاحون.

11-They are in debt and cannot repay their debts.

        إنـهم مدينون ولا يستطيعون تسديد ديونـهم.

12-He has repaid all his debts, so he is out of debt.

        إنه سدد جميع ديونه ولهذا فإنه ليس عليه ديون.

13-I am in debt to you for 1000 riyals.   إني مدين لك بـ ١٠٠٠ ريال.

14- We are worried about Ali and Nasser . They are in danger .   إنـهم في خطر.

15- We are out of danger. *We are no longer in danger.* →

        لم نعد في خطر.

16- He can't leave his home; he is under home arrest.

        إنه تحت الإقامة الجبرية.

17- A new airport is under construction. إن مطاراً جديداً قيد الإنشاء

18- Some people are at work. Take care !

19- We have to do something. They are in trouble. إنـهم في ورطة.

20- We are at war with Israel .   نـحن في حرب مع إسرائيل.

21- We are at war over the cause of the fire.

        نحن منقسمون حيال سبب الحريق.

22- He has been given the job **on the basis of** a two- year
   contract. لقد أعطي الوظيفة على أساس عقد مدته سنتين.

23- We can get useful information **by means of** the internet.
   إننا نحصل على معلومات مفيدة بواسطة الإنترنت . I am **by no**
means ready to do this job.

إني قطعاً لست مستعداً لأن أقوم بهذا العمل.

24- He has **by all means** done the job . إنه بالتأكيد قد أنجز العمل. 25- What's the
matter with you ? = What's wrong with you ? ما بك ؟ 26- It is **a matter of life and**
death.

27- إنه أمر يتعلق بالحياة والموت (أي أنه أمر غاية في الأهمية)
They live **from hand to mouth.**   28- Everything is
at hand. كل شيء قريب.

29- I got this information **at first hand** from the person who saw the accident.
حصلت على هذه المعلومة مباشرة من الشخص الذي شاهد الحادث.

30- We have this camera **on loan** from a friend.
لقد استعرنا هذه الكاميرا من صديق .

More nouns with prepositions
المزيد من أسماء مع حروف للجر

at home , on time في موعده , in time , at lunch-time , at a time
from time to time من حين إلى آخر , for the time being في الوقت الحالي   up to time مواظب ,
at the same time في نفس الوقت , at night ليلاً ,
at noon ظهراً ,   at dawn فجراً , at sun-set عند غروب الشمس ,
at sun-rise عند شروق الشمس ,   at the beginning of في بداية ,
at the end of في نهاية (الطابور- الشارع) ,   in the end وفي النهاية ,
in 1980 ,   on Sunday , in April , on April 14th ,
at the top of في قمة ,   at a height of على ارتفاع ,

at the mercy of تحت رحمة , at the expense of على حساب
at a depth of على عمق , at stake في خطر , at a price بسعر
at the cross-roads عند مفترق الطرق, at the sea-side على شاطئ البحر ,
on the beach , at variance with على خلاف مع ,
at odds with على خلاف مع , in public علناً ,
from pocket to mouth من الجيب إلى الفم , in trouble في مأزق ,
another way of doing that طريقة أخرى لقيام بذلك ,
at the expense of على حساب , at any cost بأي ثمن ,
at a loss غير متيقن – مرتبك / بخسارة (البيع), step by step خطوة خطوه ,
a great loss to the country خسارة كبيرة للبلاد ,
one by one الواحد تلو الآخر , in danger في خطر , in coma في غيبوبة ,
over the town فوق المدينة , by the time بحلول الوقت ,
by the way بالمناسبة – على فكرة , with the aim of بهدف ,
with regard to في ما يتعلق بـ , in spite of على الرغم من ,
a knowledge of معرفة بـ , interest in اهتمام بـ ,
a meeting in camera اجتماع مغلق , at your disposal تحت تصرفك
in line with تمشياً مع , in harmony with منسجم مع ,
out of harmony with على غير انسجام مع , in favour of مناصر لـ ,
in bad need of في حاجة ماسة لـ , plenty of كثير من ,
at the airport , on the street , on the floor , on the table ,
in the box , in the city , in the house , at the store عند المخزن ,
in the store في المخزن .

* Study these sentences :

1- It is nice to come **on time** .   من الجميل أن تأتي في موعدك.

 2- You have come **in time**.   لقد جئت في وقت مبكر نحتاجك فيه.   3- She always

phones **at a time** when I am busy .

إنها دائماً تتصل في وقت عندما أكون فيه مشغولاً .

4- Why not tidy the place **for the time being** ?

5- You are always **up to time** .   أنت دائماً مواظب .

6- We always meet **at the end** of every month.

7- The teacher explained everything . **In the end** , he asked us
      to prepare for a quiz next Monday.

8- I leave home **at sun-rise** and return **at seven in the evening.**

9-   We rarely نادراً sit **at the top of** the mountain.

10-   There is a rock **in the middle of** the road.

11-   You can turn left **at the cross-roads.**   بإمكانك أن

تستدير إلى اليسار عند مفترق الطرق –12– Freedom is **worth**

fighting for إن الحرية تستحق أن نناضل من أجلها

   They are worthy of having freedom.   إنهم يستحقون نيل الحرية.

13- We don't tolerate **lack of** freedom. إننا لا نتساهل مع غياب الحرية.14- He is **in**

control of some evil people.

إنه تحت سيطرة بعض الناس الشريرين .

15- There is **little control** over prices. هناك رقابة بسيطة على الأسعار.16-   The

situation is **under control** .   إن الوضع تحت السيطرة.

17-   The situation is **out of control**   إن الوضع غير مسيطرٌ عليه.18- I am **in the**

grasp of an evil person. إني في قبضة شخص شرير.

19- This point is **beyond my grasp.** إن هذه النقطة غير مفهومة لدي.20- Those **in**

power are to blame for this massacre.

إن أولئك الذين في السلطة يتحملون مسؤولية المذبحة.

 21- We are **in a position** to start the project. نحن في وضع يسمح لنا

بالبدء في المشروع.

22- He is not **in a position** to tell you his opinion.

هو ليس في وضع يسمح له بأن يخبرك برأيه.

23 – The matter is **in question**. إن الأمــر قيد النظـر. 24- His success

is **out of the question**. إن نجاحه مستحيل.

25 - Take care ! The men are **at work**. أحذر ! إن العمال في حالة عمل .

3- Verbs with prepositions : أفعــال مع حروف جر

agree with مع / يتفق في الرأي مع

disagree with مع يختلف في الرأي differ from عن يختلف / differ with

يختلف مع die of من يـموت / leave for إلى يغادر /

wait for ينتظر

ask for يطلب / appeal to يناشد - يروق لـ / add to يزيد من apologise to Ali

for coming late .

يعتذر لـ علي لمجيئه متأخراً

believe in بـ يؤمن / belong to يخص :

It belongs to me . إنه يخصني

depend on يعتمد:I can't depend on Ali for solving my problems .

إني لا أستطيع أن أعتمد على علي في حل مشكلاتي. divide into

يقسم على divide by /يقسّم إلى إلى

forgive عن يعفو: I will forgive you for breaking the door.

سوف أغفر لك كسرك للباب .

1- It is bad to **hide** food **from** your children .

من السوء أن تخفي الطعام عن أطفالك .

2- I don't **insist on** knowing the meaning of every single word .

إني لا أصر على معرفة معنى كل كلمة .

3- It is unfair to **laugh at** others.

ليس من العدل أن تضحك على الآخرين.

4- You should **listen** well **to** every word .

يجب أن تصغي جيداً إلى كل كلمة .

5- That doesn't **matter to me** .

إن هذا لا يهمني.

6- You should **pay for** your mistakes .

يجب أن تدفع ثمن أخطائك

7- We can't **protect** nature **from** factories .

إننا لا نستطيع أن نحمي الطبيعة من المصانع .

8- We **searched** the place **for** the stolen money .

فتشنا المكان بحثاً عن الأموال المسروقة .

9- We should **take care of** the environment.

يجب أن نعتني بالبيئة.

10- You don't **care for** others .

إنك لا تهتم بالآخرين.

11- We should **fight for** freedom .

يجب أن نناضل من أجل الحرية.

12- I **prefer** milk **to** coffee.

إني أفضل الحليب على القهوة.

13- Nature **provides** people **with** many necessary things.

إن الطبيعة تزود الناس بأشياء ضرورية كثيرة.

14- We **think of** Ali as a close friend.

إننا نعتبر علياً كصديق حميم .

15- I advise you to **apply for** this job.

إني أنصحك بأن تتقدم لهذه الوظيفة.

16- This rule doesn't **apply** to this case.

إن هذه القاعدة (القانون) لا تنطبق على هذه القضية .

17- We **appeal to you for** help. We are **in bad need** .

إننا نناشدكم المساعدة . إننا في حاجة ماسة .

18- I will **opt for** your way of thinking.

إنني سوف أختار طريقة تفكيرك.

19- Too many people will **compete for** this post.

إن الكثير من الناس سوف يتنافسون على هذا المنصب .

20- Poverty **leads to** crime.

إن الفقر يؤدي إلى الجريمة.

Phrasal Verbs   أفعال من أكثر من كلمة

call on يزور , call off يلغي , drop in يزور فجأة ,

concentrate on يركّز على , drop out (من المدرسة) يتسرب ,

get back يعود , insist on يصـر على , happen to حدث لـ

get along with يكون على علاقة طيبة مع , die of يـموت من ,

complain to ... about ... يشتكي إلى .. بخصوص ,

rely on يعتمد على , shout at يصرخ على , hear of يسمع بـ ,

hear from يسمع من , look at ينظر إلى , look for يبحث عن ,

set aside يتجاهل – يطرح جانباً ,

set off يفجّر – (رحلة) (شرع) يشرع ,

set out to play شرع في اللعب

set up (يؤسس) يقيم , set fire to يحرق في- يشعل ناراً في ,

catch fire يحترق – يشتعل   make for يؤدي إلى- يتوجه إلى,

make up for يعوض , look after يعـتني بـ , look out يحذر   look up يستخرج

get on (الباص-التاكسي) يركب , get rid of يتخلص من   معنى كلمة من قاموس ,

get to يصل إلى ,

get at ينتقد – يـعني – يصل إلى , get away يهـرب ,

٣٣٤

يتماثل للشفاء live on , يترجل من get off , get over, يعيش على

get out of من , يتهرب من- ينتزع من- يتنصل من

give up يترك , give in يستسلم, hand in يسلّم, hand out يوزع

depart from , ينحرف عن deviate from , يبتعد عن

distance himself from , ينؤ بنفسه عن , look at ينظر إلى

look for يبحث عن , look after يعتني بـ , look down on يزدري

look up يرتدي put on , يستخرج معنى كلمة من قاموس

put out (حريقاً) يطفئ , look forward to يتطلع إلى

pay back يسدد , dream of يحلم بـ , put off يؤجل ,

put back يعيد شيء إلى مكانه , think of (about) يفكر في ,

take care ينتبه , cut off (بلد) يعزل - يقطع ,

run out of : We ran out of food . لقد نفد منا الغذاء,

run for يحصل على ترشيح لمنصب , ,

turn on(جهاز) يفتح , turn off (جهاز) يقفل ,

take off تقلع الطائرة - يخلع (ملابس) ,

break into يسطو على- يدخل عنوة break out ينشب - يندلع ,

break down يتعطل-ينهار , break off (علاقات) يقطع-ينهي-يفسخ

break away يقطع الصلة بـ - ينفصل ,

aspire to يصبو إلى - يطمح إلى , glory in يجد لذة في .

٣٣٥

* **Study these sentences :**

1- We have to **call off** the meeting . (✔) .

نحن مضطرون لأن نلغي الاجتماع .

    We have to **call** the meeting **off** . (✔)

    We can't **call it off** . (✔)

    We can't **call off it** . (×)

2- He **dropped in** , and that annoyed me a lot .

هو زارني دون سابق إنذار وهذا ضايقني كثيراً .

3- Many pupils have **dropped out of** this school .

إن طلاباً كثيرين قد تسربوا من هذه المدرسة .

4- I **got on** the bus as soon as it stopped . ركبت الباص بمجرد أن توقف

5- It is wrong to **get off** the bus before it stops .

من الخطأ أن ننزل من الباص قبل أن يتوقف .

6-   I **asked** Ali **for** money . طلبت من علي نقوداً

7-   I must **take off** my dirty clothes .

    I must **take** my dirty clothes **off** .   . يجب أن أخلع ملابسي القذرة

8- We can **go on** learning for ever إننا نستطيع أن نستمر في التعلم إلى الأبد

4-   We **arrived in** Doha last night .

وصلنا إلى الدوحة في الليلة الماضية.

17-You can **lie to** some people, but you can't **lie to** all people

يـمكنك أن تكذب على بعض الناس ، ولكنك لا تستطيع أن تكذب على كل الناس.

11- The answer **lies in** being familiar with the grammar of the

    language . إن الحل يكمن في أن تكون على دراية بقواعد اللغة.

12- We can **contribute** some money **to improving** our roads .

نستطيع أن نساهم ببعض المال في تحسين طرقنا.

13- Poverty **leads to** illness and ignorance الفقر يؤدي إلى المرض والجهل

14- I **accuse** you **of** stealing my money. إني أتـهمك بسرقة مالي.

15- I will **remind** you of the appointment . إني سوف أذكّرك بالموعد.

16- I **approve of** what you إني أستحسن ما تقول.

17- I prefer to **deal with** honest people إني أفضّل أن أتعامل مع أناس شرفاء

18-The book <u>deals with</u> the democracy problems in this country

الكتاب يتناول مشاكل الديمقراطية في هذا البلد.

19- We **deal in** second-hand cars . إننا نتاجر في السيارات المستعملة.

20- You should **comply with** laws . يجب أن تنصاع إلى القوانين.

21- It is important to **adhere to** the agreement .

It is important to **stick to** the agreement من المهم أن نتقيد بالاتفاق

22- He has **prevented me from** entering the club .

لقد منعني من دخول النادي .

23- Ali was **admitted into** hospital yesterday .

أُدخِلَ علي إلى المستشفى يوم أمس .

24- The suspect **admitted to** his crime , and the judge **sentenced** him **to** five years'
imprisonment .

المشتبه به اعترف بجريمته والقاضي حكم عليه بالسجن لمدة ٥ سنوات .

25- The suspect **was acquitted of** all the charges and released .

بُرِّئَ المشتبه به من جميع التهم وأُطلق سراحه.

26- We intend to **leave** Doha **for** London tomorrow.

إننا ننوي أن نغادر الدوحة متوجهين إلى لندن غداً.

27- We can **leave that for another day**. يمكننا أن نترك هذا ليوم أخر.

 I **will leave it to you** to buy the food. إني سوف أترك لك أمر شراء الطعام. I will **leave
buying the food to you.**

28- If you can't do this job, you can **leave it to me.**

إذا لم تستطع أن تقوم بهذا العمل يمكنك أن تتركه لي.

29- I saw the child **falling off** the wall.

شاهدت الطفل وهو يسقط من على الحائط.

30- The thief **robbed** me **of** all my money.

سلبني اللص من كل نقودي.

31The unfair ruler has **deprived** his people **of** their political

rights for years.

إن الحاكم الظالم قد حرم شعبه من حقوقهم السياسية لسنوات.

32- You can **relieve me of** this task; it is too hard for me.

بإمكانك أن تعفيني من هذه المهمة إنها صعبة جداً بالنسبة لي.

33- **What are you getting at ?** (الفعل بهذا الشكل : ماذا تعني ؟)

You are always **getting at** me. Please stop it. إنك دائماً تهاجمني

The cat cannot **get at** the meat . إن القطة لا تستطيع أن تصل إلى اللحم .

34- We will **compensate** you **for** the injury.

إننا سوف نعوضك عن الإصابة.

ملاحظة : هناك أفعال تقبل أن يأتي الاسم إما قبل أو بعد حرف الجر. أما إذا جاء ضمير , فيوضع فقط بعد حرف الجر.

* You can **turn off** the light. = You can **turn the light off** .

* Don't turn off it ! (✗) . Don't **turn it off** ! (√)

* وهناك أفعال تقبل فقط الاسم أو الضمير بعد حرف الجر .

* Don't **laugh at** me. / You are always **getting at** me. /

He **arrived in** Doha last night. / He has **left for** London . /

We will **vote for** you. إننا سوف نصوت لك.

I can't **wait** hours **for** you. إني لا أستطيع أن أنتظرك لساعات.

Verbs without prepositions
أفعال ليست بحاجة إلى حروف جر

1- I **enjoy** reading .   إني أستمتع بالقراءة.

2- I can **defend** myself .   أستطيع أن أدافع عن نفسي.

3- We should **sacrifice** everything for our dignity .

يجب أن نضحي بكل شيء من أجل كرامتنا .

4- I can't **allow** you to smoke here .   لا أستطيع أن أسمح لك بالتدخين هنا .

5- We **celebrate** Eid Al-Fitr at the end of Ramadan , the month of fasting .

إننا نحتفل بعيد الفطر في نهاية رمضان ، شهر الصيام .

6- He will retire when he **reaches** sixty .

إنه سوف يتقاعد عندما يصل إلى الستين .

7- The Cabinet have **approved** the law .

مجلس الوزراء صادق على القانون .

8- I couldn't **recognize** Ali ; he has changed a lot .

لم أستطع أن أتعرف على علي . لقد تغير كثيراً .

9- Some Arab countries have **recognized** Israel .

بعض الدول العربية اعترفت بإسرائيل .

10- We are **approaching** the river .   إننا نقترب من النهر.

11- He was lucky. He **escaped** death.   كان محظوظاً إنه نجا من الموت .

12- I **admire** your way of doing things إني أعجب بطريقتك في صنع الأشياء

13- In a democratic country , you can **express** your ideas freely .

في بلد ديمقراطي يمكنك أن تعبر عن أفكارك بحـرية.

14- We have to **stop** building the tunnel ; it is too risky.

إننا مضطرون لأن نتوقف عن بناء النفق . إنه محفوف بالمخاطر .

15- Hani has **resigned** his job for ill-health .

لقد استقال هاني من عمله بسبب اعتلال الصحة .

16- If you **increase** prices , your sales will drop sharply

إذا زِدْتَ (من) الأسعار ، فإن مبيعاتك سوف تهبط بشكل حاد .

17- I always **answer** the telephone calls أنا دائماً أرد على المكالمات الهاتفية

18- We can **overcome** our problems . إننا نستطيع أن نتغلب على مشاكلنا

19- It is nice to **forgive** people who **offend** you .

من الجميل أن تعفو عن الناس الذين يسيئون إليك .

20- As soon as I **finish** writing the report , I will **send you** a copy of it .

بمجرد ما أنتهي من كتابة التقرير، فإنني سوف أرسل لك نسخة منه .

21- If you succeed , I will **buy** you a computer .

إن نجحت ، فإنني سوف أشتري لك جهاز حاسوب .

22- Tourism can **bring** our country hard currency , but it can **endanger** our culture .

السياحة يمكن أن تجلب لبلدنا عملة صعبة ، ولكنها يمكن أن تعرض ثقافتنا للخطر .

23- You can **do me a favour** . يمكنك أن تصنع لي معروفاً.

24- We don't **allow** hunting in this area ; we want to protect wildlife .

إننا لا نسمح بالصيد في هذه المنطقة . إننا نريد أن نحمي الحياة البرية.

25- We can say that the Westerns **have affected** our way of life

يمكننا أن نقول بأن الغربيين قد أثروا في أسلوب حياتنا .

26- I expect you to **comply with** laws.

إني أتوقع منك أن تنصاع للقوانين .

* Compliance with laws **is expected of** everybody.

الانصياع (الامتثال) للقوانين (أمر) متوقع من كل شخص.

Author's Biography سيرة المؤلف

* Born in Palestine in 1946.   ولد في فلسطين عام ١٩٤٦

* Joined Cairo University in 1963, and four years later he
  majored in English language and literature with Grade "
  Good".

التحق بجامعة القاهرة عام ١٩٦٣ وحصل منها على درجة الليسانس في اللغة الإنجليزية و آدابها
بتقدير " جيد" عام ١٩٦٧ .

* Has been a teacher of English with Qatar's Ministry of
  Education since 1967.

يعمل مدرساً للغة الإنجليزية في وزارة التربية والتعليم بقطر منذ عام ١٩٦٧.

* Sent to Britain in 1969 on an in- service training course that
  focused on teaching English as a second language.

* أُرسل في دورة تدريبية إلى بريطانيا في صيف ١٩٦٩ موضوعها تدريس الإنجليزية كلغة ثانية.

* Obtained an Education Diploma in teaching English as
  a second language from Qatar University in 1977 .

* حصل على دبلوم عام في التربية وطرق تدريس الإنجليزية كلغة ثانية من جامعة قطر عام ١٩٧٧م .

* Attended several seminars and training courses held in Qatar.

* حضر العديد من الدورات التدريبية داخل دولة قطر تتعلّق بتدريس الإنجليزية كلغة ثانية .

* Has published four books :   قام بنشر هذه المؤلفات:

- **The Sound Approach To English Grammar.**

الطريقة المثلى لقواعد اللغة الإنجليزية

- **English for Beginners** .   الإنجليزية للمبتدئين

- **Art of Writing**   فن الكتابة.

- **A Simplified English – Arabic Glossary Of Words in Use**

القاموس المبسط لكلمات متداولة

Printed in the United States
By Bookmasters

Printed in the United States
By Bookmasters